THE RACIAL DISCOURSES OF LIFE PHILOSOPHY

New Directions in Critical Theory

New Directions in Critical Theory
Amy Allen, General Editor

New Directions in Critical Theory presents outstanding classic and contemporary texts in the tradition of critical social theory, broadly construed. The series aims to renew and advance the program of critical social theory, with a particular focus on theorizing contemporary struggles around gender, race, sexuality, class, and globalization and their complex interconnections.

The Racial Discourses of Life Philosophy

Négritude, Vitalism, and Modernity

DONNA V. JONES

 COLUMBIA UNIVERSITY PRESS   *NEW YORK*

Columbia University Press
Publishers Since 1893
New York   Chichester, West Sussex
Copyright © 2010 Columbia University Press
Paperback edition, 2012

Library of Congress Cataloging-in-Publication Data
Jones, Donna V., 1964–
    The racial discourses of life philosophy : negritude, vitalism, and modernity /
Donna V. Jones.
        p. cm.–(New directions in critical theory)
    Includes bibliographical references and index.
    ISBN 978-0-231-14548-0 (cloth : alk. paper)—ISBN 978-0-231-14549-7 (pbk. : alk.
paper)—ISBN 978-0-231-51860-4 (e-book)
    1. Life in literature.   2. Race in literature.   3. Vitalism in literature.   4. Negritude
(Literary movement)   I. Title.   II. Series.

PN56.L52J66 2010
809'.93355—dc22

                                                                2009031388

Columbia University Press books are printed on permanent and durable acid-free paper.
This book is printed on paper with recycled content.
Printed in the United States of America

c 10 9 8 7 6 5 4 3 2
p 10 9 8 7 6 5 4 3 2 1

Contents

THE RACIAL DISCOURSES OF LIFE PHILOSOPHY

The Resilience of Life

Wynter

We live in a biological age. The ecological crisis has heightened our *Angle* sensibilities of the intrinsic value of the life of all species and encouraged the development of a biocentric ethics. From a different angle, the ability to generate synthetic acellular life and to prolong the life of a brain-dead human being presents us with new examples of bare life and again raises the question of just what life inescapably is.[1] The question is not only a philosophical problem, as decisions about whether to prolong or termi-nate life depend on how we understand what life is and what expressions such as "good as dead" or "a life not worth living" should mean. As life becomes the object of ever more sophisticated technical manipulation and enters the circuits of commerce, we also have new questions about how genetic engineering and therapy and assisted reproduction should be regu-lated, about whether the genome can be owned, about whether stem cells are yet a life, about whether embryos have rights, and about whether ani-mals should be cloned or made into commodities just for their hormones or parts. Today, as Nikolas Rose has laid out in a brilliant phenomenology *Rose* of the new biosociety, scientists, bioethicists, and science-fiction writers are all tantalized by the new possibilities of knowing life not simply to restore a lost normativity but to transform it at conception, in utero, and at the *in each* molecular level.[2] Such manipulation of life now overshadows biopolitical *step?* concerns like state management of bodies for docility and population for quality.

The more successful the manipulation of life (and the more lifelike our artifacts), the greater are the scientific and expert doubts about our intui-tive sense that the animate can be distinguished from the inanimate. How-ever that distinction is drawn—for example, the prototypes of each and the liminal types do vary cross-culturally; the tree is prototypical of the ani-mate for the Malagasy and the virus the chief liminal form for us—the ten-dency to want to draw a distinction between the animate and inanimate may itself be universal.[3] Yet reductionist science has threatened to undermine the fundamental ontological division even though it cannot dislodge our common-sense notion that living things are set apart by a few rather astonishing properties—autonomy, robustness, adaptability to environmental changes, self-repairability, and reproduction, to name a few of their characteristics.

Still we seem now to have fully demystified life, though not too long ago it was held to be not only a marvelous but wholly mysterious thing. As late as the early modern period—and long after the rise of mathematical physics—it was believed, for example, that toads could be generated from ducks putrefying on a dung heap, a woman's hair laid in a damp but sunny place would turn into snakes, and rotting tuna would produce worms that changed first into flies, then into a grasshopper, and finally into a quail.[4] How life—this special domain of the universe—reproduced, developed, and maintained itself was beyond any rational understanding, but life has now been put within the grasp of scientific understanding if not technical control, and in the process the animate has almost been collapsed into the inanimate.

That a reductionist understanding of life has been achieved is remarkable, since the very plenitude of life—its fullness, variety, and complexity—is one of the essential characteristics of life. For this reason, it may seem that the things "we denote as 'living' have too heterogeneous characteristics and capabilities for a common definition to give even an inkling of the variety contained within this term."[5] Yet we now know that almost all life forms—from unicellular bacteria to the higher animals—share the same metabolic processes, organized around the intricate Krebs cycle. And science has also discovered that almost all life forms, from an oak tree to a frog, express "their genetic information in nucleic acids, use the same genetic code to translate gene sequences into amino acids, and (only with some exceptions in the case of plants) make use of the same twenty amino acids as the building blocks of proteins."[6] The discovery of DNA is widely thought to have dissipated the belief that life was somehow a mysterious, impalpable excrescence that lay beyond the scientific disciplines of physics and chemistry. Life has now become nothing more interesting than a specific kind of information in an information age. As John Maynard Smith notes, "code, translation, transcription, message, editing, proof-reading, library and synonymous: these are all technical terms with quite precise meanings in molecular genetics."[7] Machines may not now or ever be lifelike, but the gap between the inanimate and animate no longer seems unbridgeable without a divine breath of life. Reduced to information, life may in fact

appear no more ontologically interesting than stardust. The French gene-
ticist Albert Jacquard drew the radical conclusion:

> We have known for some forty-five years, thanks to the discovery of
> DNA, that the boundary between inanimate objects and animate beings
> was more the result of an optical illusion than objective reality. What
> appeared three billion years ago was not "life," but a molecule that hap-
> pened to be endowed with the capacity to make a copy of itself—to re-
> produce. This capacity is due to its double-helix structure and the process
> is not particularly mysterious; it is the result of the same interactions be-
> tween atoms as those which are at work in all other molecules. The word
> "life," therefore, does not define a specific capacity possessed by certain
> objects; it simply translates our wonder at the powers these objects have:
> those of reproduction, of reaction, of struggle against the environment.
> But these powers are the result of an interaction of the same natural
> forces as those in a pebble. Like everything around us, we human beings
> are "stardust."[8]

Still, the technological and reductionist framing of life in terms of energy or information only touches life at its fringes. Even if not mysterious,
life remains what is both most intimate and opaque to us. We have an intuitive sense of what it is to be or rather feel alive, or to participate in life
or, say, a lively conversation free of stereotypical responses, but we struggle to find the language with which to describe this primal yet ineffable
sense. Rudolf Makkreel remarks that the cultural philosopher Wilhelm
Dilthey shared surprisingly with the great rationalist philosopher Imman-
uel Kant the sense that life is "simply an ultimate behind which we cannot
go" and that both thinkers repeatedly appeal to a sense or feeling of life
to elucidate their basic concepts. For example, we do not so much know
what self-sameness or the persistence of the self through change is, as we
have experience of this real category only as it arises out of the flow of life
itself. Our categories are rooted in life, Dilthey argued, and thought cannot go beyond it: life remains unfathomable to thought.[9]

One other difficulty is the word "life" itself. Just as we have no word
that expresses the unity of day and night, the unity of life and death is not
easily expressible. But as Michel Foucault has shown, drawing from the
nineteenth-century anatomist Xavier Bichat, death is dispersed within life,
and life is usefully understood as the set of dynamic functions that resists
the death intrinsic to it. As Leonard Lawlor astutely underlines, Foucault

emphasized the permeability of life by death and the co-extensivity of life and death.[10] For just as surely as almost all life shares the Krebs cycle and DNA, all life forms possess the ability to die, and we are misled by the very word life into ignoring the presence of death in life, just as the word "day" makes it impossible to think of the night as constitutive of it.

In this book, I shall be interested primarily not in the biological but the cultural and political significance of life or death-in-life. If biological life indeed consists in the sum of functions that resists death, cultural vitalism has been the name for a volatile set of doctrines that resists the petrifaction of social forms and personalities in the name of more of this unfathomable life and urges a return to raw, unverbalized lived experience through the bracketing of the sedimented categories and schema by which we reflect on and "deaden" it. Vitalism has combined cultural critique and phenomenology in complex and contradictory ways.

* * * * *

The category of life was pivotal to the visions of some of modernity's greatest cultural theorists—Friedrich Nietzsche, Henri Bergson, and Georg Simmel. The cultural importance of vitalism to modernism has certainly not gone unnoticed. Among the more important studies have been Sanford Schwartz's *The Matrix of Modernism: Pound, Eliot, and Early Twentieth-Century Thought*, Frederick Burwick and Paul Douglass's edited collection *The Crisis in Modernism: Bergson and the Vitalist Controversy*, Herbert Schnädelbach's *Philosophy in Germany, 1831–1933*, and Mark Antliff's *Inventing Bergson: Cultural Politics and the Parisian Avant-Garde*. Vitalism has also enjoyed an afterlife not only in new works influenced by the early *Lebensphilosophs* but also in the visions of contemporary theorists such as Gilles Deleuze, Antonio Negri, Giorgio Agamben, and Elizabeth Grosz.

While life has indeed proven reducible to a form of the organization of physicochemical matter, it has retained its cultural resonance and power. In the end, neither the scientific demystification of life nor the explosive emergence of the new technological and ecological questions about life has diminished the importance of the primal feeling of life to our culture. It should be remembered that scientific vitalism enjoyed validity until the early twentieth century, and it was based on the claim that life cannot be reduced to physicochemical matter and that the emergent properties of life and the ascending nature of living systems cannot be understood in terms of mechanistic or quantitative science modeled on the operation of machines or Newtonian physics. Often strengthened by such assertions of the irreducibility or autonomy of life, cultural vitalism has had at least three enduring dimensions: life is made a tribunal before which cultural and political forms are judged as to whether they serve or frustrate it; vitalism demands a new kind of realist, albeit antiscientific, epistemology or, in other words, the development of modes of perception through which life as it actually is can be known or intuited; and vitalism underwrites a personal ethics of the affirmation of, rather than resentment against or escapism from, life.

Life remains today a term of celebration and critique; it provides a perspective and is the basis of all perspective; life marks itself by gratuitous excess and can achieve itself through asceticism; it distinguishes itself through memory and recollection but strives for novelty and forgetting; it persists through metabolism but is identified with metamorphosis and ever greater plenitude of biological and cultural forms; it defies the laws of thermodynamics but cannot achieve the promise of immortality; it both singularizes itself in many lives and transcends them as one *élan vital*; it is identified with the unexpected as well as with the teleological.

Though I shall express criticism of vitalism throughout this book, there is no gainsaying that the real personal and cultural anxiety over a Medusean petrifaction or living death has been as much the source of cultural restlessness as Martin Heidegger's heroically tragic recognition of finitude.[11] As I speak to the controversy over vitalism, what I hope to add is a more sustained discussion of the complex, constitutive relation between vitalism and racialism, including here not only its anti-Semitic forms (and Mark Antliff's work has been most illuminating here) but also its defensive black forms. This book will attempt to remedy a racial gap in contemporary scholarship on life philosophies. The main argument of this book is that one cannot understand twentieth-century vitalism separately from its implication in racial and anti-Semitic discourses and that we cannot understand some of the dominant models of emancipation within black thought except through recourse to the vitalist tradition. I am therefore interested more in the relationship between the two discourses of vitalism and racialism than I am in specific authors whose respective bodies of work cannot be confined to either vitalism or racialism, much less the area in which the two overlap. I shall argue that racialism has been central to our culture and that this racialism has often been vitalist. I critically study the fabulation of the opposition between Gentile instinct and Jewish abstraction; assertions of the more life-aware nature of black cultures by the *Négritude* poets; calls for a palingenetic ultranationalism, a kind of nationalist rebirth achieved through violence; and appeals to collective racial memory.

On the connection between memory and life, it is important to remember that the animate can be distinguished from the inanimate precisely by its mnemic force or ability to condense the past. In the course of the eighteenth and nineteenth centuries, each birth came to be seen less like the engendering of a unique work of art and increasingly understood in terms of reproduction.[12] Once distinguished by its ability to reproduce, life could be defined as that which physically embodies a physical memory by means of which the present is bound to the past. Biology opened up the possibility of defining life in terms of memory, and the discovery of a deep ethnological past in the context of social Darwinian anthropology made it possible to speculate on the memories of racial groups. Life, memory, and race came to be joined in new politically charged and vitalist discourses of race. Yet my book is not only about race: not all that is objectionable about vitalism follows from its implication in racial discourses, and that vitalism has been implicated in racial discourses does not vitiate it. I have therefore attempted to rethink vitalism— even apart from its racial implications—to explain its full cultural context. In the end, I argue that *Négritude*'s grounding of black oppositional culture in vitalism needs to be handled much more critically than it has been by the scholars who have noted the connection. At the least, I hope to show that some of the dominant models of emancipation within black thought cannot be understood except through recourse to the vitalist tradition.

The implication of vitalism in racist and anti-Semitic discourses may seem surprising. Vitalism has represented the refusal to reduce life to physicochemical reactions, but racial thinking, as James Watson has recently reminded us, depends on thinking of and reducing human group diversity to sadistically imagined physicochemical group differences. That is, modern race thinking seems to have depended on both the expulsion of life as an autonomous reality from scientific enquiry and on the definition of even the human being in terms of only physicochemical substance, the stuff of DNA. To the extent that it claims a spiritual essence to living beings or the existence of a vital principle, vitalism would seem to be irrelevant to racial discourse. I shall explore, however, the modes of implication of vitalism in racial and anti-Semitic discourses. In order to lay bare these relationships, I have also attempted in the first two chapters to achieve some analytical clarity as to what life philosophy has been, in part by clarifying just what exactly this essentially reactive discourse has been a protest against.

* * * * *

As this book will show, life has proven itself a banner and a tribunal, a call for cultural renewal and the basis of cultural critique, so that despite the dazzling new technologies of life, cultural vitalism still speaks to us. It needs underlining that modern cultural theory has centered on reassertions of Life. Yet there has been little in common between the various attempts to go beyond scientific concepts and everyday notions of life with a poetry or language or art that expresses life in its concreteness and abundance, and there has been little in common among the political movements that grounded themselves in life. Vitalism has, for example, been both biologistic and spiritualist, naturalist and theological. Just as life itself may be nothing other than a name for the various ways of living, vitalism may not have an essence but only be the name for the set of multiple doctrines and movements premised on life variously understood. Before I lay out the plan of this book, I first want to suggest here the polysemy of life.

The Romantics, M. H. Abrams argued, identified themselves and the world with organic life. With the Romantics, the call to life was a call to restore the imagination and creativity against the threat of mechanistic or associationist psychology, and the Romantics tried to return us to our intimate place in the throbbing and becoming superorganism. They insisted that the cosmos had been misinterpreted ever since Galileo and Newton in the metaphysical terms of "inert matter," "measure," "quantity," and "universal law." The great work of art was also marked by organic properties. In *Natural Supernaturalism: Tradition and Revolution in Romantic Literature*, Abrams insisted:

> Life is the premise and paradigm for what is innovative and distinctive in Romantic thinkers. Hence, their vitalism: the celebration of that which lives, moves, and evolves by an internal energy. . . . Hence [also] their organicism: the metaphorical translation into the categories and norms of intellection of the attributes of a growing thing, which unfolds its inner form and assimilates to itself alien elements, until it reaches the fullness of complex, organic unity.[13]

But later nineteenth- and twentieth-century thinkers called on different meanings of "life," which became embedded in twentieth-century discourse, and we will see their varied influences throughout the book. Karl Marx, for example, reversed the idealist relationship between consciousness and the material processes. Commonly thought to have reversed the relationship between consciousness and this real life, Marx pointed to the centrality of the metabolic relationship between human society and environment as mediated by labor's use of nature's mechanical and chemical properties for its own purposes. Alternatively, Friedrich Nietzsche scorned the reduction of life to biological fitness, maximum reproduction, and the associated utilitarian ethic and wrote lyrically of a life that sacrificed self-preservation and tolerated the enmity of the resentful for the sake of creative transcendence. Henri Bergson captured the modernist imagination by combining life, memory, a layered self, and novelty. Inspired by Bergson, the French political provocateur Georges Sorel would deepen political disillusion with mechanistic and lifeless democracy, in which the sovereign abstract citizens are indifferent to one another and held together simply by an external mechanism. As Mark Antliff has recently shown, Sorel militated for disciplined, aestheticized violence for the sake of a palingenetic and organicist ultranationalism that promised to bring (at least Gentile) people together through intuitive, organic, and mutual sympathy.[14] Oswald Spengler, the early twentieth-century cultural sensation and author of the massive *The Decline of the West*, bloviated soon thereafter about the rights of blood and instinct against the power of money and intellect and their brethren philosophies of materialism and skepticism. Racial social Darwinists insisted that as the truth of living being is bio-logical, only physical race could sustain the social bond, and society was the theater of human animals' struggle of all against all and the domination of one group or subspecies over another. Of course, fascists were not content to refer just to the social-Darwinian "laws of life." To liberate life not only in a biological but also a spiritual sense, they thought it necessary to murder and destroy those who weakened life; the projection of a dystopian racial state was what the theorist of fascism Roger Griffin has called an active biopolitical project.[15]

Vitalism also encapsulated the shift in the nature of the critiques of capitalism. In the years leading to and following the Great War, the watershed event of modernity, the terms of cultural and social criticism were decisively changed, moving from Marx and Hegel to Bergson and Sorel, Nietzsche and Heidegger. If, to use Luc Boltanski's interesting categories, critics had once focused plaintively on the poverty among workers and inequalities to raise moral concerns about the opportunism and egoism of the marketplace through the contrast of *Gemeinschaft* and *Gesellschaft*, critique decisively achieved a new register in these years. Here we find the consummation of radical conceptions of modernity as a source of disenchantment and the inauthenticity of the kind of existence associated with it. We also find a focus on oppression rather than class antagonism and an appeal to the freedom, autonomy, and creativity of human beings to transcend in the name of life reified structures, impersonal mechanisms, mechanical responses, and even themselves.[16]

Devoting a chapter to *Lebensphilosophie* in his history of German philosophy, Herbert Schnädelbach powerfully brings out the irresistible force of life discourses in the early twentieth century:

> Life is a concept used in cultural conflict and a watchword, which was meant to signal the breakthrough to new shores. The banner of life led the attack on all that was dead and congealed, on a civilization which had become intellectualistic and anti-life, against a culture which was shackled by convention and hostile to life, and for a new sense of life, "authentic experiences"—in general for what was "authentic," for dynamism, creativity, immediacy, youth. "Life" was the slogan of the youth movement, of the *Jugendstil*, neo-Romanticism, educational reform and the biological and dynamic reform of life. The difference between what was dead and what was living came to be the criterion of cultural criticism, and everything traditional was summoned before "the tribunal of life" and examined to see whether it represented authentic life, whether it "served life," in Nietzsche's words, or inhibited and opposed it.[17]

Alain Badiou has also remarked that the twentieth century posed to itself as its central question whether it was the century of life or death. Nietzsche and Bergson, he argues, posed the "main ontological question which dominated the first years of the twentieth century—What is life?" And knowledge, Badiou claims, became "the intuition of the organic value of things," while the central normative question was formulated as follows: "What is the true life—what is it to truly live—with a life adequate to the organic intensity of living?" This question, he continues, "traverses the [twentieth] century, and it is intimately linked to the question of the new man, as prefigured by Nietzsche's overman." Badiou also notes, however, that this project of vital becoming is connected to "the unceasing burden of questions of race" in ways we do not yet recognize.

As I will show in detail, it was in the name of "life" that European racism was challenged from the colonies. The structuring influence of *Lebensphilosophie* is manifest in a violent way in the Sorelian politics of the early twentieth-century Peruvian radical José Carlos Mariátegui.[18] Speaking to the colonial context in the interwar years, Michael Dash has noted that whereas in the nineteenth century national-identity movements spoke of progress, industry, and participation, the nationalist movements became "Rousseauesque in their reactions," especially against modern technology and the spirit of rationality, as they became implicated in "the horrors of World War I and North American expansionism." The politics of life inspired an invention of a radical, Caribbean poetics based on an "organicist dream of the union between man and nature."[19] The *Négritude* poets Leopold Senghor and Aimé Césaire defined colonial revolt by fusing the *Lebensphilosophs* with ethnography and surrealist experimentation. The core of their poetry, a mythical founding of a unified African people yet to be, was a deep feeling for and a deep conviction of the consanguinity of all forms of life, obliterated in modern consciousness by the positivist classificatory method focused on the empirical differences of things. But with this form of life mysticism they also inherited the political dangers of life philosophy.

As I attempt to explain the predominance of life philosophies on all sides of political contestation, I am building on and correcting a large of body of intellectual history and analysis. In *Bergson and Russian Modernism: 1900–1930*, Hilary Fink has analyzed the importance of vitalism in the development of post-Kantian aesthetic theory, which influenced Russian modernism from the Symbolists to the Theatre of the Absurd.[20] This tightly argued book ends with a provocative discussion of the political implications of vitalism for a post-Stalinist society; Fink argues that an aesthetic that foregrounds the unforeseeable creativity that is characteristic of life can only ease the transition away from a closed and planned society. Ernst Bloch, however, argued that Bergson's empty self-flourishing zest was that of the entrepreneur and that it acknowledged "no suffering, no power to change, no human depths and thus no constituent human spirit over life either." Without recognition of the possible independence of spirit from life, this vitalist "aestheticism of entrepreneurial zeal" would undermine any attempt at a rational organization of important elements of social life, casting the world into catastrophic anarchy in the name of breathless, unceasing creativity and life.[21] In fact, such debates go back to Bergson's own attempt as an official state philosopher to galvanize support in both France and the United States for his homeland in the Great War against a Germany he portrayed as mechanical and said had "always evoked a vision of rudeness, rigidity, of automatism."[22] Fink's book only underlines the continuing relevance of these old debates structured around the poles of creative irrationalism and rational (or totalitarian) planning, between *Lebensphi-*

losophie and Enlightenment reason. Indeed, the contemporary interest in network society as an emergent, autonomous, and lifelike form of organization that cannot be guided from the top down only echoes yesterday's vitalism.

* * * * *

Life and death have been central to politics in ways to which traditional political theory remains blind, and they have their roots in the birth of modernity itself. A historian of vitalism, Foucault also stressed the political ambivalence of "Life." He emphasized that once life became the catchword for the critique of the social forms of modern societies whose new practice of governmentality centered on the taking charge of life by way of continuous regulatory and corrective mechanisms, life was destined to become an oppositional political concept as well. Heinrich Heine had already written that

> Life is neither means nor end. Life is a right. Life desires to validate this right against the claims of petrifying death, against the past. This justification of life is Revolution. The elegiac indifference of historians and poets must not paralyze our energies when we are engaged in this enterprise. Nor must the romantic visions of those who promise us happiness in the future seduce us into sacrificing the interests of the present, the immediate struggle for the rights of man, the right to life itself.[23]

As Stathis Kouvelakis observes, Heine had simply declared that for "life to be a 'right' is to identify it with the irreducible necessity of taking sides in a struggle. It is also to defend an unconditional right that corresponds not to a rationally grounded categorical imperative but to the fact that certain realities are subjectively intolerable."[24]

Foucault argued that as biopower was first accumulated in gross quantities by mercantilists[25] and then later qualified, measured, appraised, and hierarchized, life could then be taken "at face value and turned back against the system that was bent on controlling it":

> It was life more than the law that became the central issue of political struggles, even if the latter were formulated through affirmations concerning rights. The "right" to life, to one's body, to health, to happiness, to the satisfaction of needs, and beyond all the oppressions or "alienations," the "right" to rediscover what one is and all that one can be, this "right"—which the

classical juridical system was utterly incapable of comprehending—was the political response to all those new procedures of power which did not derive, either, from the traditional right of sovereignty.[26]

Such revolutionary vitalism was ironically abandoned explicitly by Foucault in this very book, the first volume of the *History of Sexuality*, for a preconscious *Lebensphilosophie* of bodily experience against the exercise of biopower, critically described by Habermas as "the form of sociation that does away with all forms of natural spontaneity and transforms the creaturely life as a whole into a substrate of empowerment." For Foucault, as Habermas notes, it is always "the body that is maltreated in torture and made into a showpiece of sovereign revenge; that is taken hold of in drill, resolved into mechanical forces and manipulated; that is objectified and monitored in the human sciences, even as it is stimulated in its desire and stripped naked."[27] Deleuze drew out the implications: "When power becomes biopower, resistance becomes the power of life, a vital power that cannot be restricted by species, nor by contexts and paths of such and such a diagram. The force that comes from outside, isn't it a certain form of Life, a kind of vitalism that acts as the culmination of Foucault? Isn't life precisely that capacity to resist force?"[28] While Foucault refigured *Lebensphilosophie* as an aesthetics of self-fashioning, Giorgio Agamben—as I discuss below—has traced how *Lebensphilosophie* endured a fatal inversion and became, in the forms of bare life and biopolitics, the foundation of twentieth-century totalitarian politics.

Yet Heine's vitalist legacy endures: Enrique Dussel, a leading Latin American exponent of the philosophy of liberation, insists that naked carnal subjectivity must be the material basis of all critique:

> Through the first Frankfurt School, we discovered "materiality" in the sense of living corporeality, a question that does not frequently interest those dealing with the theoretical positions of the School: "Whoever resigns himself to life without any rational reference to self-preservation would, according to the Enlightenment—and Protestantism—regress to prehistory." . . . Materiality, for the Frankfurt School, consists of an affirmation of living corporality [*sic* (*Leiblichkeit*)] as in Schopenhauer and Nietzsche, which is vulnerable and has desires (Freud), and which needs food, clothing, and shelter (Feuerbach). This anthropological materiality, a far cry from Soviet dialectical materialism, was perceptibly close to our situation in an impoverished, starving, and suffering Latin America. In

the Southern Cone, the multitude of demonstrations shouted: "bread, peace, and work!" three necessities that refer strictly to life, to the reproduction of its corporeal content (*Leiblichkeit*).[29]

Horkheimer probably would not have accepted the postulation of life as a spontaneous power and a metaphysical entity that transcends every social determination, but Dussel does remind us, *pace* strong social constructionism, that the body is not simply infinitely elastic and whatever we wish to make of it. The living body makes its own demands and requires its own forms. It is not simply the inert ship that a person occupies as a pilot. In the context of underdevelopment, the enduring political valence of the life concept is hardly surprising. As Dussel further notes:

> It would not be possible for millions of human beings to maintain and expand communal life without institutions; this would represent an irrational return to the Paleolithic era. No. We are dealing with the "transformation" (what Marx called *Veränderung*) of those institutions which began as life-enhancing mediations but which have since become instruments of death, impediments to life, instruments of an exclusion which can be observed empirically in the cry arising from the pain of the oppressed, the ones suffering under unjust institutions. Such entropically repressive institutions exercise a power over their victims, whose power to posit their own mediations is negated, and who are thereby repressed.[30]

Yet on the other side of the North/South divide we also find a rather jejune postmodern body politics, of which Paul Rabinow has given a brilliant analysis on the basis of the distinction that Giorgio Agamben makes between *zoē* and *bios* at the beginning of his book *Homo Sacer: Sovereign Power and Bare Life*.[31]

> The term life . . . encompasses too many things. In order to gain a renewed analytical vigour it needs to be unpacked. The work of Giorgio Agamben is helpful in that light. Agamben underscores the fact that the ancient Greeks had no single term to express what we mean by the term "life." . . . Rather they had two semantically distinct terms: *zoē* and *bios*. The former referred to the simple fact of being alive and applied to all living beings (animals, men, and gods); whereas the latter term indicated the appropriate form given to a way of life of an individual and group. Philosophical discussion employed the term *bios*, since the status of life

as brute existence was simply not a question worthy of extended or political reflection . . . the quality that sets men off from other living beings is found in their moral and legal community, in that supplement of political life, intimately linked to language that elevates humans above the level of animal existence. Sheer signs of life, or brute existence, that so concern us today in our ethical reflections on such issues as "brain death," would have been incomprehensible to the Greeks. . . . Life, today, is more *zoē* than *bios*; or, perhaps more accurately, many people are perfectly willing to attempt to reshape their *bios* in terms of *zoē*. The obsession with health, fitness, pre-natal diagnosis, life-sustaining systems, living wills, plastic surgery, evolutionary moralism—altruism—aggression, male bonding, gay genes, female relational capacities, Prozac, the child within, child abuse, cloning, diet, nutrition, etc., etc., etc., are indicators of that shift. Such efforts to give a form to the sheer vital dimensions of existence and to make that form a telos embodying and articulating the true, the good, and the beautiful, is nothing if not pathetic.[32]

Concerned with the ancient Roman persona of *homo sacer*, a sacralized figure whose homicide was nonetheless (and paradoxically) unpunishable, and his resurrection in the biopolitics of totalitarian regimes, Agamben in this riveting work does not, however, explore this kind of body politics in what he does recognize as hedonistic capitalism (Rabinow's reflections are thus quite illuminating). Of the *homo sacer*, on which Agamben is focused, I am reminded, however, of Aimé Césaire's identification as early in 1939 in *Notebook of a Return to the Native Land* with bare life, which is put in state of exception and exposed to sovereign control:

As there are hyena-men and panther-men, I would be a jew-
Man
a Kaffir-man
a Hindu-man-from-Calcutta
a Harlem-man-who-doesn't vote
the famine-man, the insult-man, the torture-man you can grab
anytime, beat up, kill-no joke, kill—without having to account to anyone, without having to make excuses to anyone
a jew-man
a pogrom-man
a puppy
a beggar[33]

Both Foucault and Agamben focused on the paradox of how a politics of life comes so often to imply a politics of death. If life remains a political term, so too does death. Yet why was the thanatopolitics implied by vitalism inherently racial in character? Drawing out the implications and tensions in Foucault's biopolitics, Roberto Esposito has recently argued that the immunitary paradigm is what connects life and race as well as biopolitics and thanatopolitics:

> In order for life's biological substance to be intensified, life must be marked with an unyielding distinction that sets it against itself: life against life, or more severely, the life of one against the non-life of others. . . . Not only is life to be protected from the contagion of death, but death is to be made the mechanism for life's contrastive reproduction. The reference to the elimination of parasitic and degenerative species comes up again in all its crudeness. . . . That it concerns refusing to practice medicine on the incurable, indeed eliminating them, directly; of impeding the procreation of unsuccessful biological types; or of urging those suffering from irreversibly hereditary traits to commit suicide—all of this can be interpreted as an atrocious link in the gallery of horrors running from the eugenics of the nineteenth century to the extermination camps of the twentieth. . . . Race and life are synonymous to the degree in which the first immunizes the second with regard to the poisons that threaten it. Born from the struggle of cells against infectious bacteria, life is now defended by the state against every possible contamination. Racial hygiene is the immunitary therapy that aims at preventing or extirpating the pathological agents that jeopardize the biological quality of future generations.[34]

And while we hear the use of immunitary metaphor in the discourse about immigration, it also has an anachronistic feel to it, and the suspicion is raised that the antiracist critiques of life politics are blinding us to its new dimensions. And, indeed, in his careful claims for the epochal significance of the new biotechnologies and emergent forms of life, Nikolas Rose takes issue with Foucault's (as well as Agamben's) putatively dated ideas about thanatopolitics and argues that "exclusion and elimination are [not] the hidden truth or ultimate guarantee of contemporary biopolitics." Rose also suggests that "in contemporary political economies of vitality, to let die is not to make die."[35] While I agree with Rose that Agamben's own explanations are often allusive or metaphysical (in the sense of ahistorical) and at times overwrought, I am not so sure that thanatopolitics has not a hidden or at least foundational truth; the second Bush administration has left me struck by the centrality of incarceration policies, the continuing militarization of the U.S.-Mexico border, the prison camps at Guantanamo, and the scandalous response to the disaster unleashed by Hurricane Katrina. Life remains, contra Rose, subject to a judgment of worth by the sovereign; those who can be reduced to bare life serve as not scapegoats per se but—as Césaire anticipated Agamben—liminal persons who with impunity can be tortured, killed, or allowed to die. Using the attack against illegal enemy combatants as a spearhead, the state legitimates the creation of external or interstitial spaces outside of the rule of—though paradoxically created by—the law, and it thereby prepares its totalitarian control of society as such. Bare life becomes the hidden truth of sovereignty in spite of the neoliberal project of privatization, deregulation, and risk assumption by private individuals. Our times seem to combine the strangely familiar—an old repressive biopower and necropolitics—with strangely unfamiliar biotechnology, to which the old categories of critique are indeed unsuited, as Rose has incisively and exhaustively shown. Today, an exuberant politics of life, based on a Promethean embrace of new technologies and the insubordination of life itself, is accompanied by an uncanny thanatopolitics and cultural anxieties about death and decline.

* * * * *

I shall explore each side of this polarity about today's vitalism: on one side, the new subversive politics of life, and, on the other, the resurrection of themes of death and decline, especially as expressed in the recent film *Children of Men*. In the name of a new, postmodern, and vitalist materialism, Elizabeth Grosz has recently attempted to wean the radical politics of gender, race, and postcoloniality from social critique. True political radicalism does not promise progress "recognizable in present terms" but rather seeks to transform our wants and needs "in ways that we may not understand or control." She conceives radical politics not in terms of suffering and security but in terms of aestheticism and invention:

> It is an ongoing struggle, for it is the articulation of ways of living, an ongoing experiment in the attainment of maximal difference rather than the attainment of specific goals. It is art more than a science, a mode of intuition rather than reflection, dealing with bringing into existence new social relations, distributions of force, theoretical models, concepts, and

ethical values, the likes of which have never existed before. Politics is an invention, a labor of fabrication, of experimentation with the unrepeatable, and singular, that links it more to intuition, to artistic production and aesthetic discernment than to planning, policy, or the extrapolation of existing relations.[36]

As a radical or renegade discourse, vitalism represents protest, disillusion, and hope. Life often grounds opposition today, after the political disappearance of a subject/object of history and skepticism about the philosophy of the subject in general. Anterior to subjects and systems, this pseudosubject Life, Grosz argues, cannot be interpellated. A third way, Life disallows bourgeois stasis as certainly as it makes impossible the achievement of rational controls. In fine, Life conjures up experience, irrationality, and revolt.

In the work of Grosz, Braidotti, Deleuze, and Negri, we can see that "life" has become the watchword of today's extraparliamentary politics. Today, life is mobilized in resistance to biopower and anatomopolitics, the subsumption of capital, the market, and Empire. While bare life or the impersonal aspect of life is a denuded condition for some, it remains for others the force of creative destruction, destructive of creaturely and social forms in the name of more life. Michael Hardt and Antonio Negri captured the global imagination by declaring the irreversible victory of the insubordination of life, the power of life against the power of order, suggesting that even in its dispossessed state living labor is already autonomous: "Our innovative and creative capacities are always greater than our productive labor—productive that is of capital. At this point we can recognize that biopolitical production is . . . always excessive with respect to the value that capital can extract from it because biopolitics can never capture all of life."[37]

As an indication of how little today's vitalism resembles Spengler's protofascist paeans to instinct and blood, Rosi Braidotti has rendered it lightly and even made it a parodic version of the interwar years' *Lebensphilosophie*:

That in me which no longer identifies with the dominant categories of subjectivity, but which is not yet completely out of the cage of identity, runs with *zoē* [the generative vitality of non- or prehuman or animal life]. This rebellious component of my subject position, which is disidentified from phallogocentric premises, is related to my feminist consciousness of what it means to be an embodied female. As such, I am a she-wolf, a breeder that multiplies cells in all directions; I am an incubator and a carrier of vital and lethal viruses. I am mother-earth, the generator of the future.[38]

Here Spengler's imperial totem of the *Raubtier* (bird of prey) has been replaced by the poststructuralist totem of a she-wolf.

* * * * *

The movie *Children of Men*, on the other hand, is a brilliant cultural barometer of other contemporary ideas about life and death, vitalism and necropolitics, and it brings into focus the specifically aesthetic and cultural use of life philosophies. The movie does not give expression to the Malthusian misanthropy of overpopulation checked by pestilence and war or classical eugenic fears of a declining Western population overrun by a growing immigrant population. Rather the whole human population has become infertile. England is graying, too, but dying in relative prosperity, so the rest of the world's peoples crash the gates only to be met by sadistic deportation cops. The refugees or "fugees" are indeed nothing other than Agamben's *homo sacer*, biologically alive but legally dead persons, situated in a limit zone between life and death, in which they are no longer anything but naked life and so can be killed without the commission of homicide.[39] The English state has "the capacity to establish the state of exception, to commit those stripped of the rights of bios to . . . zones, and to torture or kill those reduced to the status of *zoē* [bare life] free from the legal restraints that would designate that murder."[40] England is indeed founded on a thanatopolitics euphemized in the official slogan that "England alone soldiers on." Refugees are legally dead, and uncooperative citizens, such as the cartoonist Jasper's once-journalist wife who has been tortured, are reduced to a catatonic state, bare life whose euthanizing is ultimately humane.

Yet even the politically alive are among the living dead as well: as a conduit of life, all human persons are dead in this post-Malthusian future. Just why humanity has become infertile is pointedly unclear, but the protagonist Theo seems not to care, because humanity has made life not worth living anyway. Only a small sect—Hope for Humanity—strives to restore fertility or even understand its causes. The unknown cause for infertility seems not to be rooted in the seductions of a work-and-consume society, in the reduction of the rearing of children to the acquiring of other expensive discretionary consumer goods in a postagricultural age and in working women's calculations not to forgo opportunities for pregnancy and childbirth. Yet humans are indeed the only sterile animals in this anti-Malthusian future. Infertility expresses ultimately a uniquely human affliction, nihilism. It is not surprising that animal spirits no longer course through only human spermatozoa and ova. That these resigned humans alone are infertile suggests that the movie is an allegory about human meaninglessness and not simply about the unintended consequences of modern technology.

Theo embodies this Schopenhauerian nihilism, an immobilizing pain about the absurdity, suffering, aimlessness, and finitude of life itself. At constant war, humanity feasts upon itself and people fight each other in their futile attempts at self-preservation. Childlessness has forced everyone to confront the fact that he or she too is fighting a losing battle against time and death. Theo carries at all times a flask of alcohol. He has fallen back in his everyday life on the expedient, ataraxia, the Stoic imperturbability of the spirit, based on a sense of the triviality of the world of the senses. Adorno defines ataraxia as "the deadening of all affects, just to be capable of living at all," which reflects the recognition of everything's utter meaninglessness and ultimate insignificance.[41] Or to put the point as Franz Rosenzweig would have: Theo "steps outside of life. If living means dying, he prefers not to live. He chooses *death in life*. He escapes from the inevitability of death into *the paralysis of artificial death*."[42]

Except for his brief respites with his cartoonist friend Jasper, Theo, drunk and affectless, is never able to affirm existence—thoroughly uninspiring and hopeless as it is. Chance, however, allows him to find meaning through the affirmation of life when he is trusted to protect the first pregnant woman in decades. Life alone elevates Theo out of despair and nihilism; it provides him a superior force to which he may sacrifice his painful and finite existence, and his sacrifice allows him to achieve, as it were, immortality: the first child born in decades is to bear his name thanks to his heroic efforts in protecting the literally African Eve, a refugee. Life has incarnated itself in a mysteriously receptive body, the body of a black woman whose speech and comportment uniquely manifest genuine affect and lightness.

One is reminded here of some Romantic conceptions of life. In the late eighteenth century, magnetism and electricity were mysterious forces; the magnetic attraction between poles was so confounding as to cast doubt on the basic categories of pressure and thrust in a scientific worldview still grounded in mechanical philosophy. Electricity was understood as a psychic force, even the source of inspiration. In this context, it was conceptually adventurous to understand life itself as a force field that operates on and through those bodies that are chemically capable of reacting to life.[43]

The *Naturphilosopher* Friedrich von Schelling had developed a theory of forces, both positive (life as field) and negative (the determinate composition of individual bodies). Frederick Beiser provides a good sense of an aspect of this Romantic conception of life, which combined a quasi-occultist belief in invisible forces with quasi-scientific analogies:

> What are these positive and negative principles? The positive principle is nothing less than the universal *ether*, the world spirit itself, which is a universal medium spread throughout creation, penetrating every individual thing, both organic and inorganic. . . . The negative principle consists in the structure and chemical composition of each organic body, which is distinctive or characteristic of that body. While this positive principle is diffused throughout nature, it only animates those bodies that are capable of fully assimilating or appropriating it. There must be something about the chemical constitution of organic bodies, Schelling says, that makes them more apt to assimilate this vital principle than inorganic bodies. . . . He likens the action of the positive principle on living things to the action of magnetism or electricity. Just as magnetism and electricity are spread throughout nature, but only act on specific bodies capable of reacting to them, so life is extended throughout all of nature and only is assimilated by bodies that react to it.[44]

In *Children of Men*, life still proves itself the only antidote to nihilism and despair, the only worthy and beneficent god. But only determinate bodies can mysteriously assimilate it. In protecting the conduit of life, Theo stands apart from the state and the immigrant resistance, legal and illegal, white and black. Vitalism has lost none of its mystery and cultural power, its force as a form of and rival for theology.

* * * * *

This book will trace the continuities and ellipses in the idea of vitalism that *Children of Men* dramatizes. Vitalism was certainly the rage in the early twentieth century, and Henri Bergson was its contemporary prophet. In this book, I explore the roots and consequences of early twentieth-century vitalism, which found its apogee in the philosophy of Henri Bergson. Bergson's vitalism receives the most sustained attention in this book, as his philosophy had central categorial importance to European aesthetics and social thought, including its disturbing racialism. It became clear to me that Bergson's mnemic vitalism is the opposite of the metaphysics of change that it is understood to be. When I embarked on this book, I was trying to understand modernist poetics in the colonial world, but I soon reached the interesting and unsettling conclusion that it was often a transposition of Bergsonian philosophy to the colonial context. I then learned that Abiola Irele had long ago argued that *Négritude* remains incomprehensible outside an understanding of its evaluation of what was living and dead in Bergson's philosophy.[43] Of all the forms of vitalism, past and present, *Négritude* has often been marginalized, even though it explored this form of thought to its most productive and exhilarating ends and crashed tragically on its limits.

I shall attempt to show how vitalism, especially as transformed by Bergson, was joined not only to European racism but also to the defensive racial forms of African and Caribbean self-understanding. As George Rousseau has emphasized, this racial dimension has often been neglected in intellectual histories of vitalism:

> The progression from Enlightenment vitalism and Darwinian evolution to the new nineteenth century social Darwinism and white man's burden places an entirely new light on the crisis of modernism . . . by suggesting that Bergsonian phenomenon as well as . . . philosophers of biology cannot be studied apart from their social contexts. In this sense, the rise of biology, the cults of vitalism, and the doctrines of racism endow modernism with contexts it can ill afford to ignore.[46]

Those contexts, not studied in Burwick and Douglass's pathbreaking volume on Bergson, are the subject of the second half of this book. In our attempts to salvage great works for our thankfully more politically correct times, we are often led to ignore how self-conscious of and self-identified with dubious ideas about race great thinkers were. The idea that racialism, especially of the crude biological variety, was constitutive in important ways (even if only in the form of necessary presupposition) of great works about the human condition and metaphysics has called forth a determined opposition ostensibly worried that such intellectual critique will make fashionable once again the third-worldism that, defined against Euro-American culture, had just resulted in Weatherman ditties for Pol Pot and Kim Il Sung. I think there is very little chance of such alignments by those now working in critical race theory. Moreover, as noted by Leon Poliakov in his introduction to *The Aryan Myth: A History of Racist and Nationalist Ideas*, published in 1974, shame or fear of being racist should not allow the West to deny "having been so at any time" and thus produce a situation in which "a vast chapter of Western thought is made to disappear by sleight of hand."[47]

My study of vitalism aims to throw new light on this legacy of Western thought. It is also important to underline a paradox at the heart of this book: that the very doctrine I criticize as racialist was in fact central at least formally to the aesthetic visions of many artists who had to create under the shadow of haughty European claims to supremacy. When the connection between European vitalism and the anticolonial writers of *Négritude* is noted, the reaction today is, quite rightly, often the condemnation of both movements. Witness, for example, the reaction to a recent, unconsciously vitalist presentation by the French president Nicolas Sarkozy to the faculty at Cheikh Anta Diop University in Dakar, Senegal, on July, 26, 2007. Sarkozy effused about the black personality, as essentialized by Leopold Sédar Senghor, as animist, vitalist, and emotional. Achille Mbembe, a theorist of postcolonialism, wrote a fiery rejoinder in which he lampooned Sarkozy's aspirations at ethnophilosophy and reminded readers of the sources of the thought of Senghor to whom Sarkozy had appealed. Mbembe's biography of ideas is masterful (only Bergson, the philosophical fount, is missing, as I shall show in my last chapter), and I quote Mbembe at length:

[Lucien] Lévy Brühl attempted to construct a system out of this accumulation of prejudices in his reflections on "the primitive" or even "pre-logical mentality." In a collection of essays about "inferior societies" (*Mental Functions in Primitive Societies* in 1910; then *Primitive Mentality* in 1921), he strove to give pseudo-scientific backing to the distinction between a "western man" gifted with reason and non-western peoples and races trapped in the cycle of repetition and mythico-cyclical time.

Presenting himself—a customary habit—as "the friend" of Africa, Leo Frobenius (whom the novelist Yambo Ouologuem virulently denounces in *Le Devoir de Violence*) widely contributed to spreading elements of Lévy Brühl's ruminations by highlighting the concept of African "vitalism." Granted, he didn't consider "African culture" the simple prelude to logic and rationality. In his eyes, nonetheless, the black man was, at the end of the day, a child. Like his contemporary Ludwig Klages (author, amongst other things, of *The Cosmogonic Eros, Man and the Land, The Spirit as Enemy of the Soul*), he considered that western man's excessive assertion of will—the formalism to which he owed his power over nature—had engendered a devitalization generating impersonal behaviour.

The Belgian missionary Placide Tempels, for his part, discoursed on "Bantu philosophy," one of whose principles was, according to him, the symbiosis between "African man" and nature. In the good father's opinion, "vital force" constituted the Bantu man's very essence. This was deployed from a degree near to zero (death) to the ultimate level of those who turned out to be "chiefs." They, along with Pierre Teilhard de Chardin, are indeed the main sources of Senghor's thought, who Henri Guaino [Sarkozy's speechwriter] endeavoured to mobilize in the effort to give the presidential discourse indigenous credentials. Is he not aware, then, of the inestimable debt that, in his formulation of the concept of negritude or in the formulation of his notions of culture, civilization and even cultural blending, the Senegalese poet owes the most racist, most essentialist and most biologizing theories of his time?[48]

The power that vitalism drew from and gave to racial and anti-Semitic discourses should make us, like Mbembe, wary of its contemporary forms and of the assumptions underlying postcolonial understandings of civilizational difference. Mine is ultimately a critical book, but I have also tried to understand what made vitalism attractive and the needs to which it spoke. This is therefore also a book that delves deeply into the history of vitalism rather than simply dismissing it as racist.

Vitalism was a rebellion against the scientism of the nineteenth century, and in the first chapter I show the many ways the vital was counterposed to mechanical forms of world disclosure and self-understanding. Even though these forms were many and their specific problems various, vitalist thinkers did not disambiguate the many kinds of "mechanism" against which they rebelled. The first chapter attempts to lend some analytical clarity here; it is a conceptual exercise. The second chapter shows that the forms of vitalism were just as varied, and I present a critical study of some of its major forms and of the criticisms to which they were subject.

The third chapter is devoted not only to overturning the image of Bergson as a metaphysician of change but also to showing how his thought— audacious, profound, and hugely influential—directed artistic and political minds alike to the edge of spiritualist nationalism and racialism. I show that modern concepts of race have in fact been defined around the axes of vitalism and organicism, and I try to provide new insight into the nature and underpinnings of racial thought, usually understood as only the expression of a vulgar, Darwinian materialism. I argue that the interwar concept of race expressed life mysticism as it incoherently concatenated three tendencies—the dynamization of the racial spirit, the biologization of the will to power, and "deep holism" in the understanding of historical forms.

The fourth chapter is a study of the poetics of life in the *Négritude* movement. By stressing, even at the risk of overemphasizing, the importance of Bergson to Senghor and Aimé Césaire, I am able to clarify and criticize their vitalist commitments. Bergson's influence was emphasized by both leaders of *Négritude*. The recovery of racial memory played on the dynamics of *duration,* Bergson's key idea; the search for racial authenticity drew on the idea of *the fundamental self*, whose recovery was central to Bergson's theory of freedom; the search for experiential modes suited to the magically real, immanent in the lived experience of the Americas was based on Bergson's *critique of the intellect*; and the figure of the poet came to replace that of the *mystic* at the center of his ethical theory. It is indeed paradoxical that colonial writers would forge weapons out of the "arsenal" of this vitalist form of European irrationalism. However, in judging their achievement, we must have a thorough understanding of their history and of the resilience of the ideas they transformed.

The perceived imminent death of the West also played an important part in the development by colonial artists of life philosophy. To see the importance of that perceived death, a simple point about historical narrative should be underscored in closing this introduction. If we evaluate the past from the standpoint of the present and if we look at the past to understand what it contributed to the extant, then as the present changes our view of the past changes: different aspects of it become important. Thus— and this is the point—the writing of an absolute history requires that history has come to an end: "The logical point here could be compared with the more dramatic but essentially similar point made by Dilthey, Heidegger and Sartre about the significance of death within the life of the individual. It is only at death, when the possibility of future action for an individual is foreclosed, that we are able to begin to give final significance to what he has done in life."[49]

For the colonial intellectuals, there was confidence that the history of the West could be finally written because it had come to an end, not in the eternal present of the Hegelian triumph but in suicidal despair, not in spite of but because of the very achievements of the Hegelian *Geist*. Indeed, those features, those moments that had contributed to this specific ending, now became those aspects of the past seen in historiography. The emergence of the individual in the Greek polis, the Reformation, the creation of the modern state—the key moments in Hegel's triumphant narrative of the *Geist* before its finalization in the Prussian state—were all reevaluated, and different aspects of the past became important. For Negritude think-ers, Descartes' ascendance was considered the pivotal point. Descartes, with whom I begin the next chapter, was seen as the key figure in the emergence of the Western ideologies of mechanism and positivism that had led to the West's self-destruction. Rationality came to be understood as a narrow ideal that, far from being value free, valorized the assumptions of the tech-nologist who aimed to master, control, and use matter.

This reconsideration of the West also ravaged the dialectical theory of history, which implied that past gains are preserved in the higher stages, so that no progress is lost and that progress is cumulative. Anything worth preserving is putatively sublated. The crisis of the West then led to both a revaluation of what had to be negatively dismissed because it had not been preserved and actual study of all that had been ignored or left outside the march of progress. This provided colonial intellectuals with the confidence to embrace both vitalist philosophies discredited within the scientific West and their own real and imagined animist traditions. The Western avant garde had already come to understand its Other in terms of the very vital-ist tropes that had proven resilient in the face of the advance of mechanical science: experimental ethnography and avant-garde movements critical of modernity's reach would locate the last vestiges of animism or an en-chanted world in the cultural practices of Europe's periphery; indeed, only the non-Western subject was understood to possess the capacity to appre-ciate the creative life force at work at all levels, from the cosmos to nature to a speck of matter. Mathematical physics had devitalized the world, and Western rationality excused the nonimaginative confusion between ani-mate and inanimate only in a child or primitive person. But the extirpation of animism from the understanding of the physical world was now under-stood as epistemological violence. The dominant forms of physicalist and reductionist understanding came into question, and the place to begin this revision—here Bergson resumed the teachings of Samuel Taylor Coleridge—was in realizing that our own consciousness and freedom could not in fact be understood "by an object language which was developed to deal literally with the natural" and lifeless world.[50] The crisis in Western self-confidence that reached its apogee in the interwar years had to lead back to what had been the often implicit foundation of the sense of civilizational superiority—the distrust in life as an ontological, explanatory, and cultural category.

In the companion study on which I am at work, *The Promise of European Decline*, I discuss these ideas and vitalism more generally as a philosophy of history; there the paradox is in Alejo Carpentier's well-known debt[51] to the reactionary Spengler's historical and cultural organicism and Césaire's less well-known critical, if not inverted, appropriation of Nietzsche's polemics on antiquarian and monumental histories to the perspective of life. In this study, however, I am more interested in life philosophy as a metaphysics and epistemology.

CHAPTER ONE

On the Mechanical, Machinic, and Mechanistic

Jacques Hymans, the author of perhaps the richest history of the intellectual influences on Senghor, has shown that Bergson and the Catholic mystic inspired by him, Charles Péguy, gave Senghor the critical framework in which to question "the ability of the capitalist, individualist and mechanized West to solve its own problems, especially after the 1929 'crash.'"[1] Both the West and its colonies understood the crisis of the interwar years as a metaphysical crisis of a cold, bloodless, and mechanical civilization. A comparison of lyrical passages from the German philosopher Max Scheler and the founder of *Négritude* is quite suggestive. Scheler wishes for the first steps into a new flowering garden for the European man, who is imprisoned in a dark environment "bounded by reason solely directed at what can be measured or mechanized."[2] Senghor writes

Let us answer "present" at the rebirth of the World
As white flour cannot rise without the leaven
Who else will teach rhythm to the world
Deadened by machines and canons?
Who will sound the cry of joy at daybreak to wake orphans and the
    dead?
Tell me, who will bring back the memory of life
To the man of gutted hopes?
They call us men of cotton, coffee, and oil
They call us men of death
But we are men of dance, whose feet get stronger
As we pound upon firm ground?[3]

Senghor's African has a lesson, then, for Scheler's "European Man of today and yesterday, who, sighing and groaning, strides under the burden of his own mechanisms."[4] For Senghor, mechanism was more a metaphysic than a technology, or, rather, Western technology was a materialization of this metaphysic. In fact, Aimé Césaire would famously and disturbingly proclaim that the putative African failure in technology revealed the existence of an alternative, superior epistemology unforgotten in the course of colonial slavery, but as Senghor suggests, such technological nihilism was itself the product of the rationalization of slaughter in the Great War.[5] In this chapter, I want to explore the anxieties underlying such a metaphysical critique. There can no appreciation, critical or otherwise, of *Négritude* without recognition of the real depth of such concerns.

Upon careful study, one finds that different kinds of anxieties and critiques have been run together, and, simultaneously, one also finds that the life principle itself, no matter how primordial a force it is often claimed to be, is in fact a reactive banner and a contrastive. Despite Gilles Deleuze's attempt to understand life as positive difference, doctrinal vitalism has ironically remained a critical project, defined less affirmatively than as the negation of its own negation—the mechanical, machinic, and the mechanistic. Indeed, Georges Canguilhem would write: "The rebirths of vitalism translate . . . life's permanent distrust of the mechanization of life. In them we find life seeking to put mechanism back into its place within life."[6] To be sure, vitalism defined itself not only in reaction to mechanisms, mechanical laws, machines, and automatons; Tom Quirk has shown how Bergsonian vitalism also provided the language of revolt against the Anglo-American naturalism of the nineteenth century.[7]

But in this chapter I shall try to make sense of the common notion that Western civilization had been mechanistic not only in terms of its methods of industrial, machinic production and, after the Great War, tools of mass slaughter but also in terms of its modes of self-understanding and being-in-the-world. Opposition to such a mechanistic worldview was expressed, as noted, both within and outside the West. Machines had become man's destructive capacity, and antimechanistic ideas resonated loudly. Yet exactly what is being decried as mechanistic is not clear. The ambiguity is compounded by the fact that over the modern period these terms—machine, mechanical, and mechanistic—have not kept in the sciences or in the arts single, well-defined, and fixed meanings. In this chapter, I have tried to achieve some clarity.[8]

To begin with, the machine certainly provides us with an image of the repetition of the same operations. Regularity issues from the setting in motion of an artificially constructed group of material parts. This repeatability can be understood in terms of how the parts hold together. Mechanical science was based on the decomposability of things, not their indivisibility or individuality. Perhaps inspired by the machinists and practical tinkerers, natural philosophers or scientists were then able to discover in nature mechanical laws that described a similar regularity and determinism with regards to gross matter in general under controlled experimental conditions, whether that matter be liquids, solids, or gases. (The strict obedience of all aspects of the material world to precise quantitative law may have also been a projection onto the messy, probabilistic world of nature or the fantasy of blind submission of subjects to the law of the sovereign.) Nonetheless, processes proved to be, more or less, predictable and therefore, interestingly enough, reliable; machines built on the principles of mechanics proved more reliable and less error ridden than the human labor they replaced. Even human behavior was thought to be mechanical, that is, perfectly proportionate and typical in response to stimuli. One of the most important literary historians of vitalist thought, Sanford Schwarz, has underlined the importance to modernist aesthetics of Bergson's refusal to understand the psyche in terms of a mechanical physis in which identical causes yield identical results as positivistically described in precise quantitative law.[9] To the extent that human behavior proved amenable to such scientistic understanding, Bergson only found comedy: "the laughable element," he wrote, consists of "a certain kind of *mechanical elasticity*, just where one would expect to find the wide-awake adaptability and living pliableness of a human being."[10]

From the example of life even at the cellular level, much less the human organism, it could be argued that the reign of the mechanical was or should not be universal: life, as a zone of indetermination, is at least potentially self-directed, unpredictable, unreliable, and even free. All phenomena, in particular living processes, did not fall, in other words, under deterministic laws. In particular, mechanics as the study of the displacement of things left as a mystery the purposes of living things. Pheng Cheah draws out the destructive conclusions of mechanical causality for our sense of the essence of organic life:

> The sensible natural world is a mechanism in two senses: the movement of different parts exhibits a blind necessity or predetermined regularity that can be expressed through mathematical formulae. More importantly, no part of nature is self-sufficient because no occurrence or movement can operate without being first set in motion by something other. . . . The spontaneous self-causality of freedom is thus antithetical to mechanical causality.[11]

The mechanical worldview does not seem to accommodate the self-directedness, change, unpredictability, and freedom of life. Against his own intent, René Descartes is widely considered to have provided a reductionist, mechanistic metaphysics.

Descartes: The Animal Machine and the Human Spirit

Scholarship on Descartes' epochal importance fills many libraries; I shall be selective here. A youthful Senghor declaimed a desire to take a machete to his work. Of course, for the *Négritude* poets, Descartes represented the ontological thesis, as already suggested, that even living organisms could be likened to the interaction of material components in a machine. Such philosophical mechanism came into existence in the sixteenth and seventeenth centuries and was associated with the concepts of atomism and "matter in motion."

Mechanism itself defies simple definition. In *The Mechanization of the World View*, E. J. Dijksterhuis never once spells out a definition but traces the changing contours of the word over close to two millennia.[12] Yet for my purposes, the story does indeed begin with Descartes, whose revolutionary attempt to study reality as moving forms of space privileged the mathematical aspects of objects—their size, shape, and quantity—and emptied the natural and nonhuman animal world of animation, internal spontaneity, and purpose. All could be reduced to matter in motion and explained in terms of mechanism. The distinctions between matter and life, as well as between automatons and volitional organisms, had all been putatively proven to be otiose. The heart was not to be understood as similar to a pump but to be in fact, as we now practically know, a pump, specifically a double pump, making the analogy to pipes for circulating water exact. Mechanics simply meant that something could be imitated by a mechanical model, the iconic model being the coordinated parts of a clock. In his *Treatise on Man*, Descartes offered this well-known, yet still astonishing, analogy:

> I suppose the body to be nothing but a machine. . . . We see that clocks, artificial fountains, mills and other such machines, although only man-made, have the power to move of their own accord in many different ways. . . . Indeed, one may compare the nerves of the [animal] machine I am describing with the pipes in the works of these fountains, its muscles and its tendons with various devices and springs which serve to set them

in motion . . . the digestion of food, the beating of the heart and arteries . . . respiration, walking . . . follow from the mere arrangement of the machine's organs every bit as naturally as the movements of a clock or other automaton follow from the arrangements of its counterweights and wheels.[13]

The ontological mechanism, introduced by Descartes, worked its way from matter to the so-called lower animals to man (whom alone Descartes had raised above the mechanical, perhaps in fear of the persecution suffered by Galileo).[14] From the seventeenth century on, there emerged iatrophysicians, those who applied the general theory of mechanical activation to organic activities as digestion, blood circulation, and respiration. Technologists succeeded in the actual construction of uncanny mechanical models of living organisms, including Jacques de Vaucanson's flute-playing android and his mechanical duck, which was seen to digest food.[15] It is not easy to lose sight of the gains to knowledge we have enjoyed due to the search for step-by-step description/explanations of how the components in living systems interact to yield outcomes or processes.[16] Yet once implicated in the mechanistic worldview, physiology was reduced to a model of "corpuscles moving at a differential rates in space and exerting pressure on one another,"[17] and the internal aspects of the organism—its teleological behavior, its ability to adapt means toward given ends—are not only left mystified, but the organism should also simply wind down, even though life is also a process of self-repair and self-equilibration. Indeed, Descartes held that "life was to death as a watch wound up was to one that had run down."[18] Self-repair and other peculiarities of life—the miracle of embryonic differentiation, the complexification of astonishingly well-adapted life forms, the maintenance of heat, and metamorphoses—had long seemed to point to the existence of an immaterial vital force. Moreover, it remained true that while a machine could be taken apart and the parts assembled again into the old machine or a new one, no such reduction of the organism was, at that time, possible without the elimination of all that was living about this configuration of material parts. The living organism appeared indivisible or living exactly because it was indivisible. Nevertheless, the metaphysical mechanists attempted to take hold of the world as if there were no difference between a running clock and a growing tree or even a creative human being.

As Henri Bergson would later emphasize, vitalism at the very least served the scientific function of underlining what escaped mechanism's world view.

The vitalists' vital principle—their *vis vitalis, vis insita, vis nervosa*—all indicated explanatory limits more than metaphysical speculation. Indeed, it seemed that scientists less explained organismic phenomena, as empirically observed, than forced them into a mechanistic picture, even though organisms from beetles to humans, which actively solve problems in their environment, could hardly be reduced to automata that simply responded mechanically to stimuli.[19] Vitalism thus seemed to save the phenomena even if did posit metaphysical substances.

Indeed, it is easily forgotten that mechanical materialists were themselves forced, against all empirical evidence, into a highly speculative theory of preformation, for without a mysterious vital substance they had no other way of understanding how life itself was reproduced. Provocatively suggesting that these same mechanical materialist views survive today in new ideas about genetic determinism, Jane Maienschein has underlined the antiempiricist premises of earlier critiques of putatively metaphysical vitalist biology:

> The most important alternative to vitalism came from materialistic preformationism. It was not much that they started with preformationism, a conviction that all body parts exist from the beginning of the organism, preformed and ready to grow. Rather, materialists or mechanists began by seeking to banish all vital forces or entities from science and to account for life, as for all of nature, in terms of matter in motion. Since explaining the generation of form from unformed, effectively homogeneous matter seemed to require some vitalistic and often teleological cause that was hence not strictly material, and since this was *a priori* unacceptable to materialists, they arrived at the conviction that form must be there from the beginning. Building the form in from the beginning had the considerable advantage, therefore, of providing an explanation without invoking non-materialistic causes. The preformationists were so guided by their grounding in materialistic assumptions that they accepted the necessity of the form's existence even if they could not see it. Not seeing should not necessarily lead to not believing; in other words, for preformationists empiricism cannot provide reliable knowledge.[20]

However, Descartes himself did implicitly locate a split between mechanism and vitalism in the difference between nonhuman animal and human life. For him, even the former—*bete-machine* (beast machine)—was understood as a mechanism, an automaton, while "man, by his abilities to reason,

Reason is a u, habst '- agu fru fr Dısatrs?

to speak a language, to direct his actions and to be conscious of his cognitions is categorically not an animal."[21] That is, only man truly acted rather than re-acted; since his actions were trigged by internal mental acts rather than only by the impingement on the senses of external objects, he alone was capable of voluntary rather than involuntary mechanical actions. The correlative automatonization of nonhuman animals led the Cambridge Platonist Henry More to complain to Descartes of "the sharp and cruel blade [with] which in one blow, so to speak [you] dared to despoil of life and sense practically the whole of race of animals, metamorphosing them into marble statues and machines."[22] The Cartesian universe split matter from mind, *res extensa* from *res cogitans*, living machines from the one particular machine capable of thought and reason. As Evelyn Fox Keller writes, the deanimation of nature implicit in its mechanization "seemed merely to enhance man's own sense of animation, an animation now, however marked more by difference from than by kinship with the rest of the natural world."[23]

It proves important that Descartes has reconfigured the inside of man. As Shanker notes, "to the eye of the outside observer, voluntary and involuntary actions look exactly the same. It is only because each individual is able to see and report on his own volitions that we are able to make the fundamental distinction between voluntary and involuntary movements, and because animals lack a similar capacity they are ruled automata."[24] There are surprising connections between the internal self, in virtue of which humanity is alone thought to be alive, and race thinking, which I (drawing from an ignored gem of a paper by the philosopher Stephen Asma) shall discuss in chapter 3. Here I can say that while it would seem that the postulation of a rational soul (or what later was called derisively "the ghost in the machine") would unify humanity in the face of manifest physical differences, the soul or nonempirical self was transmuted and multiplied in vitalist thought into distinct racial essences, invisible themselves or rather only manifest or immanent in the varied histories that the putatively different races had apparently created.

But for the next several centuries, philosophical thought would be focused on Descartes' rupturing of the Great Chain of Being with his bifurcation of automatons and human life.[25] Some would try to restore the continuum by emphasizing that man's higher capacities could be found in lesser degree down the chain, in animals and even inanimate matter; however, the opposite attempt became dominant, and the mechanical movement of matter was analogized to reflex actions and then to thought itself (or, alternatively, thought and consciousness were dismissed as epiphenomenal). In such radical elimination, the mechanists became committed to the untenable view that there is less in reality than our common-sense conceptions imply and thus exposed themselves to popular skepticism that objective reality could be so radically different from the way our concepts represent it as being. Volition, choice, and purpose were dismissed as epiphenomenal; in the words of the philosophers, metaphysics had become radically eliminativist—though in a surprising twist, the development of technology is leading to the point today where the mind is now asserting itself from the body, with the "replacement of body parts—hips, corneas, hearts, kidneys and the prospect of face transplants" and "new surgical techniques that enable a person to consciously observe doctors re-engineering their organs in real time on the operating room monitor."[26]

Yet even these technological developments do not do away with the precariousness of consciousness, for it has been the development of the impersonal market economy over the last two centuries that has pushed consciousness to the very edges of an alien world, practically where Descartes had located it. Confronting institutions that had taken on the form of an ontological reality divorced from generative social praxis, consciousness had become alienated from and powerless in the world, as Carolyn Porter shows in her pathbreaking analysis.[27] Porter finds that this violent reduction of consciousness culminated in American naturalism; it drew sustenance from the challenge to Cartesian dualism in the many audacious attempts in the nineteenth century to solve the mysteries not only of sentience but of consciousness itself in terms of brain chemistry or the kinds of energy conversion displayed by the extant paradigmatic technology, the steam engine. As J. W. Burrow shows, "complementary discourses in physics, in the chemistry of life and in neurology seemed, optimistically regarded, to promise a whole series of reductions and derivations, from the ultimate laws of physics and chemistry to the functioning of living beings."[28] But, as just suggested, the mechanism and reductionism of scientistic discourse probably would not have taken hold of the imagination without the ravenous development of an impersonal market economy. The impact was at least two fold: First, the more economic forces bore down on people, the more they felt that they had become interchangeable and functional, as if their actions had been mechanically shaped to serve purposes that were not their own in much the same way that machines are made to serve purposes. Second, machines increasingly stood astride peoples' working lives as dominating masters demanding to be fed with raw materials and dictating the movement of workers' limbs and the rhythms of their work. In this context, it was easy to push antivitalist prejudice so far that even the idea that an organism may be capable of rational decisions independent of triggered responses could be easily dismissed as pure superstition.[29] It was historical conditions, more than philosophical or scientific coherence, that gave the mechanical worldview its sense of superiority to all forms of vitalism, animism, and humanism.

Eventually, the body was reductively understood as a human motor governed by the same laws of energy and entropy as an engine in a factory. Minimal amounts of energy consumption (or nutrition) and optimal utilizations of muscular force were calculated with scientific precision. Human motion was minutely recorded through chronophotography and recomposed for maximum efficiency. This history is related by Bernard Doray in *From Taylorism to Fordism: A Rational Madness* and by Anson Rabinbach in his comprehensive *The Human Motor: Energy, Fatigue, and the Origins of Modernity*. Doray underlines that for Taylor and other exponents of scientific management "the Southern Negro" was especially suited for mechanical work, given his unthinking nature.[30] Here the identification of the "Negro" with the animal or the mechanical (and Descartes had already identified the last two) continues and radicalizes the use of the term "the mechanical" to express class contempt for repetitive, knowledge-dispossessed (rather than simply unskilled), and hence easily replaceable labor. In *Keywords*, Raymond Williams notes the early elitist prejudices against the mechanical associated with manual rather than mental labor.[31] In the course of the Industrial Revolution, the mechanical came to be defined in terms of the union of the manual workers associated with the machine. Marx defined this new machine complex as the union of an independent power source, a transmission technology, and a powered tool. In representing a huge capital investment, the machine demanded continuous operation to avoid depreciation in its value; in displacing the muscle power of adult males, the machine could devour the lives of women and children and thus depress the wage of all workers; and in having its own power source, it set the pace of work and determined the motions of labor. For these reasons, modern technology can be described as alive, as a vital machine, more alive indeed than the operatives who had become interchangeable, indiscernible, deprived thus of even haecceity, any "thisness" at all. They were at best living appendages. By so reducing the human to the mechanical, the Machine Age completed the Cartesian revolution.

The industrial economy was tied discursively to the philosophy and science of mechanical materialism: the properties of the self—freedom, consciousness, creativity, self-propulsion—came to be understood as mere delusions, or those properties, which had once been the *differencia specifica* of the human mode of being, were transposed to the inanimate world of commodities and machines. Such inversion occasionally gave modern times the form of a dark comedy. Presented, however, more often as a matter of scientific fact was a newly inverted world in which the living served the inanimate: a new world of reduction, in which humanity too is reduced to a mere part of a machine. The human person had apparently been reduced to a *persona ficta*, an automaton; only those features of character conformable to technological and economic institutions were allowed to develop, and the rest were ruthlessly eliminated. American naturalism gave this reduction of character literary—as well as racial—form, for as Colleen Lye has insightfully argued, it was around the figure of the Asian coolie that naturalism found its "archetypally non-individual agencies," "entities without independent agency" who proved "useful to naturalism's representation of modernity's dehumanization of character."[32]

This ruthless "reduction of persons to objects, incapable of responding critically or creatively to world around them" would later call into question the tenets of Enlightenment thinking—the belief in "the capacity of individuals to be guided by reason and conscience," "the confidence society would be subjected to human control," and "the conviction that history would therefore be understood in terms of a humanist teleology."[33] The rise of the mass man was in reality the etherealization of persons. Human cries against the machine rang hollow and became desperate. Bergson's philosophy would come as a relief in the age of the machine.

Drawing from Bergson, the *Négritude* poets radically challenged the mechanistic view of all-being-matter-in-motion not only in terms of its social implications but also at its ontological root; their challenge was philosophical and profound. As I will discuss in the last chapter, their animist, panphysicist response to Cartesian dualism was not first and foremost a manifesto in defense of the living mind endangered by the rise of mechanistic civilization but rather a questioning whether in fact matter was dead. If in fact matter was not lifeless, then what sense could there be in reducing life to nothing more than the organization of matter? Senghor would look into modern subatomic physics for support for the notion of the dematerialization and vitalization of matter, for even dead matter does indeed seem to exhibit a force, gravity, which is inexplicable in terms of the mechanistic worldview. The point here was to make life less of a curiosity or oddity in what was understood as a material and mechanical world.[34]

If the winds, seas, and thunder were once thought to be explicable in terms of the life within—spirits, gods, and thus intentions—mechanical philosophy turned the world upside down by seeing in life nothing more than matter in motion governed by strict natural laws. The primitive was thus one who represented "the invisible forces and realities of nature as subjects, i.e., as beings who endowed with consciousness and will power, communicate among themselves and man."[35] The so-called primitive's world was thus pervaded with the attributes of man—it was anthropomorphic. Hylozoism—the belief that life was an integral property of matter that had been a fundamental principle in Western understanding of organisms from ancient pantheism through Leibniz—was replaced by "mechanistic monism," the reduction of organisms to the category of "mere matter." Cartesian mechanism thus did not separate only free men from machines and animals but also philosophical mechanists from animists and moderns from primitives.[36] This is, of course, an important component of the cultural legacy that the *Négritude* poets inherited and reworked in the interwar years.

Frühromantiks on the Mechanical State

The vitalist resistance to mechanism was both ontological and political. Senghor's vision of African socialism was also vitalist in that it expressed the rejection of a mechanical view of political association for an organic one. Pheng Cheah has left no doubt about the importance of the organismic metaphor for the politics of both German idealism and postcolonial literature in his meticulous and stimulating book *Spectral Nationality: Passages of Freedom from Kant to Postcolonial Literatures of Liberation.*

In providing an escape from physical determinism, Cheah argues, the organism allowed the displacement of the mechanical as model of society in three ways: first, the parts and the whole are integrated in an organism such that activities of the parts serve the life of the whole just as the activity of the whole serves the life of the parts; second, the organism itself is an individual, so the parts do not come into accidental relations with each other due to the pursuit of self-interest but are intimately related as part of one and the same history; and finally, a liberated society can set for itself ends, forms, and structures just as the organism is too a "natural purposive being."[37] Postcolonial thinkers could imagine the development of their societies or polities in terms of organic features such as holism, harmony, and autonomy. Cheah argues that the living organism qua natural purposive being provided an analogue for newly liberated peoples to exercise the freedom to develop, in accordance with rational ideals, their own forms of objective culture: "like organic life forms conceived epigenetically, culture is self-impelling, self-producing, and self-generating."[38] Further, Cheah adds, "through its relation to culture, the state becomes organicized. Instead of being an artificial machine imposed upon the people, it becomes united with them into a self-organizing whole imbued with organismic causality."[39] Indeed, to the extent that the actions of a people are mediated by the culture that they themselves have created, they exhibit a heightened form of freedom from natural mechanical causality that a purposive organism exhibits in its life activities. Vitalism would of course attack such cultural mediation and urge a return to raw, natural drives. But organicism is not vitalism in this sense.

Cheah notes that the organismic metaphor has indeed been understood in myriad ways and argues convincingly that it was "not inherently pathological or reactionary as is commonly assumed." Indeed, the organismic metaphor encouraged the proposal of models intended to provide "the optimal institutional basis for the actualization of freedom."[40] There is thus a need to differentiate an organicist vitalism from an authoritarian biology in which the putative governing of an organism by the *Führer* of a life force provided an analogy for such a principle in political organization.[41]

For the German idealists, the iconic mechanical metaphor of the clock was not rejected because it failed to grasp important aspects of phenomena but because it projected a despotic political ideal similar to the totalitarian one often ascribed to them. In one of the seminal political texts of German Romanticism, the sixth of Schiller's *Letters on the Aesthetic Education of Man* (1795), Schiller describes the absolutist state as mechanical because individuals are as specialized and indifferent to one another as parts in a clock, and they have been ground down to mechanical specification, as if (to put it another way) they were rule-bound pieces upon a chessboard rather than self-motivated beings:

> Once the increase of empirical knowledge, and more exact modes of thought, made sharper divisions between the sciences inevitable, and once the increasingly intricate clockwork of the states necessitated a more rigorous separation of ranks and occupations, then the inner connection of human nature was severed too, and a disastrous conflict set its harmonious powers at variance [*entzweite*] . . .
>
> This disorganization, which first started within man by art and learning, was made complete and universal by the new spirit of government

[*Geist der Regierung*]. . . . That polyp-nature of the Greek states, in which every individual enjoyed an independent life, but could, when the need arose, grow into the whole organism, now made for an ingenious clock-work, in which out of the piecing together of innumerable but lifeless parts, a mechanical kind of collective life ensued. State and Church, laws and customs, were now torn asunder; enjoyment was divorced from labour, the means from the end, the effort from the reward. Everlastingly chained to a single little fragment of the whole, man himself develops into nothing but a fragment; with his ear filled everlastingly with the monotonous sound of the wheel that he turns, he never develops the harmony of his being, and, instead of putting the stamp of humanity upon his nature, he becomes nothing more than the imprint of his occupation and of his specialist knowledge.[42]

Michael Rosen notes that Schiller suggests here that while a society composed of such fragments may maintain itself in a mechanical repetitive fashion, it cannot in fact develop: "While Greek society had the ability to grow back when damaged, this regenerative capacity (its "polyp nature") had been lost by the merely mechanical organization of the modern state. . . . Whether (and how) the social machine can be restored to its organic nature is the fundamental problem preoccupying Romantic politics."[43]

In the name of the advances of commercial society, Schiller explicitly rejected any attempt at a return to the *sinnliche Harmonie* of the Greek polis, and unlike Nietzschean Dionysianism, the individual was not to be lost in ecstatic rapture. "In contradistinction, in a genuinely organismic conception of the political body, the relationship between whole and parts can no longer be understood in terms of the soul-limbs relationship because the parts are both cause and effect of the whole and not subordinate to it."[44] Rosen underlines the barrier that organicism posed to a bare instrumentalism: "The idea that things—actions, lives, institutions—should be both means and ends seems to be one of German Idealism's most valuable contributions to moral thought. . . . The point is willfully ignored by those . . . who, for their own polemical purposes, conflate Romantic and Idealist organicism with twentieth-century 'totalitarianism.' "[45] The machine-state metaphor is more likely than the organismic one to imply that polity is, as Cheah puts it, "different from and superior to the individual wills of which it is composed."[46]

Yet between Kant's organismic theory of cultural and individual autonomy and postcolonial literatures of liberation stands the specific organicism of the Catholic Church, which had a heavy influence on postcolonial thought. While Senghor articulated what in his time was a vibrant and courageous criticism of Soviet political theory in the name of African socialism, his vision of socialism was in fact formed in his early student days through his renewed faith in Catholicism: Senghor freely admitted a debt to the contradictory interpretations of the ultranationalist mystic Charles Péguy and the integral humanist and personalist Jacques Maritan.[47] What Senghor calls African socialism echoes Catholic corporatism. Senghor writes, for example, of African society that "the person nevertheless has a chance to develop himself and to join associations, corporations, the deliberating assemblies—for palavers. . . . Equality and the sentiment of human dignity rule there."[48] If one has read the "Quadragesimo Anno" of Pope Pius XI in 1931, Senghor's vision of African socialism is simply uncanny in its similarity.[49] Senghor's organicist vision of collectivity is more indebted to the Catholic Church's view of a fallen, class-divided society in which each estate honors its obligations than to the German idealist philosophy of freedom. Where Pope Pius XI declares the incompatibility between Christian teachings and socialism (as well as communism), Senghor would later set African socialism against totalitarian forms of Marxism. What is stunning, though, is that Senghor's African socialism has the same features as papal doctrine: the respect for individual rights, the cooperation of estates, the criticism of class struggle, the insistence that private owners of the means of production be understood as trustees designated by a higher public authority, and—of course—the central importance of spiritual cultivation and immortality, or what the young Max Horkheimer would redescribe as a spiritual indulgence meant to pacify fear about bodily suffering and finitude and euthanize the driving forces for real self-help.[50]

Having inherited the idealization of organicist or corporatist social forms from the Catholic Church, Senghor did not then address three other kinds of problems attendant to it as a political theory. First, while providing an antidote to the atomistic tendencies of modern Western society, such political organicism also implied that there were no real agonistic, much less antagonistic, relations among major social groups within African society: in Senghor's view, all conflict could easily be overcome through the village palaver. Senghor implied that African society was already a virtually harmonious organic totality. Second, the conception of human cultures as individual organisms implied a monadic conception of each, and this created a tension in *Négritude*'s thought between an advocacy of the particular and the recognition that cultures are inherently mixed. Third,

[handwritten marginalia: "≠ univ-ly?   hmm - Kt's a slightly cond/nble.   Wyshon / Survuel"]

any organic metaphor (and this applies to Kant as well) is conservative in regards to social form. Once developed, an organism maintains its boundaries throughout life; it persists in its being through metabolism. For this reason, Hegel had already insisted on the nonequivalency between political and natural forms. Michael Rosen comes to a similar conclusion about the Hegelian dialectic:

> Here again however it is the disanalogy rather than the analogy between history and organic nature that is important: as individual cultures grow and die, they do so, unlike plants, not as particular examples of a species—realizations of the essentially timeless form that they embody—but as conscious expression (and therefore, developments) of the *form itself*. Thus one culture passes on to its successors a different (and higher form), in a way that in (Hegel's view) the essentially repetitive processes of organic nature do not.[51]

In other words, dialectical development has the quasi-organism go through such radical changes in its structure that it becomes self-transcendent. However, by absolutizing a social form, the organismic metaphor implies that a crisis of social form is the crisis of society itself; the metaphor implies pessimism. For example, the crisis of interwar Europe implied to both reactionary critics and colonial subjects the decline of the West as such. In other words, the organismic metaphor seems to suppress the possibility of conscious change of the social form itself, for the organism manifests development only to the point of the realization of its basic form. Marcien Towa criticized Senghor's vision of African socialism as an attempt to entrap Africans in static, apparently authentic, African forms.[52]

For reasons such as these, it is no surprise that Deleuze and Felix Guattari insisted that critical vitalism be anorganic or nothing at all: *[handwritten: "Anorganic"]*

> This streaming, spiralling, zigzagging, snaking, feverish line of variation liberates a power of life that human beings had rectified and organisms had confined, and which matter now expresses as the trait, flow or impulse traversing it. If everything is alive, it is not because everything is organic or organized, but, on the contrary, because the organism is a diversion of life. In short the life in question is inorganic, germinal, and intensive, a powerful life without organs, a body that is all the more alive for having no organs. . . . The organism is that which life sets against itself in order to

limit itself, and there is a life all the more intense, all the more powerful for being anorganic.[53]

Today's critical vitalism is inspired not by holism and stability of form but by the anarchic practice of disorganization. Indeed, critical theory is today even more likely to be motivated by anorganic vitalism than the vision of self-conscious, dialectical changes in social form. But as anachronistic as the latter may be, the former is difficult to decipher.

Deleuzean vitalism is based on the idiosyncratic idea that concrete individual and social organisms are temporary organizations of multiple machines that produce ever new sets of connection not out of a sense of lack but for the sake of production itself. Rather than seeing the organism in Kantian terms as whole and stable as a result of its parts undergoing complex reciprocal self-formative interactions, Deleuze aims to open the organism to reconfiguration.[54] The motivation not to fix life at the level of the biological individual obviously stems from a radical questioning of whether what is alive must be entrapped in the perduring identity of a given organism, a putatively lifeless form exactly because it reifies one particular arbitrary collection of machinelike parts. For this the parts have to be autonomous, more like machine parts of a mechanism. But, against Descartes, these (sub)machines are then made productive, lifelike. Deleuze's view of life thus stands outside the traditional opposition of Cartesian mechanism and Kantian organic form and is in fact best understood less positively than as a rejection of two dominant models of life—the mechanical reductionist and the organic. Life as productive force, as itself overflowing energy and plenitude, becomes an end in itself, not the Romantic vision of complex organic unity at the level of subject or society.[55] The *telos* here is not a unified person who has won greater freedom or the realization of an emancipated society in which institutions conducive to the flourishing of well-integrated individuals have been established. Deleuze revives vitalism but not the German Idealist theory of freedom. His machinic vitalism stands opposed to organicism as well as traditional political theory. Todd May puts this well:

An organism is a self-regulating whole. Each of its parts supports others, and the whole is the harmony of those parts. We often conceive biological entities as organisms in this sense, and the wonder we feel at them comes from the balance of their living elements . . . there are no such things as organisms, at least in this sense. It is not that there is no balance among various organic parts. Often there is. It is that there is always more to the parts than their balance, a more that can express itself in other directions, with other balances, or with no balance at all. . . . One way to capture this point would be to say that we should think of biological entities not as self-sustaining organisms but as mobile machines that may connect to the environment in a variety of ways, depending on how those machines are actualized. . . . To think machinically is to consider the relations of individuals to society as only one level of connections that can be discussed. One can also discuss pre-individual connections and supra-individual connections. Moreover, these connections can be seen in their fluidity. . . . Machinic connections are productive. . . . Machines do not fill lacks; they connect, and through connecting create.[56]

The idea of "machinic parts" (what are these parts, and how can they be alive outside of the organism?) strains intelligibility. Yet this vision of productive connections by which the center of the self is forever displaced directly influenced the important post-*Négritude* vision of Édouard Glissant. Challenging a vision of Antillean life rooted in a single tradition, Glissant celebrates the rhizomatic connections made in the Antilles, where a global polylinguism has developed that draws life from minor languages, dialects, and hybrids.[57]

So far, in my attempt to disambiguate the meanings of the "mechanical" against which the *Négritude* poets and others rose, I have separated the vitalist reaction to ontological mechanism from the organicist reaction to political mechanism or atomism (and then I introduced the anorganic vitalist response to organicism). However, Bergson's most famous work, *Creative Evolution*, was a revolt against Darwinian mechanism, and the *Négritude* thinkers worked both sides of this historic battle between spiritualism and materialism, French Catholicism and English empiricism, and Bergson and Darwin, as I shall now suggest.

The Natural-Selection Machine

The Darwinian revolution raises three questions in the context of this book: Is it an expression of the mechanization of the worldview? What are we to make of Bergson's vitalist critique of Darwinian mechanism? And how were the *Négritude* thinkers' ideas about race influenced by their understanding of evolutionary theory? I shall address each question in turn.

Although the idea of an organism as a machine does not figure in Darwin's theory of evolution proper, he had seemed to give a purely mechanical explanation not only of the adaptation of organisms to their environments but also to his explanations of biodiversity, patterns of extinction, the fossil record, and many other phenomena. The forms of life were seen as ground out by the mechanism of natural selection. The environment, presumably having its properties independently of the organism, forces the organism to adapt on pains of extinction.[58]

In his study of the *Frühromantiks*—*The Romantic Conception of Life: Science and Philosophy in the Age of Goethe*—Robert J. Richards has recently challenged the mechanistic interpretation of Darwinian theory and in a way pulled the rug out *ex post facto* from under Bergson's critique.[59] Richards argues that Darwin's reluctant destruction of a providentialist view of the history of life—as the creation of a caring Creator who watches over each person and all other creatures—need not take the romance out of life. Arguing for the influence of several Romantic thinkers on Darwin's aesthetic appreciation of nature, Richards underlines that if Darwin had intended to describe nature as a vast machine, he would not have paid such careful attention to the diversity and beauty of organic form. Richards contends, "If natural processes were really machine-like ought not the products be identical—same mold, same cookie? But the products of nature, characterized by an underlying theme, to be sure, were yet infinitely varied, exuding the great abundance of life." All this, Richards insists, would "seem inexplicable on the assumption of a nature clanking along in the manner of a nineteenth-century steam engine."[60] Richards argues that Darwin characterizes natural selection as such a creative force, such a higher craftsman, that its ever-novel organic products stand apart from standardized things that result from machine processes. Moreover, each variant of a species also embodies uniqueness, the stamp of a craftlike production rather than what D. H. Lawrence would call "sordid and foul mechanicalness."[61] In short, Darwin already expressed an awareness of the creativity of the evolutionary process without the positing of an *élan vital*, *vis a tergo*, or mysterious force of impulsion. In her stimulating book on the philosophy of life, Elizabeth Grosz also paints Darwinian nature as Romantic genius: "Darwin makes it clear, indeed a founding presupposition, that time, along with life itself, always moves forward, generates more rather than less complexity, produces divergences rather than convergences, variations rather than resemblances." She further contends that "in recognizing the surprising, unpredictable, and mobile force of time on the emergence and development of the multitude of forms of life, Darwin brings the concept of the *event* to the sciences."[62]

But surely Darwin's theory is not misread in mechanical terms. Life evolves, to be sure, ever divergently and abundantly. But the process, if not the products, is a mechanical though not machinic one; the materials on which the external and indifferent law of natural selection works are merely mechanical errors in copying. And because Darwinian evolution was understood as blind and mechanical, constrained by past form and indifferently violent, critics sought an alternative cosmology based on ideas of conscious and creative evolution, especially since with the mechanical worldview came the certainty that the universe would run down as a result of inevitable solar cooling.[63] For this reason, Bergson's *Creative Evolution* was widely welcomed.

Darwin's characterization of natural selection, though entirely materialist and mechanical, does have it rise above the design capacities of man. Organisms seemed to be better designed by nonintentional forces than the actual artifacts crafted by man. But this does not follow in principle. Once life is understood not to be a mysterious force but the result of a special arrangement of matter evolved through natural selection, then there should not be any barrier to man, himself, designing life. A fully materialist biology would seem to give man the ability to understand the mechanics of life and design variations in radically new ways, as opposed to natural selection's slow modification and retention of existing organs and forms. Once life is reduced to material components organized by a natural force analogized to human breeding practice, then life should become part of the material world, which the workings of the human intellect can manipulate for any desired end.

Again: once Darwinian theory allowed for a fully materialist theory of life, there were no vitalist barriers to the human engineering of new life forms. It could be improved just like the successive designs of machines. Radical transformations became possible in principle: this was indeed the logical outcome of post-Darwinian materialist biology, if not the next step in evolution itself.

Moreover, as "an engineer designing a horse-less carriage is not obliged to retain structural features that existed solely to adapt the carriage to the horse,"[64] an engineer of life should be free to import and remove wholesale new organs in the radical structuring of wholly new life forms. Like any other form of engineering, the engineering of life need not be slow and stepwise. In fact, there seemed to be no reason why La Mettrie's program would not allow Man to do Nature or God one better through the *bricolage* of the working parts from the animal world as a whole. By the turn of the century, the mechanist Jacques Loeb would argue that the understanding of life was realized in the engineering and control of it. In a review of Louis Pauly's biography of Loeb, Richard Lewontin points out that the importation of such an ideal into biological science "was the coming together of the nineteenth-century ideological commitments to materialism, on the one hand, and an optimistic progressivism, on the other."[65] The movement that began with La Mettrie reached astounding heights with Jacques Loeb, whose dreams of engineering life were the *reductio ad absurdum* of the mechanist method.

Here, then, are the contradictions of the post-Darwinian biology. On the one hand, it gives a purely materialist and nonteleological theory of life (in particular, its marvelous adaptations) and, in eliminating the need for any mysterious life force, opens up the possibility of the engineering of organic forms; on the other hand, the Darwinian revolution conceives of natural selection, the putative mechanism of the evolutionary process, as a quasi-divine law upon which man simply cannot improve. I suggest that H. G. Wells meant Dr. Moreau to embody just that contradiction: an engineer of life who not only cannot improve on the craftsmanship of natural selection but fails miserably, producing one monstrous form after another. Wells, understanding that the engineering ideal is the logical outcome of the mechanist and materialist mode of explanation of life that his friend T. H. Huxley thought Darwin had vindicated, expressed grave misapprehension about this ideal, which Loeb would extol less than a decade after the publication of *The Island of Dr. Moreau* in 1896. That life was in essence (nothing more than) matter mechanically arranged in one special form or another and thus capable of being reengineered and rearranged was greeted with dismay even as it was implicitly recognized.

While not recoiling into vitalism, Wells hesitated at the world that mechanistic science seemed to be making possible. But his horror at Dr. Moreau is not spiritualist or idealist but thoroughly naturalist. Nature was simply an unsurpassable craftsman—Wells may well have read Darwin in Richards's Romantic terms. As a vivisectionist—and the cutting up of animals while still alive (the literal definition of vivisection) was morally tolerable exactly on the assumption that they could not feel pain as Cartesian machines—Moreau was given access to the internal organs that he could directly manipulate, but he still proved incapable of matching natural selection, which in working "daily and hourly" and "whenever and wherever opportunity offers" could effect improvements for the good of the "being which she tends."[66] For Paul Rabinow, the uncompromising critic of such antimodernist reaction, Wells's Moreau should probably be understood as a Prometheus who needs be punished for ignoring the insecurity of human works, the risks linked to artificiality, and the certitude that the initial natural situation is always incomparably better.[67] Through his science fiction, Wells arguably became the first opponent of the engineering of life from the inside out. Dr. Moreau is doubtless a more important precursor of biotechnological anxiety than the crude Dr. Frankenstein.

Dr. Moreau, however, does embody some features of Darwinized nature, features that do not fit well with Richards's theory of a Romantic Darwin. While the forms that Moreau achieves fall short of natural ones, he does proceed in the same monstrously wasteful and painful way as nature: countless "experiments," proving nonviable, die brutal deaths at the laboratory table. Moreau's laboratory, known to the island's inhabitants as the "House of Pain," allows Wells to stage the merciless cruelty that Darwin thought natural processes must inflict in order to ultimately generate beautiful and diverse organic forms. In the closing pages of *The Origins of the Species*, Darwin writes:

> Thus, from the war of nature, from famine and death, the most exalted object which we are capable of conceiving, namely, the production of the higher animals, directly follows. There is a grandeur in this view of life, with its several powers, having been originally breathed [in later editions, he added "by the Creator"] into a few forms or into one and that, whilst this planet has gone cycling on according to the fixed law of gravity, from so simple a beginning endless forms most beautiful and most wonderful have been, and are being, evolved.[68]

His theory was soon interpreted as a source of metaphysical comfort to the Victorian middle class. Racializing the Great Chain of Being, Wells would imply that Moreau's nonviable forms, intermediate between animal and man, were similar to Africans. Moreau's assistant Montgomery is alone comfortable with the doctor's liminal creations—because he had spent time in the slave ports. Out of the extinction of transitional forms the most exalted creatures were to arise.

Darwinism was read as having established that submission to the cruel, indifferent, and external laws of competition and natural selection would alone allow for transcendence. In other words, Darwinian theory, hardheaded and scientific, was in fact received as a myth, though it did not have the form of a jumble of fantasy and idle speculation characteristic of so-called primitive thought. Anthropologists would sooner understand that seemingly nonsensical primitive myths had deeper and vital significance for the lives of their respective societies than they would understand that science could become the same kind of myth that performs important work for modern culture. Yet in Bronislaw Malinowski's sense, Darwinism did indeed function as a myth that "expresses, enhances and codifies belief . . . safeguards and enforces morality; [and] vouches for the efficiency of ritual and contains practical rules for the guidance of men . . . a pragmatic charter of primitive faith and moral wisdom."[69]

Darwinism provided nature with a theory of its history but then turned nature into a charter—indeed almost a legal precedent—that inculcated a magical belief in the efficacy of ritualistic competition, sanctioned extant social relations in general, and reconciled society to its contradictions. The theory became, as the philosopher of history Ernest Gellner has provocatively argued, a God substitute. The principle of natural selection rendered superfluous "the extraneous savior, redeemer and guarantor."[70] The Victorians could understand evolution as shaped by its own internal and worldly principle of natural selection to be a directional process, which in the words of the historian of archaeological thought Bruce Trigger could, against the fate of entropy, "create order and beauty out of chaos. . . . This teleological view read a moral purpose into the cosmos itself and aligned Darwinism with teleological socio-cultural evolution of the Enlightenment and the evolutionist philosophy of Spencer."[71] Though God was banished, the world was provided with the promise of salvation, "a solution to the problem of evil, the reconciliation of man to his world."[72] History had come to be deified: collective salvation complemented or even replaced individual salvation.[73]

But this theodicy via mechanical, natural processes, though it appealed to many European and American thinkers, did not appeal to Bergson. He believed that there also had to be at work in the world some kind of spiritual or conscious force, although he never did answer of whom this force is an expression. He also did not deny the fact of evolution but argued that it could not be explained in mechanistic or Darwinian terms, and his main example—and here one is reminded of today's debates on Intelligent Design—was the amazing similarity or analogy between the wonderfully intricate eyes of vertebrates and certain mollusks. Spirit alone could be such a craftsman. Bergson thought that mechanism had been refuted by this fact that life, obviously a spiritual force, had manufactured "the like apparatus, by unlike means, on divergent lines of evolution": the vertebrates and mollusks did not enjoy a common ancestor after the development of the eye began.[74] Because Bergson argued for the presence of God in roundabout ways and left the description of God opaque, his works were put on the Index to indicate that they were likely to be misinterpreted by a lay audience.[75] But his effort was doubtless the most intellectually serious attempt in his time to rehabilitate or modernize Catholicism on the terrain of scientific inquiry.

Yet the book is also at war with itself. While Bergson intimates the existence of a spiritual life force, he also argues in an anticipation of what is today called evolutionary epistemology—that the human intellect can be understood in purely naturalistic terms as a tool that has evolved for the making of tools, not for the intuiting of a spiritual life force. Bergson seems to be arguing that humanity is at once a form, though a special one, of a creative *élan vital* curiously in and out of the world and a natural being ill equipped by biological evolution to understand the very *élan vital* of which it is alone the self-conscious form. I shall return in my chapter-length discussion of Bergson to the question of why this evolutionary product of the intellect was held responsible for the inability to intuit life.

This same incoherent mix of the spiritual and the natural can be found in Senghor, too. On the one hand, Senghor accepted the Darwinian vision of evolution as a branching tree (as well as the Bergsonian vision of life, as the One that diverges creatively into the Many), for Africans could then be considered to carry in their blood and body a valid solution to their own specific physicogeographic problems. Darwin and Bergson both broke partially with the positivist vision of unilinear evolution. Senghor (though not Césaire) even toyed with the social Darwinian idea that deep differences in racial character may well have developed in the course of evolutionary history: "*nature* has arranged things well in willing that each people, each race, each continent, should cultivate with special affection certain of the virtues of man; that is precisely where originality lies."[76] Most important and insidious was the idea that to the extent that the intellect had not developed in the course of evolution at the expense of intuition to the same degree in the African, this racial type need not self-inflict the same level of cognitive violence on itself to enjoy an intuitive and participatory relationship to the life spirit. What softens the racism is that the races are not different in kind but only in the degrees to which they possess various sensibilities, and these differences should prove complementary in

WTF IS
Klus
book?,

the construction of a civilization of the universal. As Sylvia Washington Bâ insists, Senghor did not believe races to be pure and insisted that the creative capacities of each race derived from the specific way in which it was a mixture of the same basic elements. Senghor did not think the minds of moderns and primitives were categorically different: prelogicality and logicality were admixed to different degrees in different races. However, Senghor did think these differences to be deep and natural. To be sure, the achievements of other cultures were available to all, but only through a bodily ascesis of inherited temperaments. Wilder suggests that there is a contradiction between Senghor's belief in "transhistorical racial difference" and his promotion of a framework of "cultural and biological *métissage*."[77] The key to Senghor's disturbing theory of race was the belief that differences in degree could be deep and naturalistic.

Senghor's naturalist conception of race also contradicted his spiritualist outlook. Senghor was a follower of Bergson's anti-Darwinian cosmology, based on the principle of an upwardly moving spiritual life force culminating in that civilization of the universal. Senghor's *Négritude* proves an incoherent mix of racial naturalism and spiritualism and a failed and dangerous attempt to accept the putative reality of race for the sake of humane, political ends. However, as I shall argue in the last chapter, Senghor's Bergsonian antirationalism should not be carelessly dismissed as a philosophical irrationalism. Still, developed during his student days during the interwar years in France, Senghor's *Négritude* was constructed in terms of theoretical foundations not African but Catholic, Darwinian, and Bergsonian, and, ironically, the one place where he accepts mechanical thinking is in his understanding of race differences as the outcome of natural selection in various physical settings.

The Multivalence of Mechanism and Comedy

I have tried in this chapter not to define the mechanical, the mechanistic, and the machinic but to suggest their many senses. The reaction against mechanistic forms of thought and mechanical civilization has been deeply felt but little clarified. I have tried to make some effort here. It becomes obvious, however, that there is simply no one meaning over the course of history for the mechanical or the machinic. For the Romantics, the mechanical implied a form of political statis and domination. The mechanistic signified the domination by the inanimate: the Copernican revolution and the rise of mathematical physics revealed life not only to be a very small corner of the universe indeed but also to be explicable (at least partially) in terms of the categories of pressure and thrust, matter and mechanism, thereby splitting and isolating consciousness from one's own body (now understood as an automaton) and nature, in which man had once been at home, and yielding a dualism that called forth reactions (as I shall show) in German *Naturphilosophie*, British Romanticism, and the Cult of Bergson.[78]

The mechanistic has been here allied with reductionism, the reduction of all life to matter that can be explained fully by the laws of physics and chemistry, even though our actual experience of life is not of its inertness: life does not act in the predictable manner of Newtonian billiard-ball causality until the body is in fact dead. Reductionism, in turn, has led to the importation into biology of the engineering ideal, for once life is nothing other than a special organization of inert matter there is no reason why it cannot be reengineered from the inside out.

The machinic suggested the indifference and aimlessness of nature; nature has been pictured as a machine without sentiment or feeling and natural selection as the nonteleological mechanism by which the organic is adapted despite—in Arthur Lovejoy's colorful phrasing—the monstrous wastage, universal conflict, destruction, and death of those aspirants for life recklessly produced by a teeming Universal Mother.[79] In yet another sense, the mechanistic has been conflated with determinism, the absence of novelty with everything given *ab initio*; according to the laws of conservation of matter and energy, everything is already given and fixed and only rearranged; change is thus pseudochange against a background of constancy. Nothing new ever happens in and through time; there is no truly creative evolution, to use the title of Bergson's most famous book. In this sense, mechanism is also a timeless discourse. Vitalist thinkers rebelled against the scientism that left the world appearing mechanical, cold, indifferent, *geistlos*.[80]

There is yet another sense in which machinic and mechanical have been conceived. In what A. R. Lacey has dubbed "the automaton theory of humor," Bergson found the model of making something funny in "something mechanical encrusted on the living."[81] Bergson's book *Comedy* has doubtless not always been treated with the intellectual seriousness it deserves because of its subject matter, but here we find Bergson's genius at work. For example, mimicry succeeds when one can extract a repetitious form and copy it: "to imitate someone is to detach the element of automatism which he allowed in himself. This automatically makes him funny," as "life, if it is fully alive, ought not to repeat itself. Where repetition occurs, or complete similarity, we suspect the operation of a mechanism behind the living exterior."[82] Bergson also gives the example of the jack-in-the-box—here we have a bouncing repeated movement, comedy in repetition.[83] What the jack-in-the-box allows us to grasp is the difference between mere oscillation and a living adaptation or development of character, and this helps us reflect on how too many human responses are mechanical in form. As Scott Lash and Celia Lury have written, Bergson compares mechanistic matter with vitalist memory to show that "the comic, like matter, works through cause and effect. Life, and narrative drama, for Bergson comprise memory that is constituted in the interval between cause and effect, between reaction and action. The comic is cause and effect without interval. There is a depth to narrative, to the novel, which contrasts with the surface-like nature of the cartoon and the comic."[84] As Bergson himself writes:

> The rigid mechanism which we occasionally detect, as a foreign body, in the living continuity of human affairs is of peculiar interest to us as being a kind of absentmindedness on the part of life. Were events unceasingly mindful of their own course, there would be no coincidences, no conjunctures, and no circular series: everything would evolve and progress continuously. And were all men always attentive to life, were we constantly keeping in touch with others as well with ourselves, nothing within us would ever appear as due to the working of strings or springs. The comic is that side of a person which reveals his likeness to a thing, that aspect of human events which, through its peculiar inelasticity, conveys the impression of pure mechanism, of automatism, of movement without life. Consequently, it expresses an individual or collective imperfection which calls for an immediate corrective. This corrective is laughter, a social gesture that singles out and represses a special kind of absentmindedness in men and in events.[85]

For Bergson, laughter is social therapy for action that has become mechanical, machinelike. This corrective theory seems to have influenced Mikhail Bakhtin, for whom the petrifaction of official culture and the encrusted rigidity of elites creates the stage for subversive laughter at the mechanical movements of the powerful.[86] The influence is also present in the essay on humor by Rene Ménil, one of the founders and later critics of *Négritude* and perhaps the movement's most brilliant essayist.[87] Because there is explicit reference to Freud, though in an offhanded way, Ménil's reflections are often read as psychoanalytic. But they rather reflect an attempt, similar to Bakhtin's, to rework Bergson's theory in the context of a class society. Of course, Freud did understand unconscious mental behavior as akin to something mechanical, machinelike. As Eric Santner has eloquently shown, working through is the "affect laden process of tranversing and dismantling defensive fantasies, the structured undeadness that keeps us from the opening to the midst of life and neighbor/stranger who dwells there with us."[88]

For Ménil, Césaire's humor succeeds in allowing ordinary blacks to laugh, specifically, at what is mechanical in them as a result of colonial conventions. Let me emphasize that Ménil is definitely reworking Bergson's theory here, as Bergson not only evades the roots of mechanical behavior in the class and racial divisions in society but also offers racist ruminations himself. In a discussion that is disturbing and nearly incoherent (as well as ignored in the secondary literature), Bergson wonders why "we" laugh at blacks. He emphasizes that blacks are thought of as unwashed, which to him somehow means that they are thought to be appearing in disguise. He also suggests that "we" laugh at blacks for the same reason we laugh at "clowns with red noses."[89] The joke seems to be not only that the person is simply wearing the clown suit of black skin but that he cannot take it off and regain the suppleness and freedom of the underlying active white subject. Black people are for Bergson tragic comedy.

As Ménil shows, however, Césaire's humor is specifically aimed at "cultivated Caribbean circles": their "pretension numbs the mind, solemnity curbs derision, sentimentality fossilizes feelings, and self-importance prompts stiff gestures whose ridiculousness somehow escapes" them.[90] After one of the most harrowing poetic descriptions ever written of the devastating effects of poverty on the human condition, Césaire then mocks the automatons of colonial authority:

> And neither the teacher in his classroom, nor the priest at catechism will be able to get a word out of the sleepy little nigger, no matter how energetically they drum on his shorn skull, for starvation has quicksanded his voice into the swamp of hunger (a-word-one-single-word and we-will-forget-about-Queen-Blanche-of-Castille, a a-word-one-single-word, you-should-see-this-little-savage-who-doesn't-know-any-of-The-Ten-Commandments)
> for his voice gets lost in the swamp of hunger,
> and there is nothing, really nothing to squeeze out of this little brat,

other than a hunger which can no longer climb to the rigging of his
voice,
a sluggish flabby hunger,
a hunger buried in the depth of the Hunger of this famished More.[91]

Speaking of a lighter condition, Césaire's fellow *Négritude* poet, the Guya-
nese Leon Damas, mocks rigid conformity to French manners:

French man's French,
"My mother hoping for a son well table mannered . . .
A bone is eaten with restraint and discretion
A stomach should be polite
Learns not to belch . . .
A well bred nose
Does not mop up the plate . . .
Tell me about the disaster
Tell me about it"[92]

Only the oppressed, Rene Ménil argues, are able to express and enjoy "humour's bitter laughter":

The leap of the mind that escapes the futility of everyday life is nothing
but the very surge of the life instincts tugging away at and breaking the
bridle of individual and social laziness. Humour is precisely the awareness of our diminished and restrained life as well as revenge against this
diminution and restraint and the triumphant cry of the liberated mind . . .
too bad for the marionettes we are.[93]

And this theory of humor, broadly understood, is implicit in much of our
contemporary critical theory. Judith Butler's theory of drag as parody, for
example, argues that mimicry can reveal how mechanical we are in the assumption of our identities; in a way, the drag queen reveals normal men and
women to be marionettes controlled by a gender system. The laughter elic-
ited by the drag queen may well be, in Bergson's language, "a benign force"
meant "to correct the inability to be flexible" in our gender behavior.[94]

One is also reminded here of Pierre Bourdieu. Though a steadfast and
at times tiresome defender of science and objectivity, the sociologist worked
as a Bergsonian comic, for his concept of *habitus* is meant to explain how
people, in unconsciously acquiring dispositions for the reproduction of

their own class position, come to behave as quasi-automatons, as comedic performers.[95] In "Men and Machines," Bourdieu developed his key concept of habitus to explain how in the absence of actual mechanical causality in social relations purposive agents nonetheless appear as if their actions are dictated by and in conformity with their class milieu. In other words, Bourdieu's sociology of reproduction aimed to show why it was that social life actually plays out as a Bergsonian comedy. Accused countless times of holding an elitist, if not contemptuous, view of social actors, Bourdieu was able to wave away often strident and humorless reactions against his theory of "the automatisms of the practical sense,"[96] perhaps because his sociological masterpieces were never meant as a nuanced theory of action but (maybe even unbeknownst to himself) as a comedy of class society, a risible provocation.

But if for Bergson and many others the comic parodies how living beings act as machines, as mere things, then Marx parodied market society, because in it inanimate things actually appeared to have the property of active living beings. One need only refer here to Lash and Lury's recent study, just referenced, of how brand names and logos are charged with more energy and puissance than the commodity itself ever was. Marx found the transposition of life to things as well in money, machines, and land, all of which fantastically appeared to be themselves creative sources or active factors in the production of value. Money, through the mere passage of homogeneous empty time, seems to occult itself into principal and interest; capital goods or machines, though objectified or dead labor, seem to create, as a result of the illusions of competition, new value; and land, though only a magnet for extra surplus value, seems itself a source of value and is thus paid rent. Inert things seem to be the active sources of value and are rewarded as such. The market is a *mise-en-scène* in which Monsieur Capital and Madame de la Terre do their "ghost walking." Anticipating Bergson's automaton theory of humor only to reverse it, Marx's *Capital* is properly appreciated as a comedy of bourgeois society: implicit in the theory of fetishism is an animist theory of humor rather than simple irony or parody.[97]

While Marx seems to have inverted what Bergson would later describe as comedy—comedic is the conviction that there is living activity in inert things (of course, there is tragedy in Marx as well: the working class, out of the recesses of its own being, creating a system in which they are subject to cost reductions, as if they are any other physical input to the production process)—today technological development has weakened the foundations of Bergson's theory of humor, as it depends on a contrast between human life and machines that are repetitive, regular, and unchanging in their behavior. To laugh at the mechanical in us we must have confidence that we could be more supple and attentive than machines. Yet it is that very assumption which is now likely often to be the source of comedy. I think here of an episode of the American television series *The Office*, in which two paper salesmen attempt to stave off the threat of an automated Web site to their jobs. But the workers become the object of derision as their efforts to make sales through the "human touch" of gift baskets seem contrived (suggesting here mechanical) compared to automated e-mails and databases that offer cost savings, memories of past purchases, and reminders of which supplies are probably running low (and compare here the interactive and changing replies of a Web-based bookseller's automatic recommendations with the likely mechanical interaction with the staff at a local bookshop). The machine may well seem more innovative and supple in its response than the human actor. We may now suspect life of outdated machinic behavior and expect lifelike behavior from today's machines. Today, a Cartesian intuition that we are ontologically more than machines is likely not what comedy reawakens us to but what it derides. That we are in fact machines only up to a point is not an indication of our autonomy but of our failings.

CHAPTER TWO

Contesting Vitalism

Life is a concept used in cultural conflict and a watchword, which was meant to signal the breakthrough to new shores. The banner of life led the attack on all that was dead and congealed, on a civilization which had become intellectual-istic and antilife, against a culture which was shackled by convention and hostile to life, and for a new sense of life, "authentic experiences"—in general for what was "authentic," for dynamism, creativity, immediacy, youth. "Life" was the slogan of the youth movement, of the *Jugendstil*, neo-Romanticism, educational reform, and the biological and dynamic reform of life. The difference between what was dead and what was living came to be the criterion of cultural criticism, and everything traditional was summoned before "the tribunal of life" and examined to see whether it represented authentic life, whether it "served life," in Nietzsche's words, or inhibited and opposed it.
—HERBERT SCHNÄDELBACH, 1984

Nietzsche, Lukács, Deleuze

I begin this general survey of some vitalist and antivitalist ideas with this passage,[1] already quoted in the introduction, for Schnädelbach articulates concisely the truths for which the *Lebensphilosophs* struggled. In this chapter, I shall discuss briefly some of the major voices in defense of vitalism, Nietzsche, Simmel, and Deleuze, as well as two important critics, the young Max Horkheimer and the older Georg Lukács. While I shall express skepticism of vitalism, I shall also argue against Lukács' dogmatic reaction. In my opinion, Horkheimer's sympathetic critique gets it just about right, but it is tragic as well, because even Horkheimer lost confidence in the alternative he had held to vitalism—an unorthodox Marxist mixture of Hegelian rationalism and praxis-oriented materialism. I do not think that vitalism or praxis philosophies can ground critical theory today.[2] In fact, far from grounding critical theory, vitalism is likely to resume the forms it has often had in the past—mysticism and occultism.

However, life has long been a critical category, and I shall now survey some key moments in its history. In his analysis of the life concept in German philosophy, Schnädelbach writes that the *Frühromantiks* introduced the powerful contrasts between "the dynamic and the static, the living and the dead, the organic and the mechanical, the concrete and the abstract, and intuition, perception, and abstraction and the mere understanding."[3] But

Schnädelbach insists that *Lebensphilosophie* proper originated with Schopenhauer and Nietzsche. If for Hegel the passions would incite the action by which reason would manifest itself in the process of actualizing Freedom, the two *Lebensphilosphs* insisted on a dualism between will and reason, spirit and life. The fraught recognition of Life as a blind force followed upon disillusion in Absolute Idealism, in the optimistic philosophy of history that Reason was manifesting itself in the dynamic process of actualizing Freedom. In this sense, vitalism was a pessimistic philosophy arising out of the disillusion with failed revolutions of 1789 and 1848. In his countermetaphysic, Schopenhauer had already understood reason in instrumental terms. While for Schopenhauer there was tragedy in the ineliminability of the dominance of life over spirit, Nietzsche feared that spirit, though an instrument of life, "could make itself independent and turn against life itself."[4]

As Ofelia Schutte argues, Nietzsche was able to charge the Western philosophical tradition with a resentment against life and the devaluation of "its ontological analogue, temporality," by taking something other than life "as more real or worthy than life because life's 'opposite' is thought to transcend change."[5] From Nietzsche, whose influence grew with the catastrophe of the Great War, it was learned that there was no more divisive yet effective rhetorical technique than to paint one's enemies as against life, for this seemed to protect one's own views from reasonable criticism.[6] The call for the transvaluation of all values was thus unsurprisingly issued in the name of life. Now a watchword, life would become as central to early twentieth-century thought as "nature," "God," or "ego" had been in other ages. This was indeed Nietzsche's intention: "The concept of God, devised as a rival concept to life—it makes a horrible union of everything harmful, poisonous and deceitful, the whole deathly conspiracy against life! The concept of the Beyond and the true world, invented to devalue the *only* world that there is—leaving no purpose, reason or task for our earthly reality."[7]

But it was not earthly existence Nietzsche affirmed but life and indeed only those who best embodied it. Contempt for those who did not followed. Cultural forms and types of beings were brought before the tribunal of life; since, then, the truth or value of something was judged only in terms of its service to the Will or Life or the Will-to-Power—the morally empty drive of antisocial individuals bent on conquest and domination—vitalism opened the door to the unholy trinity of irrationalism, amoral power politics, and biologistic thinking, as Schnädelbach argues. To the call for justice and Christian brotherhood Nietzsche counterposed life as the action principle of a morally unencumbered noble race. Schopenhauer's linking of the will with barbarism, even though he sought escape through asceticism, represented the originary point of fascist thought, which culminated in the Third Reich's appeals to myth and *Blutgemeinschaft*. From its origins in the salubrious Romantic critiques of mechanical materialism, vitalism descended into interwar-year philosophies of reaction and irrationalism via the seminal contributions of Schopenhauer and Nietzsche.[8] Nietzsche's notorious words from *Beyond Good and Evil* are difficult to overlook:

> Life itself is *in essence* appropriation, doing injury, overpowering the alien and the weaker, oppression, hardness, the imposing of one's own forms upon others, physical adoption and at the least, at the mildest, exploitation. . . . "Exploitation" does not belong to a corrupt or undeveloped primitive society: it lies in the *essence* of living things as a basic organic function; it is a consequence of the actual will-to-power, which is precisely the life will.[9]

In *A Study of Nietzsche*, J. P. Stern has provided us with perhaps the most unforgiving critique of Nietzschean vitalism as an unsystematic and contradictory doctrine for what became the aforementioned unholy trinity. Collecting Nietzsche's scattered pronunciamento on life, Stern has written:

> But what is life? There is no single topic on which Nietzsche has so lavished his descriptive gifts. . . . "Life" . . . is a repudiation of all that is sick and near to death, it is cruel towards all that is weak and old in us and around us, a perpetual struggle waged always at the expense of another life, it is impious toward dying and perpetually murderous. . . . The assent to life entails the destruction of morality, which is nothing but the instinct to negate life (or as the Devil remarks to the hero of Thomas Mann's *Doktor Faustus*, "Life, you know, isn't fastidious, and it doesn't give a damn for morality!"). What is life? It is being different and exercising strong preferences, being unjust and partial and limited; it is full of antagonisms, for the agreement of all is a principle hostile to life; it rests on immoral presuppositions and flourishes in danger; it is not a mere desire-to-survive, but a wanting-to-grow; it is constantly being tested by the greatest possible odds and must maintain itself against the most profound

discouragements—indeed it is that testing itself. It is not peace; on the contrary, where the antagonisms of men, classes and nations are appeased, and life's enemies—the sick, the mad, the criminal and the disinherited— are cosseted, there the pith of life declines. . . . [10]

This is, of course, a far cry from utilitarianism and pragmatism, which are grounded in an evolutionary theory that has made the struggle for life the primary fact and derived from it the value of strategies and behaviors that increase the chances of survival—adaptation, piecemeal change, and parsimonious thought by which the waste of energy could be minimized. Indeed, Nietzsche understood his thought as fundamentally opposed to what he saw as the stifling implications of Darwinian ethics. Jean Gayon has recently analyzed the deep vitalist roots of Nietzsche's reluctance to accept Darwin's "struggle for existence" and "natural selection":

What [Nietzsche] ultimately disliked in those principles was that they emphasized "conservation" rather than "augmentation." Indeed, in the literature of that time, both principles were often formulated in terms of "survival." Struggle for survival, in Darwin's own terms, meant that some individuals would "survive" and others not. As for natural selection, it meant, in Spencer's famous phrase, "survival of the fittest." To Nietzsche, such a vocabulary evoked Spinoza's *conatus* (the effort by which each being enforces the preservation of its own being), Schopenhauer's *will to live*, and the moralist's trivial "instinct of conservation." In light of his romantic view of existence and life, that was the most miserable conception he could imagine. . . . Nietzsche's contempt for the vocabulary of "conservation," "preservation," and "survival" pervaded all his writings. But it probably was best expressed with greatest crudity and clarity in the *Genealogy of Morals*, in the context of the criticisms of the "ascetic ideal": "*The ascetic ideal springs from the protecting instinct of a degenerating life* which tries by all means to sustain itself and to fight for its existence; it indicates a partial physiological obstruction and exhaustion . . . Life wrestles in it and through it with death and *against* death. The ascetic ideal is an artifice for the *preservation* of life" (*On the Genealogy of Morals*, 1887, III, 13). That passage suggested that the "struggle for existence" was a conception of "degenerated," "sickly," "unhappy," "exhausted," "weak" people. That was the exact opposite of what Nietzsche meant by "struggle for power": augmentation, increase, excess, prodigality.

We can now understand what the philosopher meant by opposing "struggle for life" and "struggle for power." For the romantic and aristocratic thinker, life could not amount to merely "surviving": "Life itself is to my mind the instinct for growth, for durability, for an accumulation of forces, for *power*" (*The Anti-Christ*, 1888, 6).[11]

There are few questions more contested in humanistic studies than the nature of Nietzsche's *Lebensphilosophie*. Centered on the concept "life" and defined in various and contradictory ways (as indicated by interpretative contestation over the meaning of the closely allied doctrine of the will to power), Nietzsche's thought speaks to vitalism as a critique of metaphysics, as a philosophy of history, and as a moral politics. As already noted, Nietzsche is easily read (and I am very sympathetic to these readings) as an apologist for crude biologistic "thinking," an advocate for the destruction of the idea of the possibility of true human progress, and an enthusiast for wanton cruelty, and I am hardly convinced that he is the most important critic of a dualistic and hierarchical Western metaphysics—soul and body, cause and effect, man and nature.[12] Yet Nietzsche's influence on postcolonial artists (Césaire, in particular) was real; the troubling presence of Nietzsche simply cannot be wished away. One is led to the seeming paradox that an irrationalist, racially biologistic, eugenicist, and counterrevolutionary philosophical school—the very school that informed imperialist self-understanding—would appeal to colonial intellectuals seeking the rebirth of their cultures.

For this very reason, I would urge that vitalism be understood as a polysemous discourse, a swerving historical discourse that has many side streets (and blind alleys) to which I shall take an appropriately peripatetic approach in this chapter. Philosophical vitalism proper is best understood, however, as running along two main parallel avenues, one beginning with Schopenhauer and Nietzsche and the other with Bergson. Nietzsche will remain an interlocutor in this and the next chapter, though I shall not offer as extensive an interpretation of his thought as I shall of Bergson's. I shall argue eventually that the tension between Léopold Senghor and Aimé Césaire can be understood in part as rooted in their different conceptions of vitalism—Senghor's conception Bergsonian, Césaire's also Bergsonian but also Nietzschean in important ways (and quite surprisingly Césaire's Dionysian Nietzsche seems similar in some respects to Heidegger's debiologized one!).

With this promissory note, let me return to the analysis of vitalism. Martin Jay has sharply summarized Max Horkheimer's critique of *Lebensphilosophie*.[13] Studying the tradition of the philosophy of life from Nietzsche to Dilthey to Bergson, Horkheimer developed a dialectical analysis thereof. On the one hand, he emphasized how *Lebensphilosophie* served as an important protest against the narrowing of reason into a rigid, abstract rationalism and therefore served to connect thought back to the needs of life; in fact, as Schnädelbach points out, Marx critiqued Hegel for theorizing a pure dialectic of concepts without much awareness of how concepts and culture arose out of the needs and pressures of life. Horkheimer also found in *Lebensphilosophie* an effort to rescue the living individual from the deadening weight of conformity and law-regulated social life. But Horkheimer also critically probed the philosophies of life. While I shall return to Horkheimer's critique of Bergson in the next chapter, it is helpful to present the gist of his critique now.

First, in grounding action and cognition in life, an ahistorical force, Horkheimer argued that life philosophies threatened to eliminate the historical aspects of social life. Second, Horkheimer found in life philosophy an evasion of the material dimensions of life; as we will see, Bergson's attempt to fashion a new mode of cognition suited to life's dynamics—intuition— was an idealist response to alienation: it could only leave the world as it was. Third, and in contradiction to this point, Horkheimer argued that a critique of the narrow view of the intellect had led to an active irrationalism in the name of life. This I will show in the next chapter, but let me quote here Horkheimer on this point:

> [Bergsonian metaphysics] expresses a protest against the fixed forms of life of bourgeois society. The same historical dynamic which constrained the originally progressive parts of the bourgeoisie before and during the war to following the economically authoritative groups also changed the meaning of activist *Lebensphilosophie* and transformed it, often against the intention of its initiator, from a progressive power of social critique into an element of contemporary nationalist ideology.[14]

Aside from Jay's characteristically perceptive summary, there is very little discussion of Horkheimer's critique of *Lebensphilosophie* in the (massive) secondary literature on the Frankfurt School. (I shall return to other aspects of Horkheimer's critique in the next chapter).[15] *Lebensphilosophie* may seem to be such an anachronistic doctrine that Horkheimer's critique of it may seem no more important today than critical theoretic investigations of the vulgar, fascist apologists Gustav Klages or Othmar Spann. Yet as Schnädelbach argues, the premises of *Lebensphilosophie* never disappeared: they were absorbed first into existentialism and have remained an integral part of German philosophical and social thought, evident in as far-reaching movements as the Greens and Paul Feyerabend's anarchistic philosophy.

Why *Lebensphilosphie* only appeared in disguise is hardly surprising. As Lukács emphasized, fascist ideologists found their pivotal conception in the antithesis of the alive and the dead: demagogy took aim at the "dead" bourgeois world of "security."

> Dead was the bourgeois world of "urbanity" and "security" with all its social and cultural categories like economy and society, secure living, pleasure and the "inner life." Dead was its thinking, both that of classical humanism and that of Positivism, since it lacked intuitions and daring and was therefore—soulless, despite all the inwardness. With its sharp attacks on everything that it called bourgeois culture, militant fascist vitalism proudly declared its allegiance to irrationalistic nihilism and agnosticism, albeit in language which appeared to give them a mythical, positive element.[16]

Paradox resulted, for vitalistic fascism made the death and destruction inherent in total militaristic mobilization the basis for "an intensely lived primordial experience (*Urerlebnis*), a kind of electric shock and spasm that breaks the continuity of experience (*Erfahrung*) that is transmitted and crystallized in culture."[17] Among the most historically important polemics against vitalism, Georg Lukács' *Destruction of Reason*[18] suffers from its unabashed Stalinism (evident in its unreasoned commitment to a rigid stagist and dogmatically progressive philosophy of history and its championing of Lysenko's biology). Lukács argued that the apparent irrationality of society—its inexplicable boom-and-bust cycle, its monetary crises, and its overproduction in the midst of plenty—suggested to intellectuals trapped within bourgeois horizons that society was guided by inaccessible and enigmatic forces, which took the name of life. Pessimism and social-scientific nihilism gave way to vitalism, and vitalism in turn sanctioned in the name of life racial imperialism as a salvific response to social crises.[19]

To Adorno and others, only political capitulation could explain how Georg Lukács, who in his early work relied on Romantic conceptions of life and subjectivist Bergsonian, against objectivist, conceptions of time could write such a polemic.[20] Yet Adorno's critique is somewhat unfair, since while in *History and Class Consciousness* Lukács did question "the value of formal knowledge in the face of 'living life,' " he had also already underlined that irrationalist vitalist philosophies were dead ends to the extent that they were based on the rejection of reason: "Whether this gives rise to ecstasy, resignation, or despair, whether we search for a path leading to 'life' via irrational mystical experience, this will do absolutely nothing to modify the situation as it is in fact."[21]

In *The Destruction of Reason*, Lukács firmly located the fundamental error from Schelling to Dilthey in the appeal to intuition as a substitute for reason, which was putatively inadequate to grasp life itself. Rational explanation seemed to privilege stasis, fixity, and mechanism. The vitalists claimed that neither Darwinian mechanism nor biochemical reductionism could explain the emergence of new and complex organic types nor the process of growth and adaptation they underwent. Not only did reason fail to explain the properties of life, but it had no access to lived experience, *Erlebnis*. Reason had to deform life in order to grasp it; life remained truly apprehensible only through intuitive or expressly irrational modes. So with this, Lukács simply dismissed the Diltheyean hermeneutic program for the study of history as an irrational focus on unrepeatable lived experience and tendentiously claimed the superiority of a causal theory of the dialectical laws of history.

Hermeneutics depended, Lukács insisted, on the substitute of intuition for reason, a substitute that could only be the privilege of a few, leading to what Lukács refers to as "aristocratic epistemology," which in an amazing leap of thought Lukács argued was later made the reserve of the *Führer* and his bully boys, who insisted that life-affirming courses of action could not be defended through reason. Reason had become the enemy, the objective study of society and economics in particular was considered an obstacle to submission to life-affirming myth, and Lukács could certainly point to Carl Schmitt as the logical endpoint of irrationalism in political and juridical theory. But Lukács suggests fantastically that the roots of such fascist apologetics are in Dilthey's philosophical reflections on the problems of historical understanding.

While recognizing that mechanical materialism left many of life's characteristics unexplained and even more that *Verstand*—understood as the abstract intellect or understanding as manifested most notably in mathematical and natural-scientific thinking—had its limit, Lukács then makes dogmatic claims for *Vernunft*, by which he meant dialectical thinking. (As noted, Lukács gave as an example of dialectical thinking Lysenko's biology, which set itself against modern genetics on ideological grounds!) Again he argues that irrationalists turn the failure of nondialectical social and natural science into nihilism. Lukács' logic is difficult to follow, but the argument seems to be that once the rational understanding of life and the scientific conquest of biology were dismissed as impossible—Hans Driesch's move from biology to metaphysics is important here, as I discuss below—the stage was set for those demagogues who could claim to understand the deeper mysteries of life and race. (It is not difficult to hear resonances in the Intelligent Design debate today of such extrapolation from life's mysteries to proof of the existence of a reactionary God whose message can only be intuited by a special few authoritative teachers.) The book ends with a long chapter on racism and social Darwinism as the culmination of irrationalism and vitalism in the imperialist epoch. To give something of the vulgar character of this work, let me quote Lukács:

> The line we are tracing does not mean that German fascism drew its ideas from this source [vitalism] exclusively; quite the contrary. The so-called philosophy of fascism based itself primarily on racial theory, above all in the form developed by Houston Chamberlain, although in so doing, to be sure, it made some use of vitalism's findings. But for a "philosophy" with so little foundation or coherence, so profoundly unscientific and coarsely dilettantish to become prevalent, what were needed were a specific philosophical mood, disintegration of confidence in understanding and reason, the destruction of human faith in progress, and credulity towards irrationalism, myth, and mysticism. And vitalism created just this philosophical mood.[22]

Prolix and at times insightful, Lukács' analysis loses contact with that which was valid in life philosophy, artificially restricts the scope of vitalism to Germany (the imperialist power that the Soviet Union did fight), and caricatures the doctrine, to wit: "In fine: the essence of vitalism lies in a conversion of agnosticism into mysticism, of subjective idealism into the pseudo-objectivity of myth."[23] It is also hardly clear that reactionary thought was any more vitalist than mechanist or that any doctrine (other than nationalist and racial thinking) played an important role in the rise of fascism, though, as I hope to show, vitalism's contribution to racialism has indeed been underestimated in the critiques of so-called scientific racism.

From this all-out war against vitalism, I want now to comment on the always confounding discourse of Deleuze, who has been the major figure for the rehabilitation of vitalist discourse and Bergsonism in particular.[24] "Thinking," Deleuze writes of Nietzsche in an almost programmatic statement, "would then mean discovering, inventing, new possibilities of life."[25] But the life Deleuze has in mind here is peculiar indeed and certainly not related to the *blut-und-boden* vitalism of fascism.[26] In his recent study, *Out of This World: Deleuze and the Philosophy of Creation*, Peter Hallward finds the core of Deleuze's philosophy in his comments on the character Rogue Riderhood in Charles Dickens's novel *Our Mutual Friend*.[27] An unsympathetic figure, Riderhood is now on his deathbed. While the doctor attempts to revive the patient, those who never had the least sympathy for Riderhood find themselves moved by the struggle for life. What they are transfixed by, however, is not Riderhood's life as such but the spark of life itself. Life is conceived here as impersonal yet singular. Catherine Gallagher had already brilliantly disclosed the strangeness of the scene:

> In this episode, life takes on its pure reality and absolute value only because it has been entirely disembodied. . . . No one . . . has any interest in the fate of the man himself. . . . When that potential and hence essential life begins to instantiate itself in the particular body of Rogue Riderhood, its value dissolves. . . . As Rogue Riderhood's suspended animation clearly shows, the curious separation of life from the body is the refinement and purification of vitality itself.[28]

For Deleuze, then, life itself refers to the process by which virtuality, this spark of life, concretizes itself into actuality or creaturely forms while ever differentiating itself; actualization is inherently creative and dynamic:

> A life has quite different features than those associated with the self—the consciousness, memory, and personal identity. It unfolds according to another logic: a logic of impersonal individuation rather than personal individualization, of singularities rather than particularities. It can never be completely specified. It is always indefinite—a life. It is only a "virtuality" in the life of the corresponding individual that can sometimes emerge in the strange interval before death. In short, in contrast to the self, a life is "impersonal and yet singular," and so requires a "wilder" sort of empiricism—a transcendental empiricism.[29]

Deleuze has painted "a picture of a complex preindividual field that allows for the generation of specific individual forms but also is not bound or reducible to those forms. They posit a field of difference that outruns any specific biological forms or individuals while still giving rise to them."[30] Alain Badiou's remarks are arresting:

> The name of Being [for Deleuze] is Life. But it is so far who does not take life as a gift, treasure or survival but as a thought returning to where every category breaks down. All life is naked. All life is denuded, abandoning its garments, codes and organs. Not that we are headed for the nihilist black hole. Quite the contrary, we stand at the point where actualization and virtualization switch places, so as to be a creator. This is what Deleuze calls a "purified automaton," an increasingly porous surface to Being's impersonal modalization.[31]

So the strange idea here is that Deleuze understands life as impersonal, denuded, and purified, yet life is the basis of creativity. As Hallward has argued: "Creation always involves an escape, a fleeing, a flight, an exit. The essential effort is always to extract a pure potentiality, a virtual creating from an actual creature, such that the former can be thought of as independent of the latter."[32] In other words, life only becomes a creative force once the self abandons creaturely forms—not out of renunciation but for the sake of new productions and configurations.

And now having revived Bergson's quasi-mystical conception of the Absolute as "the great river of life," of life itself as unceasing creative action, "an internal push" that expresses itself in nature and human activity while itself being "inexpressible,"[33] Deleuze went to radical lengths to resolve this resultant paradox: if reality is inexpressible flux, then those who have made a "discursable world" must have been themselves carved out of that flux.[34] Or again: if reality is only the seamless becoming of life, and the solidified, the inert, and the lifeless are myths or only illusory reifications or processes in the way of our radical opening to what is yet-to-come, then who exactly has conjured up this world of things?[35] The key moment of Deleuze's philosophy is his attempted resolution of this paradox; as already suggested, he attempts, in dizzying yet intriguing fashion, to dissolve selves into the flux of what he calls preindividual and presocial singularities, an impersonal plane of pure immanence in which there has not yet been any making of selves marked by the molar identifications of family, clan, or nation. The possibility of new becomings out of these singularities allows persons to free themselves of the attachments to these molar identities over and between which political conflict is staged.[36] Consequently, as with Nietzsche, vitalism commits Deleuze not to a general acceptance of life in its manifold, finite forms located on a plane of immanence but to a hierarchy of living things ranked in terms of their capacity to experience and become anything at all.[37] And this in turn implies that Deleuze's object of critique must be exactly those "forms of life that are themselves against life, life that comes from life but is inimical to it."[38]

In the end, Deleuze seeks not the imprisonment of certainty through rational introspection—*Cogito ergo sum*—but abandonment of the self for the impersonal spark of life and yet more life: *Muto ergo vivo*. Focusing on the process of changing rather than on the possessor of this change, Deleuzean vitalism implies that no one possesses life, for change cannot be predicated on something that itself is not supposed to change. Vitalism in its most radical forms implies this pro-drop syntax. Even more generally, Deleuze proposes an ontology of the infinitive verb form: things are derivative, effects of verbs; subjects and objects lose substantiality.[39] Life thus strains the intelligibility of the sentence but is not for this reason itself irrational. Nietzsche's influence on French poststructuralist thought is profound. Dismissing the subject as an illusion of grammar that sets subject apart from object, Nietzsche would write that "there is no substratum; there is no 'being' behind doing, effecting and coming: the 'doer' is merely a fiction added to the deed—the deed is everything."[40] As Nik Fox emphasizes, the insight was carried over first to the radical Lacanian idea that the Subject is not an ontological datum but rather a *meconnaissance* and then to Deleuze's idea of the subject as a mere syntactical marker. While Christopher Norris writes of Deleuze's distrust for concepts and the symbolic order because of their distortion of lived experience based in the body and its drives, affects, desiring machines, and polymorphously perverse instincts,[41] Badiou argues that Deleuze's vitalism can only lead to a devaluation of our bodily needs: because we are only what we become, the path to health must be through the lessening of the self.[42]

What seems to me awry here is not Deleuze's asceticism; Badiou's own theory of the interpellation of the subject by the event reads to me as another form of vitalism. Arguing that we only achieve subjectivity through our fidelity to an event, he seems to me to have written a philosophical mandate for the intensely lived experience that comes from an infinite responsibility to that event. According to Badiou, we are only alive in our militance.[43] Needless to say, such a constricted view of vital (and heroic-male) subjectivity can only lead to neglect of and even contempt for other aspects of our lives.

My criticism of Deleuze is that there is too little room for acknowledgment in his own ascetic, transcendent vitalism (transcendent of extant forms) of what Simmel called the tragedy of life.[44] Simmel understood life as a self-continuing process, *mehr-leben*, but he also recognized the fact that life is necessarily more than life, *mehr-als-leben*. Life does not only consume materials to preserve itself; rather, it objectifies—in fact must objectify—itself in forms of art, knowledge, and religion, which then enjoy independence from life and move in accordance with their own respective laws. The point here is that life is not only more life; it is also necessarily more than life. More life requires the social cooperation made possible by more-than-life, that is, the objectivity of cultural forms. Once these forms are created, they can follow a life of their own: we are inherited by them more than we create them; consequently we are constrained by their logics. We moderns are likely to feel alienated as well by the profusion of cultural forms beyond the capacity of any one, single individual to assimilate. This Simmel calls tragedy because the alienating forms with which we are confronted and by which we are overwhelmed originate in the deepest recesses of our own being. Yet even as there comes a point at which these forms that were to serve life now imprison it, it is not a matter of will or a personal ascesis that they can be easily transcended in the name of more life or the spark of life. We can thus compare Simmel's sober tragedy of culture to Deleuze's ever-present possibility of vitalist rupture or incorporeal transformations.[45]

Hallward also presents Deleuze as the heir of Bergsonian optimism, which (he argues) given its impatience for creation and novelty can only race out of this real and refractory world into a pursuit of personal mystical experience as an end in itself. Deleuze is critiqued as an impractical and antipolitical thinker, indeed as a mystic.[46] Yet Deleuze defended Nietzsche's critique of Schopenhauer: life should be its own enrichment, a form of Dionysian intensification. And Hallward seems to equivocate: "The actual is not creative but its dissolving can be. In keeping with Nietzsche's critique of Schopenhauer, although actual or creatural forms like the I must be replaced, such replacement should proceed in and by creative individuation as such, through the power of those individuating factors which consume them and constitute the fluid world of Dionysus."[47] Hallward argues that Deleuze's philosophy is in fact guided not by renunciation, as the power of invention is valued above all else. So what kind of mysticism is this? Does the abandonment of the category of the subject and the search for lines of flight rather than social contradictions lead necessarily "out of this world" (*Out of This World* being the provocative title of Hallward's book)? Certainly Hardt and Negri do not think so. They have celebrated the new, greater possibilities of dissolution of old, fixed identities for temporary, new becomings that concretize out of what they call the multitude and cross the old lines of nation and class. In a breathtaking display of Deleuzean concepts, they refer to the "plural multitude of productive, creative subjectivities of globalization [who] are in perpetual motion . . . and form constellations of singularities and events that impose continual global reconfigurations on the system. This perpetual motion can be geographical, but it can refer also to modulations of form and processes of mixture and hybridization."[48] The problem here does not seem to be mysticism but mystification or actually a failure to understand the tragic obdurateness of our own social forms. Deleuze, I propose, should be read next to Simmel.

The call for submission to the spark of life also creates consternation on my part. Similar to Bergson in the insistence that we cannot discover the social trajectory through intelligence but must rather simply trust ourselves to that force in nature (*élan vital*) that pushes on in unknown directions, the Deleuzean feminist Grosz promulgates a kind of anti-intellectualism: "an unpredictable leap into virtuality . . . which carries no pre-given plan or guarantee except a derangement of the present order, a movement of rendering its order insecure and replaceable. This leap into the virtual is always a leap into the unexpected, which cannot be directly planned for or anticipated, though it is clear that it can be prepared for."[49] Yet it is hardly clear what is liberating about the call for blind action, which disavows any interest in planning or consequences. Even though Deleuzean vitalism obviously does not push in politically intolerable or fascist directions, one worries about the dangers of the necessary undermining of security in an already neoliberal age for the sake of the merely nebulous.

Yet Grosz does speak inspiringly of the creative possibilities of the poststructuralist philosophy of life:

> Sexual difference and racial difference cannot be understood productively except in terms of such internal difference, for they cannot be understood as the comparison of two or more already known and measured sexes, two or more given races, categories of groups. Rather, they can be

represented only as *yet-to-come*: what woman might be, what can become, what races are in the process of becoming, which cannot be known
in advance or definitively and is incapable of being measured.[50]

To experience life is to invent it, but to invent life one must not identify—
and here John Rajchman also puts his emphasis—with the molar forms or
gross identities already found in society or reduce oneself to an individual-
ization of any pure class or race within society. Grosz understands becoming other as a collective project. Yet Deleuze enjoins one to live "a life," a
life that is impersonal yet singular. While Julien Benda famously critiqued
activist intellectuals for treason against their professional creed of abstract
humanism by militant identifications with the causes of classes, races, or nations, Deleuze too excoriates the intellectual for speaking on behalf of col-
lectivities. The grounds of opposition are different—Benda speaks in the
name of universality, Deleuze in the name of singularity—but the destructive consequence as to social classes of any sort is the same.[51] And becoming singular does a violence of its own—a devaluation of the shared life one
already has with others as a result of history and the need for organized
challenges not in the name of peoples yet to come but in the defense of
peoples who have already come to be silenced, denigrated, or excluded. For
without such collective struggle by actual minorities (not those becoming
minority in the sense Grosz articulates, and here one must mean something
more by becoming other than the advertising imperative to create ever
better-defined niche markets, for today power works not simply through
the "mechanical" reproduction of identity but vitally through the production of difference),[52] individuals may not have access to the preconditions
to invent life actually, or they may understand themselves as singular, or
having become other, without in fact having become so in terms of their
actual life chances, grounded as they are in the molar categories not yet in
fact left behind. Vitalism provides the metaphysics for the Deleuzean devaluation of classes for creative minorities yet to come.

These juxtapositions of Lukács, Simmel, and Deleuze have been meant
to suggest the political multivalence of vitalism and to guard against its
simple acceptance or rejection. I remain ambivalent about Deleuze's own
vitalism and yet am unconvinced by the criticism that he (or Simmel) is a
mystic of a peculiar kind. However, I do agree with Hallward that mysticism is an important aspect of Bergson's own thought, and my criticism of
Bergson's philosophy will be less ambivalent than my judgment of vitalism
as a whole. Having discussed the political implications of vitalism at some

length, I want to explore now the mystical and occultist roots of Bergson's vitalism as a way of introducing my critique, inspired by Horkheimer. That is, I want to move from vitalism as a form of political mystification to vitalism as an expression of mysticism.

Life as Hidden Force

What was life? No one knew. It was undoubtedly aware of itself, so soon as it was life; but it did not know what it was . . . it was not matter and it was not spirit, but something between the two, a phenomena conveyed by matter, like the rainbow on the waterfall, and like the flame. Yet why not material?—it was sentient to the point of desire and disgust, the shamelessness of matter became sensible of itself, the incontinent form of being. It was a secret and ardent stirring in the frozen chastity of the universal; it was a stolen and voluptuous impurity sucking and secreting; an exhalation of carbonic gas and material impurities of mysterious origin and composition.

—THOMAS MANN

The embryologist and philosopher Hans Driesch asserted that while most functions of the living organism may be mechanically understood, it is the development of the embryo that illustrates the essential difference between the living and the inanimate. Driesch reformed the Aristotelian concept of entelechy to account for the mystery of embryological development: it was the hidden influence of a life force that "allowed the organism to survive the vicissitudes of the environment and the embryologist's knife."[53] It was an experiment in which Driesch, having divided the embryo of a sea urchin, observed that the organism proceeded to develop into two separate beings, which demonstrated this phenomena.[54] A machine, if divided into two, would not reconstitute itself into two whole machines, but splitting an early embryo into two blastula could result in the development of two full organisms. No machine would be capable of self-reproduction in a manner analogous to living organisms. Entelechy, he argued, was the invisible hand that guides an organism to its completed form; observing this processes does not grant us direct access to the "wonder of life," as many vitalists have argued, but it does allow us access to its trace effects.

This *entelechy* began as a "system of negations." As Cassirer writes: "entelechy is abstracted from the realm of spatial existence" and "describable only in negative terms."[55] It functions in the critique of mechanism,

therefore, as a marker, pointing to explanatory limits.[56] This idea of entelechy as an indication of the limitations of the mechanists' knowledge is,
in Cassirer's opinion, the most critically interesting and useful. Yet Driesch, like so many of his contemporaries, was not content with a negative
expression of entelechy; late in life he developed into a full-fledged metaphysician, and his understanding of entelechy developed into a positive
system: "it became the *ens realissimum*, the most real of all being." The
entelechy does not exist in space, nor does it belong to nature and to natural science, but for those reasons we must see in it the actual wellspring of
nature, in which "the power and seed of all activity" discloses itself.[57] "Entelechy became a supernatural positive force; in the processes of development it was this guiding 'life force' that itself chose which of the laws of
physics would allow for the realization of a complete embryo."[58] Entelechy is the force that guides and manipulates the laws of the material
world.[59] Driesch's entelechy came to be understood as the *Führer* principle
of the organism; politics was thus able to borrow from biology what it had
possibly already lent it.[60]

Vitalism and the Occult

Driesch's flight from biology to metaphysics and politics speaks to the
marginal position of vitalist thought within the established sciences of the
late nineteenth century. The positivists in the natural sciences had little patience for fanciful postulations of a "vital agent"; it goes without saying that
many scientists dismissed as vestigial superstition and religious thinking
vitalist assertions that any unseen and insubstantial agent might influence
the material world. Scholarly works that advised of the limits of science
and institutional religion were feverishly sought; the American philosopher William James and the British theologian Evelyn Underhill were particularly popular among the occultists. Excluded from the traditional sciences, vitalist thought flourished in eclectic, turn-of-the-century bohemian
circles: the occult and alternative social movements. Madame Blavatsky's
Theosophical Society, the Rosicrucians, and Aleister Crowley's Hermetic
Order of the Golden Dawn had members who were attracted to the broad
tenets of vitalism.

Bergson's work, which represented the sharpest critique of mechanist
and materialist assumptions, earned him substantial influence in these
European circles. Bergson himself had a rather complicated and intimate

relationship with the British occult movement. He was connected to these movements through marriage: his only sister, Mina Bergson, married the notorious MacGregor Mathers, a self-proclaimed mage and founder of the Hermetic Order of the Golden Dawn. Upon their marriage, Mina changed her Latinate given name to the Celtic, Moina, in accordance with the Order's Druidism and interest in Celtic cultural revival.[61] In addition to his family relations, Bergson was also a member of the famed Society of Psychical Research, an elite organization made up of a rather impressive collection of internationally renowned scientists whose initial vocation was to investigate the unexplained laws of nature and the psychical powers latent in man. However, as occultism grew in influence and the Society of Psychical Research attracted more skeptics and scientists, its focus shifted to debunking the extravagant claims of occult leaders.

It was the literary figure T. E. Hulme who introduced Bergson's work to both the British occultist circles and the Anglo-American modernists with his introductory essays and his 1913 translation of Bergson's more rigorous *Introduction to Metaphysics*. As R. C. Grogin has shown in *The Bergsonian Controversy in France, 1900–1914*, the occultist revival created fertile ground for the reception for Bergson's philosophy, at whose center were life experiences and life forces that were not discursable but accessible solely through other more mysterious means.[62] Despite the ready availability of his work, the occultists did not engage with the details of Bergson's critique of positivism; rather, they selected key concepts to give a philosophical imprimatur to their mystical doctrines. Regardless of their superficial interpretations, however, elements of Bergson's work did indeed overlap with occultist doctrine. Himself a member of the Groupe d'Études de Phénomènes Psychiques (Group for the Study of Psychic Phenomena), Bergson's notion of the *élan vital*—the life force that permeates all things, attainable only through our higher intuitive faculties, proved to be the most important conceptual appropriation.[63] For the occultist, it became the philosophical evidence of a universal energy that surges through and connects all things—matter, humanity—with the cosmos. The *élan vital* gave substance to the occultist projections of "cosmic energy" and divine forces. The principal goal of spiritualist and occultist practices was to enable its participants to reach higher planes of consciousness; their doctrines either recommended that one delve within, maximizing one's inner experiences, as in the case of the occultist, or, as in the case of the spiritualist, that one look without, channeling this universal force through the will to manipulate the external world.[64]

Occultism and mysticism stood at odds against a society newly obsessed with consumption and production. In an industrial and commodity society, the material—that is the tangible and apparent—constituted both the ontological and the valuable. Such a world is devoid of deeper, inaccessible mysteries. It is through these spiritualist movements and not scientific debate that vitalism gained its widest exposure, so that by the interwar years the language of "life" would need little clarification to the public at large. Unlike the discourses of the sciences, the occultist and spiritualist movements attracted participants from a wide spectrum of European society. The British occult societies illustrate best this broadening. Although they were decidedly marked by the class biases of their times—top-heavy in upper-class leadership and virtually devoid of working-class participation—these societies did nonetheless manage to popularize and circulate current philosophical and social thought to the petit bourgeoisie.[65] Influential figures and freethinkers, artists and intellectuals of the burgeoning symbolist and modernist movements, Irish and Indian nationalists, and various other social and political reformers traveled through the occult circles along with the most ordinary professionals. The list of renowned members of these societies is numerous: W. B. Yeats and Bram Stoker were members of the Hermetic Order of the Golden Dawn, the composer Erik Satie was an associate of the Rosicrucians, and George Bernard Shaw and the countless Fabians, most notably Annie Besant, were followers of Madame Blavatsky's Theosophy.

The popularization of vitalism through the occult underlines a key element of vitalist discourse: the belief in inner and hidden causal factors. Occultism provided a perfect vehicle through which the contradictory vocation of a science of the "unknown" could be practiced. The rituals of these secret orders bore the mark of theatrics, performances through which the "determining essences" of men could be realized. The Golden Dawn, which reached its peak in popularity during the interwar years, focused on a mangled version of the Nietzschean will to power, offering complex and often violent rituals that claimed to endow initiates with the power to exert pure will on others. Aleister Crowley, the movement's grand mystic, embodied this fantasy of absolute control in the his doctrine of "do what thou willst." The Russian-born seer Madame Blavatsky made similar claims to influence and vision, focusing less on harnessing the will of initiates and more on tapping into the great reserves of "racial memory." What is most notable about Blavatsky's writings is her division of the world into a complex racial hierarchy, with each group laying claim to its own animating power. It is, of course, little surprise that this hierarchy and the attributes of talents mirrored the racial hierarchy of the imperial imaginary—with Europeans endowed with superior talents and the colonized with base functions. Blavatsky reserved special animosity toward native Australians, whom she viewed as a demonic race. As we shall see later, so much of even Bergsonian modernism proper emerges out of occultist interpretations and their focus on hidden substances, race memory, and intuition as a privileged state of consciousness.[66]

CHAPTER THREE

Bergson and the Racial *Élan Vital*

Pure speculation will . . . benefit by this vision of universal becoming. . . . What was immobile and frozen in our perception is warmed and set in motion. Everything comes to life around us, everything is revivified in us. A great impulse carries beings and things along. We feel ourselves uplifted, carried away, borne along by it. We are more fully alive. . . . The more we immerse ourselves in it [*durée*] . . . we participate . . . not [in] an eternity of immutability but an eternity of life.

—HENRI BERGSON, "THE PERCEPTION OF CHANGE"

While Driesch's entelechy arose out of the mystery of embryological development (how like produces like, how a horse begets a horse and not a rabbit), Henri Bergson's vitalist principle was said to underlie the creative unfolding of the multitudinous forms of life. Bergson's critique was thus aimed just as much against mechanism, the idea that sufficient computational power made the future predictable from given, initial conditions, as it was against finalism or teleology, which rendered process as fully determinate and predictable as mechanism. As much as Bergson appreciated Driesch's experimental proofs of the putative breakdown of mechanism and the model of mathematical physics in the face of life, he understood life in fundamentally different terms. In a way, Driesch opened the door for a full-scale vitalist philosophy, which reached its apogee in Bergsonism.

Bergson was also perhaps the first celebrity philosopher; his concepts were ironically taken up in the new networks of mass culture, reduced, popularized, and made consumable to an eager and easily bored middle class. Bergson's philosophical influence was unparalleled in the first quarter of the twentieth century. Perhaps no philosopher since has had the same cultural standing. Bergson's thought exists at the intersection of several lines; his most famous title was *Creative Evolution*, and his great concept was *durée*, which expands in his early books from a description of psychic life to become a cosmological postulate in his most successful work, the one with which the metaphysical arsonist ignited the modernist imagination. As a philosopher, Bergson began—and here William James hit the mark in his remarkable lecture, "Bergson and the Critique of the

Intellect"—with the problem of time implicit in Zeno's paradoxes and central to the French philosophy of his day; he wanted to show the limits of scientific and discursive thought in our understanding of ourselves as situated in the flow of time and to validate our intuitive sense of our own freedom.[1] He strove, therefore, to undermine the idea that the continuously evolving world could truly be understood in terms of laws in which identical consequences follow identical causes; moreover, he wanted to show that the world of things is not what actually is and that dematerialized flows were ontologically fundamental. As Suzanne Guerlac has shown in her masterful presentation of his ideas, Bergson grappled with the latest developments in physics to undermine the mechanistic worldview (the breakdown of the atomistic and corpuscular ontology; the collapse of the commonsensical, mechanistic worldview in the face of the unpredictability and discursive intractability of the subatomic world; and the reluctant and incomplete discovery of the irreversible flow of time).[2] Because his thought reintroduced the Pauline distinction between an illusory world of solid bodies (including, of course, the flesh) and the impalpable yet truer spiritual world, Bergson spoke powerfully to the crisis of the Catholic Church in the Age of Positivism, appealing to those exploring spirituality in the nontraditional, occult movements of his time. Ongoing political crises turned his name into a palimpsest: he was put on the Index, calumnied by Action Française, claimed by reformers in the Catholic Church, invoked by syndicalists and fascists, and cited by defenders of the new physics and champions of the idealist reaction against science.

The diversity of uses to which this Bergsonian vision was put—anarchosyndicalism, mysticism and occultism, aesthetic modernism, fascism, pacifism, literary subjectivism, environmentalism, scientism and antiscientism, etc.—astounds.[3] As Judith Shklar noted, while the syndicalists called themselves the "Bergsonian left," the meaning of the term was even unclear to them. Through their main organ, *Le Mouvement Socialiste*, they sent out a questionnaire to leading philosophers asking their views on the political implications of Bergsonism. "There was no trace of agreement among the correspondents. Some answered that there was no political meaning to be found, others saw a trend towards some religion of feeling or towards Catholicism in his ideas. Even the greatest of the syndicalist thinkers, Georges Sorel, an avowed 'Bergsonian,' admitted at one point that his real debt to the philosopher was limited to borrowing his 'phrases.'"[4]

In stating concisely the core of the Bergsonian vision of intuition, creative process, spiritual life, and metaphysical oneness, Richard Lehan also makes it clear how and why Bergson would and could be claimed by so many conflicting parties:

> Intuitive intelligence is thus the highest form of cognitive power as well as the force which drives man ahead of it. When the weight of this force carries the totality of the past to the moment, we have memory—and the creation of both the universe and the self in Bergson is inseparable from the functioning of intuition and memory. Thus, for Bergson, mind both directs and accesses life. With this idea he undid the notions of mechanism and teleology, undercut both Enlightenment and Darwinian assumptions, gave weight to the modernist belief that art is the highest function of our activity, and helped establish the modernist belief that the universe is inseparable from mind and that the self is created out of memory. If the moderns did not have Bergson, they would have had to invent him.[5]

I shall argue for a more critical perspective on Bergson's thought and vitalist philosophies in general, as I believe they have generally unpleasant implications, even though almost all of the work on Bergson today is sympathetic. And indeed Bergson himself was most often sympathetic. Though he did not join Emile Durkheim in the campaign for Dreyfus, he did condemn the verdict; he also fashioned his antimechanistic philosophy as the expression of a moderate and open ethos of good sense congenial to the Third Republic. He would also work for international peace. But he was not the best practitioner of his own thought; Sorel was ultimately convinced that Bergson had not understood the mainsprings and implications of his own thought. Just as Heidegger's philosophy cannot be condemned simply on the basis of his political commitments, neither can Bergson's philosophy be embraced in light of his own generally humane and moderate politics.

As I shall argue, Bergson's epistemological thought is indeed at times insightful but collapses into irrationalism, his philosophy actually discounts rather than affirms novelty, and he opened the door to the spiritualist racialism to which European thought succumbed in the interwar years. Bergson's two most famous disciples, who wrote admiring and lucid introductions to their master's thought, did not draw emancipatory political conclusions from his thought. Eduard Le Roy drew from Bergson to rehabilitate a reactionary Catholicism through the combination of Thomism and idealism of Berkeley. Jacques Chevalier, under the Vichy government, was put in charge of the Aryanization of French education. I shall argue that they both were not unfaithful to their master. This chapter circles around Bergson and some of his disciples and intends to encourage a more critical contemporary discussion of what I shall characterize as Bergson's mnemic vitalism. However, I shall be less concerned with the actual historical reception of Bergson's ideas than with its conceptual relations to irrationalism and racialism (including its anti-Semitic forms).[6]

I must also underline that I do not attempt to offer a comprehensive analysis of Bergson's thought. First, I do not evaluate how prescient Bergson's critique of the physics of his time proved to be. It may be—as Suzanne Guerlac argues—that Bergson was precocious in grasping the implications of statistical thermodynamics or subatomic physics or that his metaphysics proved to be less an obstacle to the assimilation of the latest advances in physics than the image of science dominant in his time. One also finds such a defense of Bergson in the second half of Milič Čapek's *Bergson and Modern Physics*. Second, I do not focus on Bergson's dualism between a brain, which serves as a filter for perception of images, and an immortal memory, or, to put it another way, his argument for a difference in kind between perception and memory in light of today's cognitive science. Bergson's curious theory of a spiritual memory can also be understood in terms of its cultural implications, and that is what I do here. Third, I do not comment on the scientific importance of Bergson's critique of Darwinism. Surely it did not reflect scientific bad faith to challenge what is today called ultra-Darwinism by pointing to the organism's own active creation of the environment to which it then was adjusted by natural selection, though Bergson does more than that. In what is one of the more careful and open-minded sympathetic studies of Bergson, John Mullarkey has argued that Bergson had already outlined a view of life in terms of energetics as a far-from-equilibrium structure that takes up and dissipates energy in order to maintain structural integrity.[7] And while Bergson does indeed speak in terms of the accumulation and release of energy flows in forms of life whose structures are entirely contingent upon the kind of solar energy and materials that happen to be available on Earth, he does not reduce life and its forms to physical and chance terms.[8] First, Bergson insists that life is fundamentally a psychical force—a variegating reality to which the concepts of unity and multiplicity apply no better than to the flow of our consciousness. Second, he claims that life proceeds with missionary zeal to beat back matter and even death and would have found a perfect vehicle in humanity, were humanity not marked by its own earthly evolutionary history, over the course of which cognitive capacities for the sake of instrumental control of nature have eclipsed the intuitive capacities that exist only at the fringes of our instincts. The mysticism implicit in the *élan vital* cannot be wished away.

My focus in this chapter will be on the cultural and political implications of Bergson's mysticism.

Bergson's Last Interventions

The place to begin such a commentary is with Bergson's last book, *Two Sources of Morality and Religion* (1932). While Bergson put his philosophical system to nationalist use in the First World War by arguing that French culture was infused with an *élan vital* that the mechanistic German culture lacked, he would soon thereafter work for international peace through the League of Nations and identify in this last work the elusive concept of *élan vital* with an open morality, in a bid to undermine the closed tribal and nationalist commitments that had kept the world on the brink of a Second World War. However, one finds little critical commentary on Bergson's faith in mystics and heroes for inspiring efforts to dissolve social boundaries in the name of life as a creative, transcending force. Bergson's characteristic argument about the limits of analysis and intellect was preserved in his belief that the creation of more complex forms of international cooperation depended in the last instance on a leap out of the closed moral systems by which groups defined and defended themselves in contradistinction to other groups. Though Bergson would a few years later courageously risk pneumonia to stand as an old man in the cold rain to register as a Jew in Vichy France, he had claimed in his final book that the only complete inspiration for universal openness could be found in Christian mysticism and mythology.[9] He explicitly criticized the insularity of the Judaic religion (and caricatured Eastern forms of mysticism). So it is important to note that in contrast to Bergson, Ernst Cassirer found, as Donald Verene has recently reminded us, in Judaism the first historic break with the taboo and totemism of closed primitive societies for self-conscious ethical ideals and explained Hitler's Judeocide as an attempt to extirpate the living source of ethical universalism, rationally based.[10]

Karl Popper popularized the distinction between open and closed societies but like Bertrand Russell would have had no truck with Bergson's Christian mysticism. However, there was nothing manifestly unscientific or unrealistic in Bergson's call for remythification, since having scientific

reasons to believe in the power of the myths of closed morality on the human mind (groups that had instilled loyalty through myth and ritual had
been more successful in the course of evolutionary history; that is, humans
susceptible to myth have been successful in a positivist Darwinian sense),
he called for the co-optation of such susceptibility by those myths and rituals that instilled loyalty to humanity as such. Reason and science were not
antithetical to myth but rather allowed for an appreciation of the real role
that it plays in human society. Where human intelligence threatened to un-
ravel the social cooperation that other animals enjoyed as a result of instinct, pure and simple, myth and custom had to succeed.[11]

However, rather than following the roles and customs that maintained
a closed society in static equilibrium, humanity could dynamically extend
the scope of sociability. Yet this would require the power of mystics. But
Suzanne Guerlac writes:

> An explicit appeal to the social values of mystical experience in this study
> [*The Two Sources of Morality and Religion*] appeared to vindicate those
> who had criticized Bergson all along for being simply a mystic. And yet
> the title of the work, and the basis for the notion of closed and open soci-
> eties, derive from scientific, not mystical discourse. They refer us to an
> opposition between closed and open systems in Sadi Carnot's theories of
> thermodynamics.[12]

Yet, as I read Bergson, he does not base the opposition between closed and
open societies in thermodynamics but in sociobiology. Having rejected
reason as means to political and social insight, Bergson predicated tolerance
and peace not on rational interfaith dialogue but on the success of Christian
mystics calling us to one putatively universal faith. He thus leaves us with no
obstacle to intolerant, authoritarian, and evangelical leadership.[13] Appealing
to the wish to overcome the atomism or monadism within closed groups
and the conflict between them, Bergson valorized intuition as the means to
access the principal ontological category of the universe or the whole, the
life principle or *élan vital*. Individuals are to be united in the unfolding
whole but now only as means or expressions of the whole: the individual is
deprived of ontological dignity. To the extent that the individual is recognized, he takes the form of the spiritual hero or mystic only. Here atomism
and conflict have given way to a universal and totalistic vision in which
there is no dialectical interplay between individuals and community. Bergson counsels his readers to await and give themselves to a mystic whose in-

terpretation of Christianity is not to be disciplined by anything other than his intuitive sense of the creative life force. All this said, Bergson actually consigns himself in the end to the inevitability of international conflict, given the voracity built into human nature and the scarcity of resources. His message, the message with which he concludes, is the consolatory promise of the afterlife. For this reason, critics did indeed have reason to believe that Bergson's theory of the independence of the memory and the spirit from the body was indeed meant to establish the possibility of immortality.

The Unique

Yet Bergson's philosophy is not obviously a political one at all, and his mysticism most often focuses on individual experience. For example, it is not difficult to see, as Eric Matthews notes in his short perceptive commentary, why Marcel Proust would be influenced by Bergson's attempt to intimate subjective experience underneath language and concepts that only abstract that which is expressible in mutually comprehensible and thus public form and thereby fail to express that which makes experiences exactly personal: "Language cannot express what is unique in something by the use of terms which refer only to one instance, because there are not and could not be such terms. Language can identify particulars only by the use of general terms, including terms of spatial and temporal location. It seems a natural conclusion that intuition of the unique as such is inexpressible in language."[14]

The rejection of the realm of universal and impersonal validity need not result in a wholesale irrationalism, as Lucio Colletti and others have claimed. Bergson's skepticism of the intellect, which proved so important for the development of modernist aesthetics and its epistemological value (I mention here again these excellent studies: Sanford Schwarz's *The Matrix of Modernism*, Mark Antliff's *Inventing Bergson: Cultural Politics and the Parisian Avant-Garde*, and Frederick Burwick and Paul Douglass' edited collection *The Crisis in Modernism: Bergson and the Vitalist Controversy*), gave confidence that there was in fact a real difference between

the use of language for "scientific," fact finding purposes, in which the important thing [is] to secure a shared reference for terms by means of already accepted rules (Bergson's "fixed concepts") and a use of language for more expressive purposes, in which what is to be conveyed [is] what

[is] unique about someone's experience, so that success in communication depend[s] on the speaker's skill in finding appropriate expressions, combined with the hearer's responsiveness to what the speaker [has] to say (Bergson's "fluid concepts," capable of following reality in all its sinuosities). . . . Science and common sense take for granted a view of the world as detached from our experience of it (and conversely of our experience as belonging to a detached, purely internal, world of subjectivity). But this view of the world is not reality. . . . It is derivative from "real reality," which is given to intuition, and which can properly be described only by means of "fluid concepts." The proper method of metaphysics, as the study of "real reality," must therefore be intuitive, rather than intellectual.[15]

Bergson resisted epistemological violence. Living beings achieve individuality (or nonidenticality) in and through a real temporal process, that is, by way of history and memory in its genetic, immunological, motor, and psychological senses. And as Matthews argues, our language, especially formal, intersubjectively objective scientific discourse, is bound to crush what is unique and assimilate what is novel. The individual (or at least aspects of the individual) is incommunicable, and the novel nonconceptual. For Bergson, the memory of a rose or a madeline, however, is an essentially personal one, associated with a concrete individual's singular childhood memories and inexpressible in common language. Bergson, in other words, is not simply limiting the reach of conceptual and scientific thought; he is showing that such thought creates a veil of abstractions that then interferes with the passion for the real experience of *durée* as recovered in the artwork. Sanford Schwartz argues quite insightfully that Bergson differs here from Nietzsche, William James, and T. E. Hulme, who understood both scientific cognition and the work of art as reorderings of the perceptual field so that objective aspects of reality that would otherwise be lost in the sensory flux could be brought to consciousness. Bergson's philosophy, in contrast, privileges the artwork over the scientific model and the subjective over the objective.[16]

But Bergson does not reject the possibility of mechanistic psychological explanation on the grounds of subjective, concrete individuality making impossible universal laws. He is willing to grant that because people do make sense of the world in shared ways, not only do they not contravene causal order, but they establish it. Bergson critiques science in the

Kantian sense of delimiting the boundaries of its validity. Of those moments outside the scientific imagination he writes in *Time and Free Will*:

> But the moments at which we thus grasp ourselves are rare, and that is just why we are rarely free. The greater part of the time we live outside ourselves, hardly perceiving anything of ourselves but our own ghost, a colourless shadow which pure duration projects into homogeneous space. Hence our life unfolds in space rather than in time; we live for the external world rather than for ourselves; we speak rather than think; we "are acted" rather than act ourselves.[17]

Yet it seems to be sheer metaphysical prejudice to find the deeper truth or reality in what is incommunicable rather than shared and mutually understood. We are told that deeper truth is grasped by withdrawing from action and intuiting our own inner duration. The contrast with Hegel could not be sharper: "And the ineffable [*das Unsagbare*] feeling and sensation is not the most excellent and true but the least important, the least true." And "what is called is the ineffable [*das Unaussperchliche*] is nothing but the untrue, irrational, the merely believed [*Gemeinte*]."[18] Why indeed should we understand ineffable subjective experience as reality? In effect, why equate the extralinguistic with the supralinguistic?

Bergson's powerful idea is that while individuals appear to be acting from self-interest, they are unaware that the self whose interest they try to promote is constructed for pragmatic social and instrumental reasons; unaware of this, they identify with this "self" as something truly individual and personal—in short, as "themselves."[19] To be sure, Bergson captures especially in his generally ignored book *Comedy* some aspects of the surprising alienation of modern life. While freed from the ascriptive and heredity roles of a traditional society (for example, the self-sacrificing roles of a woman or serf), modern subjects still assume personae that are defined socially and even juridically. The roles are institutionally and coercively enforced, and society seems to be occupied already in advance of mechanization by automatons (the malaise about which has been created by the flattening of social roles rather than the advance of technology, the development of which depends on the mechanization of action in the first place). The fear of "becoming automaton" haunts Bergson's thought from beginning to end. Bergson speaks allusively to modern self-alienation, and through depth psychology he attempts to plunge below the apparently only apparitional self (although, as we are learning, the wearing of masks can come to redefine even biologically the actor in its own image—what Judith Butler has called the installation of the ontological).[20]

However, thinkers as diverse as Arthur Lovejoy and Georg Lukács argued that in making claims about truths and levels of reality that by their very nature could not be subject to norms of universal and impersonal validity favored in democratic and open discussion, Bergson had in effect introduced a kind of aristocratic epistemology. However, Bergson seems never to have suggested that intuition was only available to a select few, even as he emphasized (as I discuss below) that intuition was not available without immense and concentrated effort. In fact, this seems an ungenerous reading or rather a tautology that the truth and the real can only be found in the impersonally valid and not in the irreducibly subjective really intuited or truthfully expressed.[21] Leswak Kolakowski seems hardly incorrect that one finds more than an anticipation of the major themes of Adorno's *Negative Dialectics* in Bergson's critique of the intellect.[22] Of course, Bergson invited controversy (and the famous stinging reply by Bertrand Russell)[23] by privileging intuition over the intellect as a mode of cognition and devaluing the truly cognitive value of the latter. Here Schwarz is correct to compare Bergson unfavorably to Nietzsche and James in particular. The hierarchies in Bergson's thought left their unfortunate mark on the *Négritude* thinkers.

Intuition and Absolute Knowledge

For Bergson, as I have already suggested, the function of the intellect was not truth but rather practice. The intellect carved up and classified the world in order to control it efficiently: objects are abstracted from a processual reality in terms of those aspects that allow them to be classified in general terms and thus handled in terms of set behavioral patterns, matter is handled under abstract categories of mass and energy in order to better manipulate it, and truly indivisibly continuous motion is broken into moments in order to intellectually control it under the sign of mathematics and the differential calculus in particular. In a Nietzschean formulation, Bergson declared: "Purely logical thought is created by life, in definite circumstances, to act on definite things"; by what power then could it "embrace life, of which it is only an emanation or aspect?"[24] In fact, the very idea of matter itself—what Bergson's refers to in *Creative Evolution* as the corpuscular theory of solid and impenetrable bodies—is itself an ontological projection we have learned to make onto the world in order to control and shape it toward our ends.[25] This we do out of "necessity," toward the preservation and maintenance of the biological self. The ontological presumption then comes to inform our very idea of the logical. For example, the logical principle of noncontradiction is simply the spatial idea that no two spatial bodies can exist in the same place at the same time. For Bergson, however, the duration in which our consciousness exists freely has the past, present, and future interpenetrate in violation of the canons of logic. Moreover, all things that have life are changing, transforming; they both are and are not. One need only point to a metamorphosizing plant, as did Goethe and Hegel. The law of the excluded middle rules out "precisely the indivisible middle phase we seek to capture at which the plant is neither a seed nor not a seed . . . but is ceasing to be a seed . . . as equally coming to be a seed-leaf."[26]

As Bergson's follower Vladimir Jankélévitch exclaimed: "Life jeers at contradictions which are the despair of the intellect. Becoming, a mélange of being and non-being, is the escape from the principle of the excluded third."[27] Rejecting the logic of identity, that $A = A$, Rene Ménil, one of the founders of *Négritude*, would exclaim: "Aristotle's logic? A practice of things or corpses / Thought is bio-logical—or does not exist."[28] In short, life escapes logical thought; in particular, while a machine is always itself, living things are dynamic entities, constantly in a process of change in violation of the canons of logic. Not only does poetry alone have the power to imagine such change—we speak not conceptually of a plant's metamorphosis but poetically of its bursting forth, bending back on itself, or recoiling upon itself—but metaphoric language is itself a force of incorporeal transformations. Poetry also has the power to transform things though metaphor and simile: poetry is life, prosaic thought the dead classificatory logic of inert things.

Conceptual and scientific thought enable mastery and control, but they are achieved at the expense of intuition of duration, process, change, and becoming. Nowhere more than in the mysteries of our own consciousness and memory and in amazing processes of embryonic differentiation and in phylogenetic complexification—in the features of life—did the intellect modeled on mathematical physics seem inadequate. By shifting attention to biology, Bergson hoped to show the limits of intellect in the grasping of the real and the whole and life in particular.[29] In this way, Bergson hoped to explain the current disillusionment with positivism and justify his belief that it had abandoned true knowledge of reality for lifeless intellectual symbols. As Jacques Chevalier, Bergson's principal interpreter wrote:

> The intellect, intoxicated by its discoveries in this domain of the material, bestrides the entire physical and moral universe, measuring tape in hand, and since matter alone is measurable it endeavors to translate everything into the terms of matter: movement to the space which subtends it, sensation to the physical *stimula* which incites it, thought to the cerebral process which conditions it, liberty to the fixed symbols or dead forms in which it expresses itself.[30]

In place of this relativized, abstract, and symbolic view of reality, Bergson offered a new metaphysics, which, submerging human knowledge into the flux of existence, would thereby achieve absolutely true knowledge of existence: "*What is relative is the symbolic knowledge of reality by pre-existing concepts, which proceeds from the fixed into the moving, and not the intuitive knowledge which installs in that what is moving and adopts the very life of things*. This intuition attains the absolute."[31]

What seemed to be the modern conquests of knowledge, for example, the parsimonious symbolic statement of physical laws, was thus understood by Bergson as no more than *techne*, a way of projecting the world as inanimate, solid, and fixed for the purposes of its technical manipulation. While extensive magnitudes could be analyzed by the mathematical science, Bergson left to philosophy and literature the exploration of what he called the intensive magnitudes at the basis of personal experience. On one side was space, mechanism, and extensity; on the other side was time, vitality, and intensity. It is hardly surprising that Bergson was received as a savior by humanists and theologians in the age of science.

Bergson's duration was defined by an irreducibly qualitative intensity and, in fact, not a quantitative magnitude at all. Instead, it was a qualitative experience to which science and practical industry had lost all living contact in its suppression of the language of qualities and affects for a quantitative fetishism and measurement rather than appreciation of experience. Unlike Schopenhauer, who had also derived the higher functions from the will but who sought transcendence in renunciation, Bergson sought escape in a nonrational mode—intuition—the truth value of which he defended on grounds of its practical worthlessness!

Horkheimer protested that Bergson, unlike Hegel, simply eliminates the conceptual tools of the intellect from the realm of philosophical truth, which "relegates them to the 'merely' material field, to the science of objects, belittles their usefulness in terms of knowledge."[32] In other words, Bergson's hierarchy in forms of thinking only expresses the hoary prejudice for the pure intellect over thought engaged in the material transformation of nature, now disqualified from an understanding of deeper realities. The young Horkheimer is suggesting that Bergsonism is indeed the retreat of an aristocracy to the pathetically powerless province of philosophy in which it lays claim, unchallenged, to deeper truths. The irony is that Horkheimer and Adorno's later critique of instrumental reason would only echo Bergson's metaphysical distrust of the intellect. While Bergson understood the intellect as a naturally evolved prosthetic or organic tool of the human for survival and reproduction, Horkheimer and Adorno would speak of technological reason, which "forced all things to correspond to thought, to equal it, to be ad-equate to it" and which had become, in their estimation, a theoretical basis and legitimation for any totalitarian project."[33]

Bergson, however, did not share the epistemological modesty of Adorno's *Negative Dialectics*, in which the object retains its exteriority. Bergson's intuition was absolute in its promise—the transcendence of the seemingly impermeable split between subject and object; intuition would allow one to know the object from within—to grasp it via intuition. In *Introduction to Metaphysics*, Bergson wrote:

> Our intelligence . . . can place itself within the mobile reality, and adopt its ceaselessly changing directions; in short, can grasp it by means of that intellectual sympathy which we call intuition. . . . To philosophize, therefore, is to invert the habitual direction of thought. This inversion has never been practiced in a methodical manner. A profoundly considered history of human thought would show that we owe to it all that is greatest in the sciences, as well as all that is permanent in metaphysics. . . . But metaphysics, which aims at no application, can and usually must abstain from converting intuition into symbols. Liberated from the obligation of working for practically useful results, it will indefinitely enlarge of the domain of investigations.[34]

Bergson had argued that only by self-intuition could one apprehend actual process, change, and creativity without intellectualist parsing into discrete, frozen, and solid entities out of which continuity could then never be reconstructed. Creative duration, after all, "is the foundation of our being, and, as we feel, the very substance of the world in which we live."[35] In fact, for Bergson creative duration is life itself; hence time for Bergson implies life. From our own creative temporal oneness we can become one with nature. Self-intuition allows one to understand by analogy nature itself as the same kind of never-repeating, continuous, ever-creative process.[36] Bergson defines life as a kind of time-space, a temporal organicism: life is defined in terms of a temporal unity of events and as a self-production of self-enclosed space. This remarkable passage, in which Bergson states more clearly than anywhere else his understanding of life, has been overlooked, as it appears in what is wrongly considered to be one of his lesser works, *Comedy*:

> Life presents itself to us as evolution in time and complexity in space. Regarded in time, it is the continuous evolution of a being ever growing older; it never goes backwards and never repeats itself. Considered in space, it exhibits certain coexisting elements so closely interdependent, so exclusively made for one another, that not one of them could, at the same time, belong to two different organisms; each living being is a closed system of phenomena, incapable of interacting with other systems. A continual change of aspect, the irreversibility of the order of phenomena, the perfect individuality of a perfectly self-contained series: such, then, are the outward characteristics—whether real or apparent is of little moment—which distinguish the living from the merely mechanical.[37]

I want to focus now not on life as perfect individuality but as forward-moving temporality. Bergson emphasizes the irreversibility, processual nature, and creative force of time in his identification of living processes. He argues that the temporality of life escapes the intellect. But first I want to abstract his conception of time to argue that he makes a fetish of it. Now one cannot understand Bergson except in light of his thoroughgoing revolt against the curiously atemporal sense of time in mechanics. The movements of the planets in abstract homogeneous time can as easily be retrodicted as predicted, run forward as backward. But it is not simply the irreversibility but the productivity of time itself on which modern Bergsonians insist. Thermodynamics proved a revolutionary development, although Guerlac suggests that Ludwig Boltzman thwarted the recognition of a dynamic ontology of irreversible temporal processes. And she argues that doubts about the principle of the conservation of energy does not make it scientifically suspect that time could itself be a form of energy, a force or efficacy.[38] But this particular argument seems not to be grounded in actual *[handwritten marginal note: NA! This is his point! w/o scien (which you to knu, it's false?]*

scientific theory, at least as far as I can follow.[39] It seems to me that Bergson has in fact simply fetishized time—in other words, made it in itself the magical source of transformation that find its bases elsewhere. Indeed, one is reminded of the Bergsonian Péguy's dismissal of the notion of time as itself a force, an idea he dismissed as the banker's self-serving yet hegemonic practicotheoretical belief that the passage of time itself yields money interest. For Péguy, Bergsonism was not meant to give metaphysical grounds for the delusive belief of the mere passage of time as in itself productive but to critique just that banker's fetishized conception of time in the name of a time conception marked by fullness as well as emptiness.[40] I suggest, however, that the mere passage of abstract homogeneous time is fetishized by Bergson as a result of his making it out to be the hidden force that allows, in apparent violation of the conservation of energy, more to appear in the consequences than in the antecedent conditions. Such a time fetish is grounded in the practical illusions of rentiers and bankers, not (as far as I can understand the case) in twentieth-century physics.

Bergson also insisted that *durée* itself is refractory to the analytical intelligence. Time is only discursively present in terms of spatial images, yet in *durée* the moments are interpenetrated, making it misleading to think of time as any kind of succession of images or form of space (as I shall soon elaborate). Real (especially psychological) time cannot thus be understood in terms of visual images, spatial metaphor, language generally, and scientific theory in particular. In referring to what he called the cinematographical illusion, Bergson could thus be said to have invented *the strobe light theory of the intellect*; that is, the intellect prevents appreciation of motion and the interpenetrated unity of qualitatively changing unfolding duration. While the senses allow us to perceive fluidity, movement, and life, the intellect can only recompose it out of the halting moments into which it has been broken. *[handwritten note: No No No, 1st lines of Mythr + Mem]*

Bergson's solution to the alienation of the subject from itself and the object world is idealist and aesthetic through and through, for it is only by intuitive participation in the temporal flow of life that the *élan vital* can itself create through one as its conduit. As a materialist Hegelian, the early Horkheimer had proposed that labor, coded as dialectical materialism, could reconcile subject and object because it developed both the subjective mode of thought and manipulated external objects. Horkheimer had thus replaced intuition with the more active and material principle of labor until, as already suggested, his belief in the capacities of working-class action was shattered, and he came to understand labor in an instrumental sense closer to Bergson's sense of the reifying intellect than in any emancipatory sense. The crisis of confidence in the Second and Third International led Critical Theory and the whole of Western Marxism back into the orbit of Bergsonism.[41]

And here there was promise: Man was to become once again one with the universe through intuition—the implication being that analysis, unable to apprehend motion and thus ultimate reality, results in the destructive paradoxes of Zeno. Through the philosophical elaboration of the conception of intuition, Bergson, working in the idealist tradition of *Naturphilophie*, had hoped to provide a connection between man and the natural world so that the individual need not regard herself as living in, on the whole, an alien natural environment but rather as having arisen out of and thus being one with nature, every bit of which is now imbued with cosmic significance.[42]

> As the smallest grain of dust is bound up with our entire solar system, drawn along with it in that undivided movement of descent that is materiality itself, so all organized beings, from the humblest to the highest, from the first origins of life to the time in which we are, and in all places as in all times, do but evidence a single impulsion, the inverse of the movement of matter, and in itself indivisible. All the living hold together, all yield to the same tremendous push. The animal takes its stand on the planet, man bestrides animality, and the whole of humanity, in space and time, is one immense army galloping beside and before and behind each of us in an overwhelming charge able to beat down every resistance and clear the most formidable obstacles, perhaps even death.[43]

Horkheimer would read this promise of participation in eternal life as an insidious attempt to "console humans about that which befalls them on earth with make-believe stories about their own eternity."[44] That is, Bergson resurrected the mythological belief that if what had been alive is now dead, something had to have departed from the dead body. That "something" was for Bergson the *élan vital*. In theological fashion, Bergson denied or at least qualified the prospect that the death of a human being represents his final and complete extinction. Bergson even held séances, hoping to communicate with the ghost souls that had animated person's bodies and had survived the body's death. For orthodox Marxists such as Georges Politzer and the dean of critical theory Horkheimer, the renascence of spiritualism was altogether reactionary.

Yet for Bergson, the methods of mathematical physics, which had alienated man from the universe, prove grossly inadequate to the comprehension of temporal, organic processes, and the ceaseless creativity of which in the flow of time remained the greatest of mysteries. The mimetic tradition sets up conflict between perception and object, however realistic representation may be. Intuition allowed a way out, or rather in—into the self and objects by way of intuition, not intellectual apprehension. In *Bergson and Russian Modernism*, Hilary Fink insightfully explores the aesthetic reaction to Kantian epistemology, which by foregrounding the subjective framing of the object left it unknown and unknowable as a thing-in-itself.[45] While not insisting on actual Bergsonian influence on Russian modernists, Fink does emphasize their affinity with Bergsonian epistemology, which through intuition (a nonrational mode of cognition) allowed understanding to penetrate the object and thus make knowledge absolute. This suggests (Nelson Goodman would later protest) that since there is only one true way that reality is behind our representations, there cannot in fact be many ways the world is, with multiple right versions capturing one of the many ways the world is.[46] For Bergson, however, since the representation we form of the images that we sense are always diminutions of the images we started with, science, language, perception, and philosophy can never be utterly faithful to the world as it is. Since representation does not simply give a partial but a distorted, "spatialized" view, Bergson suggested that we never achieve an even partially faithful portrayal of the way the world is. Dismissing the relative and limited value of the symbolic or conceptual comprehension of the real, Bergson had given the promise of what Cassirer would call the "paradise of pure immediacy" to those who could decipher the mystery of his thought.

It is to this mystery at the heart of modernist aesthetics to which I now turn. I begin with a discussion of D. H. Lawrence.

Immediacy and the Art of the Detour

The intellect is only a bridle. . . . All I want is to answer to my blood, direct, without the fribbling intervention of the mind, or morals, or what not.

—D. H. LAWRENCE

The intellect is characterized by a natural inability to comprehend life.

—HENRI BERGSON, *CREATIVE EVOLUTION*

As Richard Lehan has shown in an insightful reading, the figurine of the African Goddess often becomes "a kind of icon in Lawrentian fiction."[47] In *Women in Love*, Birkin contemplates a statuette of an African Goddess:

> She had thousands of years of purely sensual, purely unspiritual knowledge behind her. It must have been thousands of years since her race had died, mystically: that is, since the relation between the senses and the outspoken mind had broken, leaving the experience all in one sort, mystically sensual. Thousands of years ago, that which was imminent in himself must have taken place in these Africans: the goodness, the holiness, the desire for creation and productive happiness must have lapsed, leaving the single impulse for knowledge in one sort, mindless progressive knowledge through the senses, knowledge arrested and ending in the senses, mystic knowledge in disintegration and dissolution, knowledge such as the beetles have, which live purely within the world of corruption and cold dissolution. This was why her face looked like a beetle's: this was why the Egyptian's worshipped the ball-rolling scarab: because of the principle of knowledge in dissolution and corruption.

I include more of the passage than Lehan does to underline that Lawrence is not a simple primitivist. The "primitive" culture, of which this statuette an embodiment, is understood to have lost a creative union with the universe for the kind of instinctual knowledge that the beetle or scarab is taken to symbolize.[48] The African statuette possesses a faint power, a mere shadow of its animistic potency, and is, as a result, depicted in a state of impotency. What power it has comes only from its ability to inspire reflection and prompt anxieties. The statuette becomes a *tabula rasa* onto which Birkin reads his own alienation, his own inability to achieve not only a supporting, life-giving union with Ursula but also with feminine principles through which the life force works. While Birkin may fantasize about an empathetic relation with a statuette imagined as an actual woman, the statuette has become a vehicle for a narration of decline, cognitive truncation, and that loss of an intuitive unison with others and the cosmic life force.

The Bergsonian influence can be felt here in the implicit tripartite distinction between intuition, instinct, and intellect. Bertrand Russell had famously charged Bergson with devaluing the intellect for instinct, which is "seen at its best in ants, bees and Bergson."[49] It may not be an accident that Lawrence's metaphor for instinct is an insect, as he is attempting to set his search for intuitive understanding against the instinctualism into which Bergson's critics had collapsed it.[50] It simply would be incorrect to read Lawrence's iconization of the African statuette as an example of the valorization of an instinctual racial primitivism. In order to fend off such an interpretation, Lawrence has Birkin indulge in a rather racist stream of consciousness, in which the African statuette is at once taken to represent an actual African woman, embody a civilization, and portray its lapsing into instinctualism at the level of insects. At the same time, an often racialized primitivism and misogynist instinctualism frequently seems to be for Lawrence a "vitalist" antidote to an English industrial culture in which he no longer has confidence. In *The Plumed Serpent*, his overwrought meditations on phallic vitalism and power are expressed through the supernatural sexual prowess of his Mexican protagonist, Don Carlos. His works focused on Britain fare no differently. Reared in the austere rural culture of the Midlands, Lawrence also held a deep fascination for the fundamentalist practices of the primitive Methodist church. He is particularly enamored of their "chapel men," who hold a "wild mystery or power about them" as if they "had some dispensation of rude power from above." They were in complete accord with the forces of life; for Lawrence this was evident in the way they effortlessly controlled "their" women. In his final work, the jeremiad *Apocalypse*, he posits the convictions of these rural churches as a model for social transformation. There, in "strange marvelous black nights of the north Midlands," emerged the quasi-Nietzschean religion of life, power, and absolute male authority, the remnants of Britain's lost phallic cult: "a religion of self-glorification and power, forever! And of darkness. No wailing 'Lead kindly Light!' about it."[51] Ernst Bloch would memorably characterize Lawrence as the "sentimental penis philosopher" who "sings the wilderness of the elemental age of love, which to his misfortune man has emerged from" and "seeks the nocturnal moon in the flesh, the unconscious sun in the blood."[52]

Yet in the passage cited above, Lawrence seems to be counterposing Birkin's bridle of the intellect *and* the statuette's intimation of "mindless sensuous knowledge" with true intuition. Only the last enables integral or absolute knowledge. And the path to such knowledge lay not in rationalist epistemology but rather in the renewal of intuitive capabilities. As Bergson put it in *The Creative Mind*: "We call intuition here the sympathy by which one is transported into the interior of an object in order to coincide with what there is unique and consequently inexpressible in it."[53] Just as Lawrence sometimes conflated one nonrational mode with another, instinct with intuition, Bergson often failed to distinguish clearly the two forms: the distinction between instinct and intuition remains vexed. Of instinct he gives the example (insect as instinct again) of a wasp that somehow knows how to paralyze a caterpillar, keeping it alive so that the wasp can feed its larvae. For Bergson this represented, as A. C. Lacey sharply puts it, "an uncanny way of letting its possessor know what is not accessible by ordinary means of knowing."[54] Yet it was not an instinctual relation to the world that Bergson's philosophy was meant to achieve. In a heroic effort to defend the validity of said distinction, Milič Čapek has developed a subtle reading of the relationship between the immediate and the intuitive in Bergson's philosophy.[55]

Čapek argues that for Bergson the immediate was exactly not what constitutes our sensory data, as in empiricist philosophy, but only that sensory data as "freed from irrelevant and extraneous elements which, so to speak, 'mediatize' it." For example, an intuitive plunge into a melody—and, as Fink shows, the intuitive experience of music was the highest form of modernist aesthetics—requires that a listener free herself from fleeting thoughts about notes as "graphical symbols," the "visual image of the orchestra," and "tactile reminiscences" of the instruments (if she is musically trained). It is all too easy to dismiss as irrationalist modernist aesthetics—and, I shall argue, *Négritude* poetics as well—if we do not appreciate the (paradoxically) counterintuitive sense in which Bergson theorized intuition. Čapek's analysis of the intuitive appreciation of melody is wonderfully concrete and warrants quoting at length:

> The cluster of these heterogeneous images [graphical symbols, images of the orchestra, tactile reminiscences] is in a sense immediately present to [the listener's mind]; yet, it would be wrong and misleading to confuse this kind of immediacy with the immediacy of musical experience which appears only when all accessory non-musical images and recollections are radically eliminated. By not doing it, we confuse the auditory data with the visual and tactile ones, and even run the risk of losing sight of the central nucleus of musical experience, although we may still continue to *talk* about it. It is true that the "audition colorée" may be very effective in poetry or even in subjective interpretations of musical experience, as the case of Rimbaud and Baudelaire clearly showed; but epistemologically it always means a translation of the auditory data into visual terms. In other words, it means a transition of the experience whose salient feature is temporality into terms which, if not entirely devoid of

temporal character, are at least preponderantly spatial in nature. The search for immediacy here means a search for *epistemological purity*, i.e. an effort to avoid the confusion of heterogeneous strata of experience. If the Bergsonian notion of *immediacy* is understood thus, there will be little danger of misunderstanding the Bergsonian *intuition*; both terms are almost synonymous. . . . It is thus clear then that what was designated by the word "intuition" is a very complex process which had nothing in common with emotion and instinct, and which certainly does not go on effortlessly and passively.[56]

In other words, Bergsonian epistemology is subtractive. It is an active mental operation meant to demediatize experience. This is not a form of irrationalism, much less instinctualism (it will be important to remember this in considering Senghor's valorization of emotion as African, and I will return to this passage). An appreciation of Bergsonian intuition allows us to prevent what Michael Löwy and Robert Sayre have called the "short-circuiting" of the difference between "the irrational and non-rational (that is, between the programmatic negation of rationality and delimitation of psychic spheres that are not reducible to reason)."[57] While Čapek captures well the concentrated effort that intuition—unlike instinctual behavior understood as an unlearned action carried out without any knowledge of the end the action serves—requires, he tends to treat it as a mode for understanding individual, self-enclosed experiences. The larger point here is that through discourse there can be no absolute knowledge of not only music and personal experience but also the external world deformed by the spatial logic of the intellect. The achievement of absolute knowledge depends on the quasi-mystical acts of intuition and intellectual sympathy.[58] Best poised to understand life, flux, interpenetration, and creativity, Bergson's intuition could promise transcendence of the split between subject and object.

However, the rejection of mediatization has pointed in far too many cases in a troubling direction. Vitalism can be reduced to the proposition that neither one's own life nor the cosmic life force immanent in nature can be understood through the mediation of the logic of solid bodies and the concept in general: to life corresponded its own cognitive mode, intuition. As György Márkus puts the point: "In general, consistent proponents of *Lebensphilosophie* identified creative subjectivity, which they opposed to the mechanical world of things and material relations, with the irrational and incommunicable stream of psychical experience, purified of all traces of the conceptual."[59] In this way, vitalism represented the destruction of the objective idealism of the *Frühromantiks*, for whom (Schiller in particular) play represented man's essential nature, precisely because it lifted humanity above the world of "Life" qua reflex actions and blind drives and represented the culmination of "Spirit." As Cassirer emphasized, Spirit allowed for creative formation—the breaking of the chain of instinctive responses. As the antithesis of Life, then, Spirit was understood as "the art of the detour"—the ability through the development of language, the use of tools, and the honing of artistic and conceptual representations to set the world aside and retreat into a world of unreality before reality was conquered—and it was only to the extent that man's response to stimuli was mediated by his own symbolic systems that he broke from his heteronomous determination by nature and thereby achieved a measure of freedom that vitalist movements threatened to obliterate. For Cassirer, the theorist of symbolic forms, aesthetics was not the only sphere in which man comes to his own through play. He was insistent that the detour, in some form, was inescapable, and his critique of vitalism strikes the deepest of all:

> Indeed, if we pass in review the whole series of accusations which the modern "philosophy of life" has raised against the usurped supremacy of the Spirit, one objection immediately obtrudes itself. Who exactly—it must be inquired—is the plaintiff, and who the defendant in the trial here getting under way? It seems as if Life were here brought to the bar against the Spirit, in order to defend itself against the latter's encroachment, against its violence and its conceit. And yet this impression is deceptive—for Life is self-imprisoned, and in this self-imprisonment is speechless. It has no language other than that which Spirit lends it. Hence, wherever it is summoned against the Spirit, the latter in truth is always both assailant and defendant, plaintiff and judge in one. The real drama takes place not between Spirit and Life, but in the midst of the Spirit's own realm, indeed at its very focus.[60]

As I shall suggest in the next chapter, Césaire had a profound understanding of this philosophical problem. As Goodman put it: "Since the mystic is concerned with the way the world is and finds that the way cannot be expressed, his ultimate response to the question of the way the world is must be, as he recognizes, silence."[61] However, Césaire did not escape into silence or speechless intuition as the medium through which life could be understood; nor did he say, with Cassirer and Goodman, that Life has no existence outside of conceptual or discursive form, similar to the way that the unconscious can only appear in disguise. As we shall see, Césaire holds to the power of poetry, given a proper audience response, to intensify the sense of life without representing it.

For both Bergson and Césaire, the life forces that they hoped people would intuit in themselves and then see everywhere at work in a bountiful universe were quite different in nature than the life impulses that were featured by the virulently irrational forms of vitalism. Bergson's critique of the limits of reason and the understanding in the domain of life did itself, however, prepare the ground for an aesthetics of the irrational. In this regard, Ezra Pound, who advocated a poetics of immediacy, can be productively read as a vitalist, albeit a non-Bergsonian one.[62] This is evident through the full stretch of his career, from his early interest in the Troubadour tradition, in which poetry transmits the "true gift" of love to its intended, to his Imagist period, in which the poetic lends the artist direct treatment of the thing, and, finally, to his lifelong utilization of Chinese ideograms, which provided the means to condense maximum meaning into the single phrase.

Nowhere is Pound's antipathy toward mediation more forcefully or rather obsessively expressed than in his economics. Pound understood money as akin to the prolific obstructions of metaphoric and figurative language; money in the form of specie and gold stands in the way of authentic, virtuous, and life-giving activity. People could produce and exchange concrete things and thereby reproduce life, yet a shortage of circulating money, often the result of usury, could stall the movement of goods and the reproduction of life because, after all, people produce for money, not for life-giving exchange with others. If for the vitalists culture and reason had rendered man incapable of being moved immediately by actual life-giving stimuli, Pound also lamented that producers did not act within the sphere of immediate and social need or in accordance with their creative impulses; their actions did not originate from themselves, or need, or the concrete but were rather teleologically oriented toward abstraction: the making of money.

Money thus mediated between man's life impulses and his actions. Life was on the side of use value, need, and natural impulse; death correlated with exchange value, money, and abstraction.[63] Where Herbert Schnädelbach analyzes the vitalist pessimism expressed in German philosophy about the spirit's domination over life in the realm of culture, we can see Pound expressing anxiety about the domination of money as the analogue of

spirit over life in the realm of economics. Schnädelbach writes: "Nietzsche's idea that spirit, as an instrument of life, could make itself independent and turn against life itself became a watchword . . . the idea of the
self-alienation of life in the spirit was combined, as early as Nietzsche, with
cultural criticism based on a theory of decadence, in which a denunciation
of rationality was connected in a striking way with an appeal for an awak-
ening to a new culture of life."[64]

Money, which had arisen as an instrument of exchange and interconnection, had turned against man. For the vitalists, culture and reason, which
were to mediate between living impulses and actions, had come to petrify
man, just as the mediation of economic exchange by money had come to
atrophy productive powers. As the cultural vitalists reacted against the
spirit, economic vitalists called for the end to the mediation of social relations by money, which had given excessive power and control to those
who controlled its supply. Interpreting Pound's poetics as a continuation
of a vitalist and Romantic revolt against rationalist abstraction and conceptual mediations—that revolt manifested as well in his defense and use of
the ideogram—adds weight to Richard Sieburth's wonderfully insightful
examination of Pound's economic thought.[65] As Sieburth writes, the monetary system facilitated the "alienation of the symbol from the thing. . . .
The arch criminal for Pound is the man who makes sure that value is detached from its concrete embodiment and then 'plays the gap' between symbol and object, between abstract money and embodied wealth."[66] "Playing
the gap" for Pound is usury, collecting interest—making money off time
and achieving wealth from the unproductive realm of abstraction rather
than through unmediated acts of creation: "Bank creates it ex nihil . . . / No
man hath natural right to exercise profession / of lender, save he who hath
it to lend."[67] Usury is the most dire symptom of Western decadence; in one
of his famous "economic Cantos," XLV, he stages usury's effects as deadly
and degenerative:

> With usura the line grows thick
> With usura is no clear demarcation
> And no man can find site for his dwelling.
> Stone cutter is kept from his stone
> Weaver is kept from his loom
> WITH USURA
> Wool comes not to market
> Sheep bringeth no gain with usura[68]

Usury not only obstructs and hinders production; it depletes, corrupts, and slowly kills life, leaving sterility in its wake. "Usura slayeth the child in the womb / . . . lyeth / between the young bride and bridegroom / CONTRA NATURUM / . . . Corpses are sent to banquet at behest of usura."[69] To end the power of money and to restore life to the community, Pound is attracted to the schemes of monetary cranks such as the interwar-year economist Major Douglas's social-credit schemes and the German monetarist Silvio Gesell's idea of *Schwundgeld* (disappearing money): "a currency which loses its value every month it lies idle or unspent," thus making it impossible to hoard or lend.[70] Vitalism's cultural reaction against the spirit was matched by its economic revolt against money: irrationalism and antimonetary demagoguery, and its correlate of anti-Semitism,[71] ultimately paved the way for the Judeocide.[72]

If Pound's vitalist aesthetics combined the romantic revolt against quantification and rationalist abstraction in its critique of mediation through money—echoes of which we hear in today's movements against globalism and reactions to the financial crisis—Gertrude Stein's immediatism was of a different kind. Stein has been painted with the broad brush of Bergsonism, most famously by Wyndham Lewis, who cast her along with the popular novelist Anita Loos as the high priestess of his loathed "Time-Cult," which included any movement that challenged linearity, sequence, and causality.[73] However, Stein's understanding of immediacy had nothing of Bergson's epistemological import. Frederic Jameson has read Stein's characters as precursors to the Deleuzean schizophrenic who enjoys nether continuity with the past nor anticipation of the future. Stein, however, enlists not the schizophrenic but the figure of Melanctha, a black woman, to explore what she names "the continuous present."[74] Jumping from the incorrect assumption of a singular tense, that is, of the continuous present in black dialectic, Stein has been read as intimating that blacks themselves, in a world of immediate sensation and amnesia, had no real cognitive appreciation of time or history. Immediacy could then refer to the process of cultural or monetary de-mediation; it also referred to the construction of time. The "Jew" represented mediation, and the "Black" embodied immediacy.

Having explored the imbrication of the race concept with Bergsonian intuition and immediacy, I shall attempt similar readings of memory and duration, on the one hand, and the *élan vital* on the other. Vitalism pitted the regenerative gifts of the non-European "primitive" against the ennervating "Jewish" abstraction of high culture.[75]

Racial Memory

Mark Antliff has related in brilliant detail how Bergsonian intuition was appropriated by opposed political tendencies. On the one hand, intuition was said to provide access to the pure subjectivism that expressed itself in anarchoindividualism; on the other hand, Bergsonian intuition was heralded as the mode for the apprehension of a creative organic racial or national spirit that—presumably as without spatiotemporal location and extension as the Cartesian soul—dissolved under the light of analysis and intellect. As Antliff argues, those who appropriated Bergsonism for a racial organicism and a Celtic nationalism in particular valorized intuition for the access that it allowed to a creative racial or national spirit, which, to use Bergson's metaphor for the *élan vital*, was like the absent center from which a display of fireworks emanates.

Antliff splits Bergson from Bergsonism, of which the said appropriations are examples. But Bergson's own pronouncements about his philosophy do little to resolve diverse and contradictory interpretations of his doctrine. To understand how an intuitive politics of racial memory and spirit was inspired by his philosophy, we have to go to its foundations. The fundamental challenge that Bergson had put before modern philosophy was that of "revising our categories and reconstructing our conclusions by substituting the *se faisant* for the *tout fait*, the idea of a reality which is actually and literally making itself moment by moment as it goes along in place of the idea of a reality which—even if it be supposed to be temporally and successively experienced—is yet regarded as already *made*."[76] Bergson's cosmic vision is most often understood in the following way: the emergence of new forms and processes is not possible as the effect of external forces alone (mechanism) or from the influence of a predetermined end (teleology). Moreover, each moment is the site of creativity or marks a fresh beginning exactly because no other moment *condenses* the same past that precedes that specific moment. For example, the repetition of notes in a refrain carries with it the just-played, self-same notes, thereby changing the effect of those notes and producing a novel effect, even if those notes in symbolic or abstract terms are the same.

Notes are, after all, an abstraction; they can be repeated over and over again, but the melody as heard is the real fact and in the real fact notes are never heard again. The effect depends on the changing process, the melody, of which they are part. Their flavor grows out of the whole of what has gone before, and since this whole is itself always growing by the addition of more and more "later stages," the effect can never be the same twice over.[77] Bergson thus avoids the triviality that each moment is a fresh beginning by bringing the whole past to bear on it and thus ensuring its qualitative uniqueness, as each new moment is preceded only by its own specific past. Since scientific laws predict consequences from identical conditions, and since conditions can never be identical, life itself cannot be governed by an external and indifferent law. Even the repetition of the past in the present marks novelty, because the apparently self-same can never be preceded by the same past. If mathematical or clock time is endlessly repetitious, as it indeed *is* a string of homogeneous, infinitely divisible moments juxtaposed and mutually external to one another, the refrain is evidence of time's dynamic, heterogeneous multiplicity of succession without separateness.[78] Even the repetition of notes in the same homogenous unit of time introduces a qualitative change, since time is experienced not as discrete multiplicity or as juxtapositions in metaphoric space but as continuity, as interpenetration.[79] The secret to time is thus to be found more in the tense structure of verbs than in prepositions, prepositional phrases, and conjunctions—before, after, earlier than, later than, and so on.

Yet this is a heavy burden to assume for the sake of qualitative uniqueness. If one recognizes that antecedent conditions never repeat themselves—for even if they do, memory of the previous now enters in their apparent repetition and calls forth novel responses and consequences—then Bergson is surely correct to argue for nonpredictability and thus freedom of action on the basis of the nondestructability of past experience. But as Lovejoy long ago pointed out (although mention of his fierce anti-Bergson polemics from 1912 and 1913 seems to have disappeared from the burgeoning new literature on Bergsonism),[80] Bergson has now ensured that the character of any present moment is made chiefly up of the vestiges of the past, though it may not be a necessary assumption that "the components of any moment— the old and the new—are proportional to their quantity."[81] But this is certainly how Bergson's duration was understood by many, thus revealing the possibly profoundly conservative nature of Bergson's philosophy despite its fame as the ontology of novelty and indeterminism.

For example, even a thinker who celebrates a radical Bergson emphasizes that:

For Bergson the emphasis is on the virtual character of time, in particular
of time's past which always "grows without ceasing," meaning that there
is no limit to its preservation (it possesses an infinite capacity for novel

reinvention). It is in this context that he outlines his conception of memory, which is to be understood neither as a drawer for storing things away nor as a faculty. Whereas a faculty works only intermittently, switching on and off as it pleases, the reality of the past is a deep and productive unconscious that evolves automatically. We thus arrive at the definition: the duration "is the continuous progress of the past which grows into the future and which swells as it advances."[82]

And Todd May readily admits:

> Our experiences do not simply drop away when they are over; rather, they accrete in us, they sediment into a thickness that orients us in some ways and not in others. Certain futures become open to us based on our past; others do not. Certain personal styles become ours; others do not. The past is swept into the future, coloring and directing it. The future is where the past is taken up, where it has its effects.[83]

As Deleuze succinctly puts it: "Bergsonian duration is, in the final analysis, defined less by succession than by coexistence."[84] But the problem runs even deeper. For if life is essentially a mnemic force—indeed, if living being is memory in its genetic, immunological, motor, and psychological properties, then any entity is constituted through its history. We should be able to understand (though not necessarily predict) what an entity will do in the present only from a study of that particular entity's past; moreover, if we suppose that each new entity through some heredity mechanism has as its virtual memory its species' history, then we may learn from its species' history what the future chapters of the life of the creature before us will likely be. There is simply no obvious point with which to begin our understanding of any organism. Again, there is no necessary reason that the species has to be necessarily a biological or a racial one rather than a social class or a nation. Still, Bergson's own philosophy does not clearly guard against a biologically reductionist reading and in fact encourages it at many points. Having analogized the living being to a thoroughfare through which the impulsion of life is transmitted, Bergson has the individual carry his entire past, a past that extends back to his earliest ancestors and that is augmented with the passage of time:[85]

> These memories, messengers from the unconscious remind us of what we are dragging behind us unawares. But, even though we may have no distinct

idea of it, we feel vaguely that our past remains present to us. What are we, in fact, what is our *character*, if not the condensation of the history that we have lived from our birth—nay, even before our birth, since we bring with us prenatal dispositions. Doubtless we think with only a small part of our past, but it is with our entire past, including the original bent of our soul, that we desire, will and act. Our past, then as a whole, is made manifest to us in its impulses; it is felt in the form of tendency, although a small part of it only is known in the form of idea.[86]

Here we enter a debate about how truly radical Bergson's theory of novelty and creativity are. Lovejoy argued that by locating the self in duration, Bergson had delimited the scope of creativity. In fact, he argued that Bergson was no theorist of novelty at all, for he did far more than *explain* the present on the basis of the past: he *reduced* and even subsumed the present to the past with which it was made continuous. Bergson may have imagined that he was keeping the gates open for the future, but only on the condition that the philosophical demon called *durée* allows only the swelling past to flow through.[87] To use William James's expression, the speciousness of the present as a discrete moment in clock time—for, as Heidegger underlined, the present indeed conceals the transpired and the anticipated—gives way in Bergson's thought to the overburdening of the present with the past.[88] Indeed, Jacques Chevalier, Bergson's principal interpreter and later Vichy collaborator in the Aryanization of education, read Bergson not (in today's happy jargon) as a temporalist of radical becoming but as a revolutionary retrievalist underwriting the display of Gallic symbols and the consecration of kings. Antliff's studies show just how commonplace such racial-nationalist Bergsonism was.[89]

Suzanne Guerlac has recently written about Bergson's identification of the self with its whole past, quoting him from *Time and Free Will*:

When feelings are considered concretely, in their real depth of feeling, they can be said to freely express the whole person; they are fused with all one's other feelings in what Bergson called a confused multiplicity. "Confusion" literally means *with fusion* here, since feelings are fused together; they overlap such that each lends a particular coloration to the other. "It is from the whole soul that the free decision emanates." Bergson describes the superficial layer of consciousness as a kind of crust of language and symbols that covers over living feelings. At moments of strong passion, our energies break through the crust. "The self rises up again to the surface. The outer crust bursts. It is at these moments that we act freely. Our actions tumble from us in a way a ripe fruit drops from a tree. They cannot be rationally explained."[90]

Thus, for the past to determine then how we act there must be, as J. W. Burrow has noted, "a concentrated act of will to, as it were, gather and focus our whole self in order to act freely and creatively. . . . It is like the Idealists' concept of the true, higher, integral self, but built now out of the fashionable materials of the flow of existence and Unconscious Mind."[91] Not only does this theory of free action seem excessively inward and irrational, but it burdens the self with having to act in the flow of existence and true to character in order to act freely. Putting freedom in "time, considered in its radical difference from space, that is as duration" makes for less of a theory of the possibility of freedom than a delimitation thereof.[92]

Keith Ansell-Pearson states the problem well, though he argues, implicitly contra Lovejoy, that the self's freedom is only located in duration:

> The dispute is not, it perhaps needs to be noted, over the reality of the new but precisely how the production or creation of the new is to be thought. For Bachelard and Badiou the new is, almost by definition, that which exceeds prior conditions and which cannot be explained in terms of them. The quarrel with Bergsonism appears to rest on the claim that the new cannot be genuinely new if it is bound up with, in however a complicated fashion, the past. Bachelard, for example, sought to reject completely Bergson's attachment to continuity because it appeared to him, this meant that the present was inscribed in the past: the "solidarity of the past and future and the viscosity of duration" mean, he argues, that "the present is never anything other than the phenomenon of the past." . . . For Badiou the event has no relation to duration, it is a punctuation in the order of being and time (if it can be given a temporality it is only of a retroactive kind).
>
> For Bergson, and Deleuze, following him, however, the new is bound up with a creative evolution. . . . It cannot be conceived outside of duration. Contra Badiou, Deleuze argues that to think the new, or the event, otherwise is to reintroduce transcendence into philosophy and to talk of the production of the new in terms of an interruption of a founding break is to render it mysterious and almost inexplicable. In this essay I want to demonstrate . . . how it is possible to conceive duration as a condition of novelty.[93]

Ansell-Pearson warns against a cult of novelty predicated on a theological belief in a transcendent and miraculous, godlike, infinite power for the transformation of the world's forms and conditions.[94] Yet actual change may simply result from nothing more earthly than our having to invent, innovate, and create in order to resolve and sublate immanent subjective and social contradictions as they mature and develop over time. There is nothing transcendent about such change because, while it is in important aspects discontinuous with the past, there are always limits on the novelty that can be produced. Pearson moreover misses exactly why Bergson located the "novel" not over and against but in duration. The key point for Bergson is that we are free only when our act springs spontaneously from the intuition of the whole continuity of our personality, including our virtual memories, which may include the race's as well, as it has evolved up to the moment of action. If this spontaneity is absent, our actions are simply stereotyped or mechanical responses. In these cases, we behave like automata, and our behavior would have the character of *réaction machinale*, a phrase repeated throughout *Matter and Memory*. Walter Benjamin arrived at an importantly different kind of identification of life and memory through his studies of Edgar Allen Poe and E. T. A. Hoffmann. As Michael Löwy has noted:

> The repetitive, meaningless gestures of the worker grappling with the machine . . . are similar to automaton-like gestures of passers-by in the crowd, as described by Poe and Hoffmann. Both groups of people, as victims of urban, industrial civilization, no longer know authentic experience (*Ehrfahrung*)—based on the memory of a historical, cultural tradition—but only immediate life (*Erlebnis*), and in particular "Chokerlebnis" that produces in them a reactive behavior, akin to that of automata "who have completely liquidated their memory."[95]

Automata today are of course not incapable of memory, and one should underline that for Benjamin memory was ultimately called on to recall failed revolts against and thus inspire a break with the continuum of history, not synchronize the self with the flow of *durée*.

Bergson introduces two kinds of memory, the first being habitual memory: the memory of the automata, which fixes objects out of the flux and can be fitted into preexisting categories and treated in terms of preset behavior. But there is also a personal or episodic memory, which does more than provide us with patterns that allow us to recognize and adapt to objects to which we are unable to respond to by rote. Indeed, for Bergson life is simply memory as an interval between reaction and action. Personal memory also preserves all experience, thereby providing a foundation for the persisting sense of self-identity and the endurance of fundamental inspirations and ideals. Only to the extent that the subject recovers his true self in duration and thereby brings his whole and true self to bear on the present can he act freely, as more than inert matter in motion, as more than a semiconscious automaton. But this is a heroic act. It requires the recovery of an integral self, but since that True Self has to be in its duration, the scope for truly creative action would seem to be limited.

Grosz states the point as well:

> If habit-memory repeats the past in the present, memory proper recalls it, represents it, just as perception represents the material image. For Bergson, this distinctive recollection of the past occurs only when our attention is drawn away from the present and immediate future, when our attention is in a state of relaxation, or makes a specific effort to direct itself to the past. The past itself is "fugitive," fleeting, accessible only through the movement of turning away from the present.[96]

In other words, Bergson stipulates that the temporal horizon of the freely acting subject be unified, encouraging us to understand retrospectively our experience as con-fused (in Guerlac's specific sense) and continuous.[97] But then continuity would not be an immediate datum of experience at all; it would be a construct of that kind of depth psychology that serves to conserve identity and suppress in the name of the recovery of the singular profound self the possibility of the dissolution of the self into multiple, discrete personalities.[98] Through a plunge into duration, the self could then be unified at any point in time as well across time and (as I shall point out) generations as well. In this way, the self recovers his true *inheritance* and becomes true to *his* character. Jonathan Crary writes that Bergson's normative model of the self is an "impossible counter-model of dissociation: a synthesis of all the fragments of lived time into an experience of wholeness so rich and intense as to be an antidote to forms of alienation and reification in a contemporary social world."[99] While a self true to character in this way may be less likely to lose in himself in the commodity demands of novelty and obsolescence, this Rousseauian conviction of truth and authenticity of inner subjective experience is hardly the basis for the more appealing positivity of internal difference and becoming minor but rather the basis for any wealthy heir to understand his individuality as continuous with and grounded in acquired wealth in all of its doubtless sordid history. In *Deleuze: The Clamor of Being*, Badiou levels a similar criticism against his philosophical rival, whose real teacher, he claims, was Bergson. But Deleuze does allow (though does not theorize the material conditions) for the proliferation of selves against the colonization of the human subject by a dominant ego in the service of the Oedipus complex or exchange socius. Deleuze is in fact a utopian visionary of the multiple.[100] Badiou misfires in applying an old critique of Bergson to Deleuze, who is indebted only to those philosophers whom he has reinterpreted in his own idiosyncratic image. For example, he makes Bergson out to be a thinker of difference when he is in fact a philosopher of the one. Unlike Deleuzean multiplicity, Bergsonian con-fusion is indeed not free in its becoming but neurotic in its past attachments.

Even the coherence of Bergson's theory of freedom as being in character can be questioned. Guerlac wants us to focus on our own preverbal, affective experience as the arbiter of the question of whether we have acted con-fusedly or freely (that is, whether our action flowed from the unified and whole soul), but then we are not given any criteria to determine when we have understood our own experience correctly. How do we know that we have applied the word "freely" correctly to our experience? Guerlac argues that we can just feel it—hence the centrality of affect in this interpretation. But can't we be misled? One wonders, then, whether Guerlac's profoundly inward or private theory of freedom indeed founders on something like Wittgenstein's private-language argument. I think Leonard Lawlor has Bergson right here, but he too does not pause at the radical inwardness he discovers in Bergson's thought:

> If philosophy therefore, for Bergson, is to turn to the true experience—to turn to true, and not relative knowledge—it must turn its back on social life; hence, his loneliness in *Matter and Memory*. Bergson says in fact in *The Two Sources* that Robinson Crusoe is still social. The philosopher must therefore inhabit a world without others more radical than the famous Robinson Crusoe. . . . As we have already seen, intuition is a sort of experience of death, a turning away from the external in order to pay attention, to spirit.[101]

Just as Jünger located in the limit experience of trench warfare the mainsprings of life, Bergsonian vitalism calls for social death in the name of an inward life, and that inward life is not necessarily conscious, personal life. Bergsonian duration is, in other words, not only the subjective apprehension of one's self in the flow of time. There may seem to be no room for an organic memory with biological and racial resonance or a collective racial memory of which the individual is simply a conduit, but there are clear indications (as I have noted) in Bergson's own writing that by duration he meant the whole virtual field not only of a single subject's memory but of the race to which he belonged, which now finds its home not in society but on the inside.

Elizabeth Grosz does not shy away from this radical conclusion:

> As living beings, we *are* the accumulation and concretion of our history, of what has happened to us and what we have done, perhaps even before any personal or subjective existence. The past, including one's personal life, the past of one's parents, one's cultural history and even biology, are carried with every living being. The history of all living beings is contained not only in its full detail as world history, the past; it is also contained within all beings, compressed in their genetic lineage, in the living remnants of earlier times, their continuing inheritance from their earliest ancestors. Although we think and perceive with only the most immediate layer of the past as it straddles the present, we always act with the whole of our past, which is, in a sense, our "identity," our "personality," the only stability that is possible in living organisms. The past does not determine our present action . . . for our present actions spring directly from and in continuity with our past. The present is not the repetition or completion of the past but its prolongation.[102]

May credits Deleuze for having completely depersonalized the Bergsonian conception of the past:

> Bergson uses the image of the inverted cone to describe the past. The summit of the cone intersects with the plane that is the present. "If I represent by a cone SAB, the totality of the recollections accumulated in my memory, the base AB, situated in the past, remains motionless, while the summit S, which indicates at all times my present moves forward unceasingly, and unceasingly also touches the moving plane P of my actual representation of the universe" (*Matter and Memory*, 152). The imagery here is of psychological memory: *my* memory, *my* actual representation. For Deleuze, however, Bergson is already on the ground of the ontological

past. It is not merely *my* past that exists like a cone in relation to the present: it is *the* past. My past is a particular perspective on the ontological past in which it participates.[103]

Here a sociological reading becomes possible, as the profound unease with the loss of the past as a living force has become palpable. As Frederic Jameson has perceptively argued, Bergson's duration allows a culture that is incompletely modernized and in which the premodern in the form of a *pays*, or local village, retains concrete reality to keep open the artistic and cultural channels from the past to the present.[104] Indeed, Maurice Barrès, the most virulent of the anti-Dreyfussards, uncannily echoed the same notion of freedom as that of his classmate. For Barrès, free action depended on an intuition of French ideals that lived still only outside of Paris; he thus counseled the youth to leave the metropole in order to return to their *pays natal*, there to walk among *La Terre et Les Morts* (Barrès's auratic fields and cemeteries), so that they could once again achieve a sense of oneness with their dead and the soil. Only once this feeling was deeply experienced could the young achieve freedom through emotive identification with the national organism whose (racist) boundaries the youth would enforce and whose (rapacious) growth it would serve. Bergson thus laid the philosophical foundation for a redefinition of freedom away from the abstract and juridical rights for which the Dreyfussards had fought and away from the human need of living bodies and toward a mystical idea of living freedom that, grounded in *durée*, would also set the limits of action on themselves as Frenchmen.[105] Needless to say, the depth and seriousness of this theory of the fundamental self, with its manifold aesthetic and political consequences, makes a mockery of contemporary identity politics usually mobilized around flat bureaucratic categories.

In this theory, the return to one's *pays natal*—of course the theme of Aimé Césaire's epic poem—is a turning back not simply to a location. Here we have more than a geographic metaphor and also a call to move out of an inauthentic space back into time, into one's living heritage. This idea of return is located in Bergsonian duration. As we will see, Senghor was an open admirer of both Bergson and Barrès. The central paradox of Bergsonism, if not Bergson's own thought, became freedom's dependence on the intuition of racial memory. Heine once joked about Kant that only a German could conceive subjection to the law as true freedom; the idea that creativity depended on the summoning of one's mythical racial past seems *prima facie* no less absurd, yet, as Bergson reasoned: "It is into pure duration that we plunge back, a duration which the past, always moving on, is swelling unceasingly with a present that is absolutely new. We must, by a strong recoil of our personality on itself, gather up our past which is slipping away, in order to thrust it, compact and undivided, into a present which it will create by entering."[106]

Antliff's brilliant study documents in disturbing detail the importance attached to memories of racial organicism in the self-conception of the Parisian avant-garde. Drawing from Eugen Weber's historical research, Antliff writes:

> "The nation" was "the new slogan" that met their [the avant-garde's] needs; furthermore, "in the eyes of the nationalist, the nation too is a living organism; and if it is, it cannot be patched up as one might an engine; it has to be magically healed and revived by an appeal to its roots, not just of existing society but of life itself." Thus, while reactionaries like Sorel or Valois did not believe in "logical discursive thought," they "did believe in energy, in force, in unthinking passions" evoked in the name of the mythic "purification" and revival of a class, nation, or a "race" that had a task to perform . . . or a destiny to fulfill.
>
> For the Futurists, that destiny took the form of a regenerative war between proletarian and bourgeois nations, between intuitive and rational societies. For the Puteaux Cubists, the purification and revival of the nation called for a return to its Celtic roots in the face of Cartesian and Germano-Latin cultural incursions. For the Rhythmists, it was Celtic and Latin roots that made up the French cultural mix, to the exclusion of other racial configurations. But for all these movements, Bergsonism, with its attendant antirationalism and biological collectivism, was at the nodal point of their reactionary politics.[107]

The nationalist quest for a mystical, panoramic vision of the past could find sustenance in the astounding facts of hypermnesia, which seemed to show that no phase of our past is ever completely destroyed. An impressive number of testimonies suggested that in some instances of extreme danger the entirety of our past is glimpsed at once, more accurately, in a present moment that is contemporary with a very short interval of public time. Such "panoramic vision of the past" (*la vision panoramique du passé*) had been discussed extensively at the turn of the century; Bergson focused on it in *Matter and Memory*. From the premise of the immortality of the past it followed that the past was fully present, if only virtually so.

Where Nietzsche counterposed *Lebensphilosophie* to historicism and the dead weight of the past, objectively and minutely recorded, Bergson paradoxically located (again in one reading) the very possibility of creativity in the location of consciousness in continuous duration, in the interpenetrating of past, present, and future in consciousness. While it is common to read both Nietzsche and Bergson as vitalist philosophers, their arguments could hardly be more opposed. One seeks life, novelty, and freedom in forgetting; the other locates creativity and indeterminism in duration. Freud, too, saw the past as a burden, as a source of neurosis and the primal crime of patricide repeated in the murder of Moses, but Freud was pessimistic about a simple overcoming of the past to the extent that he believed the memory traces of the primal crime could be ascribed to a phylogenetic heritage.[108] James Arnold argues persuasively that Freud's most dubious ideas about racial, phylogenetic heritage in *Moses and Monotheism* may have appealed to Césaire, as the Freudian myth of a biologically given, archaic memory opened the possibility for "the poetic exploration of the unconscious to unlock the treasure of symbolic knowledge" and for "the disinherited sons and daughters of colonialism and slavery" to "travel a short route to their ancestral past."[109] Yet the crucial difference remains: the racial memory of *Négritude* accesses not a putatively real traumatic event that is the source of neurotic return but the source of one's vital and productive difference. In its understanding of memory, *Négritude* is thus, in my estimation, more Bergsonian than Freudian.

Grosz is clear about the productive role of the past in Bergsonism:

> The past is not merely psychological but also ontological. It exists, whether we remember it or not, and it exerts whatever is unexhausted in it only through access to the present. This is indeed the primary political relevance of the past: it is that which can be more or less endlessly revived, dynamized, revivified precisely because the present is unable to actualize all that is virtual in it. The past is not only the past of *this* present, but the past of every present, including that which the future will deliver. It is the inexhaustible condition not just of an affirmation of the present but also of its criticism and transformation. Politics is nothing but the attempt to reactivate that potential, or virtual, of the past so that a divergence or differentiation from the present is possible.[110]

Just as Bergson's philosophy made (in one reading) memory of the virtual the *sine qua non* of creative spontaneity, the results of the revolutionizing of man's conception of the past—the discovery of humanity's deep, ethnological time and thus the vast possible store of virtual memory—were being assimilated in popular discourse through the anthropological fantasy of long-evolved racial differences despite the evidence of humanity's common point of origin.[111] As Archbishop Abbott Ussher's dating of God's creation at 4004 B.C. was pushed back, racial differences were thought to have had time to evolve, and the task of assimilating each race's deep, ethnological past was aided by a theory that made continuity with one's whole past the basis of freedom.

Moreover, racial spirit—its natural impulses, its strivings, its rhythms—was something one could only know through aesthetic experience or deeper and immediate self-knowledge, knowledge that could not be conceptually and rationally presented. The interwar-year conceptions of race thus often combined pseudoanthropological interpretations of the meaning of deep ethnological time, the philosophical concept of duration, and the existential search for the authentic self.

Historicity was not simply given in a living, organic tradition; it had to be retrieved actively through exceptional aesthetic experiences that allowed for a recovery of authentic existence in a world of mass conformism and decadent consumerism. Aesthetic exceptionalism often went hand in hand with vanguardist political violence, and both depended on Nietzsche's, Sorel's, and Spengler's supplanting of a naïve optimism for a pessimistic *stimmung* in order to call forth heroic sacrifice, violence, and even self-immolation. Conservatism became a violent, elitist, and revolutionary project. What we have here is less Jeffrey Herf's reactionary modernism than revolutionary traditionalism. The possibility of palingenesis hinged on the recovery of original roots.

Simon Critchley has recently put just this reactivation of heritage at the center of his justly celebrated analytical history of continental philosophy. I shall quote from his most recent formulation; the initial articulation was posed—and this proves important—in a discussion of the ethnocentrism of the Western philosophical tradition. His most recent understanding is quoted at length:

> The appeal to tradition need not at all be traditional, insofar as what the notion of tradition is attempting to recover is something missing, forgotten, or repressed in contemporary life. As such, the appeal to tradition

need not be some conservative acquiescence in the face of the past, but can rather take the form of a critical confrontation with the history of philosophy and history as such. Such a critical conception of tradition is what Heidegger calls the *Destruktion* (de-structuring) or *Abbau* (dismantling) of the history of metaphysics. . . . Tradition can be said to have two senses.

I. As something inherited or handed down without questioning or critical interrogation.

2. As something made or produced through a critical engagement with the first sense of tradition, as an appeal to tradition that is in no way traditional, a radical tradition . . .

Heidegger's conception of *Destruktion* is precisely not a way of destroying the past, but rather of seeking the positive tendencies of the tradition and working against what Heidegger labels "baleful prejudices." *Destruktion* is the production of a tradition as something made and fashioned through a process of repetition or retrieval, what Heidegger calls *Wiederholung*. . . . In the period of *Being and Time* (the late 1920s) Heidegger articulates the relation between a received tradition and a destroyed one in terms of the distinction between tradition (*Tradition*) and heritage (*Überlieferung*). This does not mean, however, that tradition merges with some sort of heritage industry; rather Heidegger is playing on the senses of the German verb *überliefern* (to hand over, or deliver over), to suggest that the authentic existence requires as its precondition a radical and not received experience of the past.[112]

There are surely important differences between Bergson's and Heidegger's revolutionary traditionalism; however, for Heidegger in *Being and Time*, the activity of *Dasein* is characterized by "being ahead of oneself" only by incorporating one's past in a resolute act that makes oneself present,[113] Bergson, however, had woven together the ideas of retrieval and authenticity well before Heidegger's solemn Germanic formulations.[114] At any rate, we are again at the foot of the paradox that the philosophical call for a renewal of the lost heritage of a West in distress and crisis would resonate with colonial artists.[115] The student of *Négritude*'s first great document, *Notebooks of a Return to My Native Land*, is struck by how the idea of return has achieved a revolutionary significance.

As a result of its Bergsonism, *Négritude* did indeed share the syntax of a revolutionary traditionalism, the attempt to recover a sedimented African tradition, though Césaire's reactivated tradition, unlike Senghor's, was quite constructed and constructive. Which tradition can one recover, after all, if one's heritage is made up of African retentions in spite of the violent history of slavery, the innovations of *Creolité*, and a first-class European education? To be sure, Césaire may have found congenial Walter Benjamin's deployment of the constellation through which tradition, sedimented or otherwise, was not to be recovered but instead rendered as explosive unrelated moments amalgamated and charged with *Jetzzeit*—speaking here of moments such as humanity's prehistory of primitive communism, failed rebellions, or martyrdoms. As I shall discuss in the next chapter, Césaire at times misunderstood himself as a redeemer of a sedimented African tradition.

To such a revolutionary reactivation of tradition Critchley counterposes his own Derridean form of deconstructed traditionalism, which he argues has been most creatively practiced by Paul Gilroy in his black modernist defense of tradition as a changing same. The difference on which Critchley insists is not at all clear: deconstructive thinking for Critchley has to take place within the linguistic and conceptual resources of the Greco-Roman *tradition*, making excessively difficult the drawing of one's poetry from the future. Why, as Critchley seems to be suggesting, should Socrates' solipsistic and rationalist form of argument found and close the tradition of philosophical critique? Indeed, to stave off charges of Eurocentrism Critchley is willing to accede to Martin Bernal's arguments about African and Semitic influences on ancient Greece. Yet, however black Socrates may have been (and it is not race but the critique of monadic conceptions of culture that is Bernal's concern), traditionalism is still a conservative closure, as Critchley himself fears. One also balks at Critchley's enlistment of Gilroy as a traditionalist of any kind when one considers how profoundly he has reworked and loosened the very idea of the black tradition through his unforgiving critique of the ethnic absolutism of Afrocentric thought and his brilliant embrace of the forward-looking (yet often disturbing) Richard Wright, for whom tradition was no longer a guide for the creative aspirations of black artists but had in fact become the enemy.[116] Gilroy, however, does defend an idea of a "nontraditional tradition," defined however so negatively that the addition of the inverse and the term leaves us nothing, puts us nowhere, atopia: "The term 'tradition' is now being used neither to identify a lost past nor to name a culture of compensation that would restore access to it. It does not stand in opposition to modernity, nor should it conjure up wholesome images of Africa that can be contrasted with the corrosive, aphasic power of the post-slave history of the Americas and the extended Caribbean."[117]

Resurrection! Who is this language (any Kran!

This was not Bergson's tradition. Here the recovery of *la vie* hinges on *la sur-vie* (living on, survival) of the past. The very condition of the possibility of the vital in this tortured philosophy of a distressed culture was the weighing down of the past on the heads of the living: life philosophy became a transcendental argument for the resurrection of an inheritance, in which the living and the dead crisscrossed in an imploded temporality. Bergsonism is indeed a traditionalism, as Lovejoy argued, but of a peculiar sort. In the next section, I consider another aspect of racial Bergsonism.

Noumenal Racism

By creating a philosophical basis for a subjective racial self—what Stephen Asma has called a "noumenal racism"—Bergsonism may have contributed more to racialism than even social Darwinism, which posited the differences of each group not in terms of internal racial essences but in terms of diverse adaptations to differential external environments.[118] If once the positing of an inside self allowed for the claim of common humanity despite apparent physical differences, the turn to the internal came to put race beyond science and disconfirmation in a way that social Darwinist discourse would prove not to be. In his important but neglected piece, Asma writes:

> Thus a progression can be traced from the Cartesian non-empirical self, through the Romantic apotheosis of manifested will to Nietzsche's criticisms of Darwin. The common thread throughout this progression is the attempt to preserve a notion of the self that is free from the determinism of external natural processes.
>
> This tradition asserts the autonomy of the individual by conceptualizing it as "uncaused cause." The whole orientation of the internalist tradition is to deny the self a causal history, for such a history would make it an enslaved "effect" rather than a free agent. That is to say, the self is seen as the cause even of its own representations; the self, immune from external contingencies, causes its physical manifestation and causes history. According to this internalism, if contingent history and physical laws cause the self, then the free agency of the individual is evaporated.
>
> After the Darwinian revolution, the empiricist and externalist model has even greater grounds for reversing the relation, for arguing that the self is caused by contingent history and physical laws. Natural selection is the

creator of the human intellect and will. Darwin suggests that our "innate ideas," for example, are simply well entrenched products of our ancestral past. Internalist thinkers are correct in seeing Darwin, then, as a radical opponent.

The idea of "race" is, for the externalist tradition, like the wider notion of "self," bound up in the contingent and accidental nature of Darwinian adaptation. Race is an adaptational effect of contingent racism. But a noumenal racism, where physical traits and customs are expressions of some internal occult quality, claims that race is a cause of history, not simply an effect.[119]

I have already tried to show how Bergsonism brought to a culmination the internalist metaphor of race. Bergsonism makes a further contribution in the language that it provides for the reconceptualization of race as a dynamic essence. I suggest that there is a certain isomorphism between a conception of God as an *élan vital*, as an incomplete force that realizes itself in the world only through pain and suffering (the crucifixion thus understood as a necessary stage in God's own development), and race not as a fixed essence but as a force that realizes itself through ever more complex and powerful concretions. That is, Bergsonism banishes both from theology and racial essentialism "the recognition of any self-sufficient, and perfect reality either transcendent of time, or logically antecedent" to the evolutionary process.[120] In *The Great Chain of Being*, Lovejoy would write of how Schelling's similar conception of God would strike his contemporaries as blasphemous. Yet as Bergson unabashedly writes almost one hundred years later: "God has nothing of the already made; he is unceasing life, action, freedom." George Bernard Shaw in *Back to Methuselah* understood Bergson well in claiming that what is "back of the universe" is not an omnipotent perfection but an aspiring will, a developing life force"; Shaw urges that we think of "God as a great purpose, a great will, and further—more as engaged in a continual struggle to produce something higher and higher." Shaw then pictures this force as "first lacking instruments, and then needing something to carry out its will in this world, makes all manner of experiments, creating birds, reptiles, animals, trying one thing after another, rising higher and higher as one instrument after another is worn out."[121] Shaw would later advocate eugenics as a coming to consciousness and direction of this evolutionary upsurge. The evolutionary process is thus making itself God. Creation does not begin with God, a personal being who is already perfect. No longer a transcendent being, God is conceived as not only immanent in the world but also dynamically so.

My argument is that once the conception of Spirit or God was so revolutionized and dynamized—the triumph of Asma's internalist metaphor presupposed this—God was soon replaced by race in this evolutionary schema, which we too often equate with social Darwinism. But it is closer to Asma's noumenal racism. The consequence of the whole evolutionary process was not to have fortuitously created deeply different races; rather the whole point of the evolutionary process is in the first instance to realize various dynamic racial essences, a process that can be understood neither in predictable, mechanist terms nor in the terms of finalism—the very dualism (mechanism/finalism) that foreclosed true creativity for Bergson. The organism is not the mere adaptation of the inside to the outside, like a fluid shaped by the container into which it is poured; rather the ever-evolving organism, conceived here as a racial culture, is the ever-differentiating expression of the inside, an entelechy more dynamic than Driesch's. Adding to Asma, I have emphasized that the victory of noumenal racism depended on a dynamic reconceptualization of the inner essence, which thus became serviceable as the foundation of a reactionary worldview.

The reconceptualization of race as a dynamic essence gave it the character of Spinoza's substance as understood by Deleuze. May, for example, writes:

> This is not a static picture of substance standing behind a set of attributes that it has brought into existence. That would be a picture of attributes as created by or emanating from substance. That is the picture most of us would likely have in mind, since it is one that has dominated the philosophical and religious tradition. For Deleuze, there are two differences between this picture of substance and attributes and Spinoza's. First, substance is woven into the attributes that express it. They are not separate from it. Being is univocal. Second, substance is not like a thing gives birth to other things. It is more like a process of expression. Substance has a temporal character. It is bound up with time. To understand this temporal character will require the introduction of Bergson's thought. But we must already remove ourselves from the temptation to see substance as an object or a thing if we are to grasp the Spinoza that Deleuze puts before us.[122]

Because technology could be understood as an extraorganic organ or prosthetic, it could be assimilated as the expression of the nondiscursable inner spirit of Faustian or Western man. Technology, in other words, was an attribute woven into a racial substance. The anterior life force that defied conceptual thought was thought to be embodied not in the creative artist but in the technologist, *homo faber*. Here I think light can be drawn on what Jeffrey Herf has called "reactionary modernism." Technology was not justified in fascist thought in terms instrumental reason, that is, utilitarian grounds or efficiency considerations, or Comtean banal optimism.[123] The Futurists, for example, fetishized and sought to employ the destructive capacities of the new (war) technologies—radio, automobiles, and aerial bombardment—in an effort to destroy the remnants of the moribund past. Centuries of idyllic attachment to the human form, particularly as it was glorified in figure of feminine beauty—"the sentimentality drenched . . . ideal of Woman-beauty"—would be violently severed. Indeed, the human form itself, the most obtrusive barrier separating the subject from an authentic experience of life, would be eradicated and replaced by the new mechanical being. As the poet Enrico Cavacchioli writes: "if you want to live, go get a mechanical heart, / inhale the red-hot blast of furnaces / and powder your lovely face with chimney soot; / then shoot a million volts into your system!"[124] In this articulation of the life principle, vitalist thought incorporates the machine, subsuming and elevating it to the status of an ideal conduit for the life force; technology alone is capable of providing the fullest expression of the Will in all of its creative and destructive capacity. The work of Ernst Jünger best illustrates the ability of life philosophies to construct a mythos of a life-serving technology, technology that extends an *unmittelbarlich* (unmediated) experience and which functions as the material externalization of identity and the "Will." Writing in reaction to both the Marxist and bourgeois figuration of the worker, which position the machine as the object through which the worker experiences alienated and *mittelbar* (mediated) relations of production, Jünger not only celebrates and encourages the workers' submission to new technologies, both destructive and productive—the metallic armor of modern warfare and immense, syncopated machines of the production line—but reframes technology as the means through which the worker "mobilizes the world." "Der Technik ist der Art und Weise, in der die Gestalt des Arbeiters die Welt mobiliziert."[125] In vitalist technophilia, the body qua vehicle for life is transcended as a conduit for the life force. It is for this reason that we encounter the motif of the destroyed body replaced by the superior machine. Fascist thought must stage and restage the sacrifice of the body at the altar of the machine as empty insensate conduit for the Will.

ARG 1 - *Bergson* is about *Nature* or *individuals* view of God (Evolution by activation of internal dynamic racial essences) → racial movement

Bergson and the Racial *Élan Vital* 121

As Spengler exclaims in *Man and Technics*, subtitled *A Contribution to the Philosophy of Life*, the technologist's "passion . . . has *nothing whatever* to do with its consequences"; rather, it is the Faustian urge to "triumph over difficult problems" and to build a world *oneself*, to be *one-self* God." Once race is understood as the Bergsonian God of the evolutionary process, vitalism is no longer a form of primitivism; it is rather a form of reactionary—nay racial—modernism.[126]

Racial Modernism

The philosopher David E. Cooper writes that vitalism or *Lebensphilosophie* went through a definitive transformation in the interwar years. While Jeffrey Herf explores the importance of "reactionary modernism"— the ideological outpouring of the era's most controversial thinkers, Oswald Spenger, Carl Schmitt, and Ernst Jünger—in the "aetiology of National Socialism," Cooper considers it from the point of view of the development of "post-Kantian" philosophy. As Herf is troubled by the contradiction between these thinkers' embrace of technological rationality and their resolutely Romantic opposition to Enlightenment reason, Cooper attempts to show how irrationalist commitments arose not paradoxically but logically out of the antinomies of Kantian philosophy. In short, Cooper attempts to defuse the paradoxical in Herf's neologism: the outburst of the irrational was not an interruption of the tradition established by the Enlightenment. What of course distinguishes my attempt to do the same is the greater emphasis that I put on race thinking or rather the changes in race thinking that made possible the marriage between technological Romanticism and the assault on Enlightenment reason.

Cooper's lucid demonstration of how irrationalism arose out of real problems of Kantian philosophy does allow one to see some other ways in which space was created for a vitalist concept of race in the very domain of Enlightenment rationality. This interwar reactionary modernist concept of racial vitalism was the concatenation of three tendencies—the said dynamization of the racial essence, the biologization of the will to power, and "deep holism" in the understanding of historical forms. Here, I shall briefly examine how the last two arose out of the antinomies of Kantian idealism. Once, Cooper argues, Kant had accorded an a priori status to the concepts by which our experience is organized—causality, two-valued logic, space, time, etc.—the source of these concepts immediately came into question. For example, Kantian "a priori" may not in fact be transcendental, as they arise out of the practical process of manipulating matter, or they may be in fact truly innate, as a result of a prior evolutionary process (both ideas can be found in Bergson). In this latter case of evolutionary epistemology, the a priori of the individual is in fact an evolutionary a posteriori of the species or race. Moreover, the idea that the subject itself forms experience—Kant's "Copernican Revolution"—raised the possibility that our knowledge is not cognitive but instrumental; it is, at any rate, humanly forged "perspectives" that constitute the world—the only one there is—as we experience it.

How did the problems that arose out of the Kantian conception of reason open the door to race thinking? I think Cooper's own discussion of Nietzsche and Dilthey—two thinkers whose engagements with Kant Cooper believes have been underestimated—explicitly and implicitly provides some important answers. Nietzsche, for example, did not take what we shall see to be Dilthey's route of historicizing the a priori categories but rather understood them as products of physiology and psychology. Cognitive capacity is shaped by the in-dwelling demands of self-interest, the almost biological demands of self-improvement and personal happiness; our perspective is not so much under cognitive command as a response to eudaemonic *demand*. Nietzsche had turned vitalism into the basis of epistemology. For Nietzsche, however, there are different breeds of men who organize the world differently based on their respective frames and schemes. For Nietzsche, the highest form of man (it goes without saying European man) understood the reality of this epistemological relativism (that is, the absence of grounds or cognitive truth value for organizing schemes of thought). For Nietzsche, the artist best transcended hoary epistemological myths. He would most freely choose those frames that served life. At the least, the biologization of the will meant that people experienced and came to know the world differently. In a sympathetic reading of Nietzsche as a *Lebensphilosoph*, Robert Wicks writes:

> Kant claimed, almost as a matter of obvious definition, that human beings can know things only within the framework of the human perspective, and that outside the manageable and managing constraints of this human perspective, we can prove nothing at all. The saving grace of Kant's view, as far as Kant himself believed, is that because we are all human beings, we must interpret all things in the same human way. Our limited human standpoint remains a shared one—one which coordinates our individual

interpretations with each other from the very start. Human nature might stand in the way of ultimate knowledge, but it keeps our community intact and in interpretive harmony. For Kant, we may be barred forever from entering the garden of absolute knowledge, but we can rest with the philosophical certainty that we think in concert. . . . Whereas Kant rested content to articulate a single, universalized, human perspective, Nietzsche looked carefully at the specifics that govern people's perspectives, case by case, group by group, and among these he considered differences in physiology, environmental conditions, and temperamental conditions, and he developed typologies of the stronger and weaker types, utilizing these discriminations to analyze all sorts of cultural phenomena. For this reason, there is much talk throughout Nietzsche's writings, where he compares and contrasts these groups to their various survival styles. Nietzsche expressed the need to consider as well all moral imperatives as the linguistic embodiments of varying physiological conditions which he considered more basic than conscious states of mind.[127]

Kant's anthropological writings may reveal that he was not the universalist Wicks makes him out to be, leading us to important questions about the achievement of Enlightenment universal humanism not in spite of but through the racial exclusions by which (European) men achieved their commonness, the shared attributes in terms of which man was defined and others dehumanized.[128] Or, as Fanon understood the consequences, "Leave this Europe where they are never done talking of Man, yet murder men everywhere they find them, at the corner of every one of their own streets, in all the corners of the globe."[129] Senghor's position is unique: he positively embraces the thesis that differential racial physiology makes impossible shared, universal assumptions, but he finds in the African mind the frames and schema necessary for absolute or universal knowledge. In other words, Senghor sought the possibility of absolute knowledge through Bergsonian intuition grounded in Nietzschean terms in differential African physiology. In Wicks's term, Senghor is thus the through and through anti-Kantian, holding to the possibility of absolute knowledge and rejecting the existence of shared internal cognitive controls.

For Dilthey, the organizing schemes of human thought were not physiologically grounded but were, in Cooper's words, "historical episodes." By writing that "the human type melts away in the process of history," Dilthey challenged both Kant and Nietzsche and located the a priori at the level of historically unique cultures. Cooper argues that Dilthey becomes here less a vitalist than a deep holist for whom monadic cultures are enclosed within their own organizing schemes (thus validating cultural relativism) and individuals stamped by them. Just as the concept of culture was conceptualized in supraorganic terms, the will to power or vital force was conceptualized as anterior to the living organisms it temporarily inhabits and uses as relay points in its infinitization. Cooper argues that the key to reactionary modernism was to make

> the real basic loci or centres of the will to power . . . Gestalts, the cultures which "stamp their characters on so-called individuals." Or matters can be put the other way around: the reactionary modernist vision results from superimposing a doctrine of the will to power on Dilthey's theory of Gestalts. For Dilthey himself, we saw, the primary sense in which a Gestalt constrains people is that of limiting the range of meanings available to them. If, instead, each Gestalt is thought of as the expression and locus of an underlying, blind will to power, the primary constraints imposed take on a different aspect, so that people may now indeed be described as subject to a "raging process" or as "inscribed by a Gestalt which is the medium of a will independent of individual control."[130]

As Cooper points out, the Faustian culture of reactionary modernism is believed to be organized by the technological scheme; technology becomes the way of revealing reality exactly because it best conduces to the expression of the will to power as an end in itself, as endless expansion of its domain of activity.

The nineteenth-century philosopher of history Dilthey, on the other hand, removes the normative concept of a priori from the understanding of historical development and in its stead introduces the concept of "Life." In Dilthey's revision of the movement of history, historical subjects are not free agents beholden to transhistorical and universal demands; they are on the contrary deeply immersed in their respective historical "age." For Dilthey, life implies historical rootedness in a historical whole or an age such that fundamental preconditions of knowledge and experience are not timelessly inherent in the nature of the mind or the will.[131]

This, in turn, raised the possibility that the "will to power will be manifested by different perspectives according to the kinds or 'breeds' of man adopting them."[132] Cooper could cite here Lucien Lévy-Bruhl, who argued in his early quasi-anthropological philosophy that the primitive mind did not respect the principle of non-contradiction, so that for example the same person could occupy two bodies at once, as in leopard men, or insisted on intentional invisible forces where we moderns understand only the probabilistic or chance outcomes of essentially mechanical processes, for example, the wind blowing off of a roof some shingles, which may happen to strike to death a passer-by. About the suspension of causal logic in the primitive mentality, Lévy-Bruhl wrote:

> As we understand it, the connection between cause and effect necessarily unites phenomena in time, and conditions them in such a way that they are arranged in a series which cannot be reversed. Moreover, the series of causes and effects are prolonged and intermingled to infinity. All the phenomena of the universe, as Kant says, have universally reciprocal influence; but however complex the system may be, the certainty we have that these phenomena are always arranged in causal series, is the very foundation to our minds, of the order of the universe, and, in short, experience.
>
> The primitive's mind views the matter very differently, however. All, or nearly all that happens, is referred by him, as we have just seen, to the influence of mystic or occult powers, such as wizards, ghosts, spirits, etc. In acting thus, his mind doubtless obeys the same mental instinct as that which guides us. But instead of both cause and effect being perceptible in time and nearly always in space, as in our case, primitive mentality admits only of the two conditions to be perceptible at one time; the other belongs to the sum-total of those entities which are invisible and imperceptible to sense.[133]

Thanks to Robert Bernasconi's very important recent work, we are now only beginning to understand the influence that Lévy-Bruhl's theories had on the development of continental philosophy by Husserl, Merleau-Ponty, Derrida, and others.[134]

In his stimulating work on the relationship between *Négritude* and Bergsonism, Messay Kebede calls attention to what appears to be Bergson's critique of Lévy-Bruhl's theoretical apartheid between the modern and primitive mind. Yet to Lévy-Bruhl's racist comedy about how the Congolese would ask for compensation from doctors who had cured them, Bergson "empathetically" recalls how his childhood dentist would slip him paper currency upon removing a tooth as if he had to pay not for young Henri's silence but for the privilege of operating on him. While Bergson would then seem to reduce the so-called primitive mind to the child's, Kebede leaves this and other (as we will see) passages aside and insists that

Bergson on the whole attempts to show that the kinds of mental structures are not so different as to be closed on to themselves, respectively. And, sure enough, Bergson does attempt to show how we moderns too are not content to explain events that have tremendous human significance only in mechanical or probabilistic terms. Kebede claims that Bergson insists that the primitive mind respects natural causality up to a point and makes use of supernatural explanations only to account for tragic events as they relate to humans, events that are often more beyond their ability to explain mechanically or probabilistically than ours.[135] That the primitive mind is perforce more interested in the meaning of events related to humans than it can be in their naturalistic explanation is, Kebede convincingly argues, a foundational premise of Senghor's epistemology:

> This involvement of the human translates the evolutionary distinction between pre-logical and logical stages into two different approaches to reality, the intuitive and the intellectual, the former being interested, to use Senghorian expression, in the "meaning of the object and the latter in its 'form.'" In . . . transposing Lévy-Bruhl's discrimination between prelogicality and logicality into distinct forms of knowledge rather than into hierarchical moments of the same process, Bergson provided *Négritude* with all the premises legitimizing its conceptions of dissimilar races that culminate in the opposition between European civilization and the African Negro civilization.[136]

What is surprising is that neither Senghor nor Kebede mentions what Bergson had to say not about only those aspects of the primitive mind that are said exist to some extent in the modern mind but about primitives as they actually are. What Bergson writes here is actually more racist and insulting than anything he quotes from Lévy-Bruhl. Bergson reminds us of the missionary stories full of detailed accounts of childish and monstrous deeds. He implores his readers not to forget that primitives, having lived as long as moderns, "have had plenty of time to exaggerate and aggravate" the irrationalities of the once more humane, primitive mind. These are also societies that have not known progressive leadership, Bergson informs us. These societies, "marking time," only "ceaselessly pile up additions and amplifications," so that "the irrational passes into the realm of the absurd, and the strange into the realm of the monstrous." Bergson then plunges the racist dagger even deeper by denying that such retrogression required any (negative) innovative capacity at all: "These successive extensions must also have been due to individuals, but here there was no longer any need for intellectual superiority to invent, or to accept the invention. The logic of absurdity was enough."[137]

What has never been pointed out is that Césaire's *Notebook* may well have been in part the tragically anguished response to the insult and humiliation Bergson visits in these exact pages upon so-called primitive peoples. Consider here one of the most famous passages from the *Notebook*:

> Eia for those who have never invented anything
> For those who have never explored anything
> For those who never conquered anything
> but yield, captivated, by the motion of all things
> ignorant of surfaces but captivated by the motion of all things
> indifferent to conquering, but playing the game of the world
>
> truly the eldest sons of the world
> porous to all the breathing of the world
> fraternal locus for all the breathing of the world
> drainless channel for all the water of the world
> spark of the sacred fire of the world
> flesh of the world's flesh pulsating with the motion of
> the world!
>
> Tepid dawn of ancestral virtues![138]

Césaire assumes the "wild and wilder" voice Bergson attributes to the primitive, for how else could he have been recognized and heard? Rather than challenging Bergson's calumny that his people or people "like his" (Lévy-Bruhl speaks, after all, of the primitive mind) have invented nothing, not even monstrosity, he defends their mental capacities in the valorized Bergsonian terms as superbly intuitive, rendered here as a yielding to and captivation of things in motion as the essence of what they are in themselves. All that is objectionable in even Césaire's *Négritude*—the racial essentialism, the technophobia, the irrationalism, and the self-hatred—has no other source than the overpowering and destabilizing racism to which colonials were subjected by Europe's great thinkers in the Age of Race as it was about to turn inward.[139]

Epistemological diversity, as we can see in Bergson's putative critique of Lévy-Bruhl, was usually adduced as strong evidence of ontological divisions in humanity; even if the conclusion was not explicitly drawn as it was in Bergson's work, it was implicit, a kind of racist common sense. Or rather, racist common sense fixed the a prioris in the human mind: different a prioris were fixed for different kinds of human minds. In this way, the biologization of the Will from Schopenhauer to Nietzsche did close down, as Cooper argues, the path to a true historicization of cognition, which was later attempted by Dilthey, though in such a way that the individual mind, though historical, was enveloped in a gestalt, thus creating the basis for another kind of biologization, a racial supraorganicism of which *Négritude* was an expression, as I shall argue in the next chapter.

CHAPTER FOUR

Négritude and the Poetics of Life

If the Dutchman Baruch de Spinoza was the *marrano* of reason, hiding his rationalism, then the Martinican Aimé Césaire was the African of Life, openly affirming his existential vitalism in the face of centuries of humiliation and degradation and in response to the reduction of black humanity in juridical terms to lifeless means of production, to a mere *instrumentum vocale*. There is little less surprising than the vitalism of the enslaved, and it is certainly not a mystery that a volcanically aggressive and liberating voice emerged from Martinique, which, as Michel Rolph Trouillot has noted, imported more slaves than all the U.S. states combined, despite being less than one-fourth the size of Long Island.[1] As a result of this relationship between slavery, colonialism, and the vitalism of the oppressed, the study of *Lebensphilosophie* simply demands that we also become scholars of colonial literature.

Césaire, Léopold Senghor, and their fellow *Négritude* poets were, to put it sharply, poets of a black ancestral myth by which they hoped to reawaken a latent feeling of affinity for the common descent of all Africans who had long become separated into seemingly independent groups. They hoped to redefine all blacks as persons joined together in the same familial group.[2] Through intense collaboration, the *Négritude* poets tried to recover the core of their fabulated common ancestry and to unite themselves around certain shared metaphysical and stylistic assumptions. In his introductory comments to Césaire's *Cahier d'un retour au pays natal*, Abiola Irele has incisively identified these core assumptions as a vitalist hyperromanticism—"a vision of restitution to wholeness of experience promised by a reconnection to the life-enhancing values of an ideal Africa, the peasant continent par excellence."[3] In his essay "The Spirit of Civilization, or Laws, of Negro-African Culture," Senghor would explicitly introduce the concept of *la force vitale*: "It is the ultimate gift . . . the expression of the vital power. The Negro identifies being with life; more precisely with the vital force. His metaphysics are an existentialist ontology."[4] In her study of Senghor's poetics, Sylvia Washington Bâ has also underlined the vitalist basis of his commitments: "The moral philosophy and ethical system of black American civilization are based upon participation in and communication of the supreme value, life. Respect for life is projected back in time to include parents, the dead, ancestors, spirits, God, maintaining an unbroken line of communication that remains intact with varying in degrees of life force."[5] In a monograph on Senghor, Janice Spleth argues persuasively that his aesthetics are fundamentally vitalist as well:

> The importance of rhythm in African societies has a metaphysical basis related to the concept of vital forces. The energy of these forces, which animates all beings, manifests itself in the form of waves whose ebb and flow appears as the weak and strong beats of music or poetry. The act of creating rhythm becomes a means of participating in vital forces of the cosmos. Senghor distinguishes between Western art, which imitates nature, and African art, which is not only social, he tells us, but vital. This is true of all forms of rhythm including the dance, which figures so importantly in religious ceremonies. Unless there is rhythm in poetry, words do not in themselves constitute a creative force. Senghor emphasizes that it was the *parole rhythmee* by which God created the universe, not by the world alone.[6]

These judgments echo Jean-Paul Sartre's introduction to the *Négritude* poets in his *Black Orpheus*. Giving a sociological analysis of *Négritude* as the vitalist expression of a peasant culture in revolt against the engineering culture of the West, he drew on Bergson to describe black epistemology as intuitive of the *inner life* of things as opposed to intellectual, which only grasped the surface of things. He also compared the unity of vegetal and sexual imagery in the *Négritude* poems to images of mineralization of the human in French poetry. So profound was the sympathy for life among the *Négritude* poets that they were taken beyond the chaste and asexual intuition of Bergson, and Sartre quickly descended into an offensive, hyperbolic description of *Négritude* as a "spermatic religion . . . like a tension of the soul balancing two complementary tendencies: the dynamic emotion of being a rising phallus, and that softer, more patient and feminine, of being a plant that grows."[7] However exaggerated Sartre's description, *Négritude* did indeed represent an attempt to plunge deeper than the reactive identity that blacks had formed in response to colonial humiliation and recover a vitalist and romantic personality putatively common to those who understood themselves as Guadeloupians, Martinicans, Senegalese, Malians, and other African groups.

It is not surprising that there has been a recovery of *Négritude* among African minorities in neoliberal France today, given the shared sense of disenfranchisement. "Césaire is in my lyrics, and I was upset when people misinterpreted what I wrote as anti-white because *Négritude* is the affirmation of our common black roots," said the twenty-year-old Youssoupha, recently profiled in an article in the *New York Times* about how *Négritude* and Césaire have made a comeback. Having earned a master's degree at the Sorbonne only to find himself stuck in low-level work, Youssoupha has taken to writing music. "*Négritude* is a concept they just don't want to hear about," he raps in "Render Unto Césaire" on his latest album, *À Chaque Frère* (To Each Brother).[8]

Then, as now, the *Négritude* poets offered Africans the Bergsonian promise of rebecoming who they really are, at least in terms of a return to traditional values if not traditional structures. At the same time, though, the mythic foundations posited and the unity achieved were not timeless but specific products of colonialism in two ways: the *Négritude* poets accepted colonial stereotypes only to valorize, and not transcend, them, and the unity they imagined was not in fact a product of blood or ancestral values but political opposition to colonial rule. The *Négritude* poets, intent on reconnecting blacks around ancestral values, could not properly emphasize their dialogue with the European thought, with which they had profound engagement.

As an important exception to this neglect of European roots, A. James Arnold produced a monograph to show the centrality of Césaire's engagement with European modernism rather than the Muntu tradition on which the Africanist Janheinz Jahn had focused.[9] European influences are sometimes admitted, but in the case of the German Romantic anthropologist Leo Frobenius, the debt was highlighted by the *Négritude* thinkers themselves, for Frobenius had essentially only given ethnographic validity to their claims of a core ancestral African identity. To the extent, then, that the ancestral myth is accepted, it is more difficult to admit the importance of the dialogue between *Négritude* and modernism and European anti-intellectualist philosophy.

I shall bring out in this chapter a four-fold debt to Bergson: the dynamics of *duration* provided a framework for the recovery of racial memory, the idea of *the fundamental self* formed the basis of the search for racial authenticity, Bergson's *critique of the intellect* laid the basis for *Négritude*'s search for experiential modes suited to the magically real immanent in the lived experience of the Americas, and the poet came to replace the *mystic* at the center of Bergson's ethical theory. A genealogy of postcolonial and modern New World literature cannot fail to engage with Bergson. While my genealogy of the life concept has been intended to lead to Bergson, my discussion here is meant to suggest how paradoxical it is that colonial writers would "forge weapons" out of the "arsenal" of this vitalist form of European irrationalism and counterrevolutionary thought.[10]

I shall argue that *Négritude* has been too often caricatured as simply irrationalist and culturally particularist and that a more nuanced reading of Senghor and Césaire reveal both a subtle vitalist epistemology and a complex theory of culture. Indeed, they both developed profound ideas about participant reason and cultural morphology. However, for all their efforts to recover a shared identity, there are important differences between Césaire and Senghor. Senghor openly embraces the life mysticism of race theory, and I shall attend at some length to these reactionary aspects of his vitalism. My focus will then turn to the now well-known differences between Senghor and Césaire in their respective understandings of vitalism: while Senghor's philosophical basis was the Bergsonian traditionalism discussed in the last chapter, Césaire's life philosophy also drew from Nietzsche's vision of Dionysian experience. Unlike Nietzsche, however, Césaire vision was, in the end, affirming of the existence of all blacks rather than affirming of only what is most intensely vital or healthy in African culture. Because Césaire dared to affirm the whole of black existence—and his great poem *Cahier d'un retour au pays natal* is just the laying bare of the painful journey to this *terminus ad quem* that is a new point of departure—he had no truck with the elitism, eugenics, and thanatopolitics implicit in Nietzsche's *Lebensphilosophie*, even though he could not escape its spiritualization of the biological and its biologization of the spiritual. It bespeaks of Césaire's humanity and greatness that he affirmed the real existence of blacks without blinking at tragic and damaged lives, and as we see, his towering contributions to the flourishing of black life live on after his death at the age of ninety-four in 2008.

What Is Living and Dead in Senghor's Bergsonism?

My analysis of the influence of the *Lebensphilosoph* Henri Bergson on Léopold Sédar Senghor has two motivations: I want to rethink critically the effect of the vitalist forms of antipositivism and antirationalism on colonial and postcolonial theory, and I want to suggest lines of criticism of today's renascent Bergsonism, of which Senghor was a brilliant and self-conscious exponent.

While Bergson's faith in creative evolution, guided by an *élan vital*, was shattered by the Great War and the decline of the West it had seemed to engender, Senghor exuded optimism over the fate of African humanity, whose renaissance, he believed, would guide Europe out of its own calamity. Senghor attempted to give intellectual confidence to not only the validity of African culture but also the immediate cultural possibilities for the intuition of absolute knowledge, the reconciliation of man with nature, the possibility of communion with the living and the dead, and the immortality of the human spirit. In all these efforts, his language was Bergsonian.

In a historically rich account of the cultural contradictions of French imperial rule, Gary Wilder has recently emphasized Senghor's philosophical roots in vitalist philosophy:

> Senghor maintains that blacks are organically connected to the natural world that they represent poetically. . . . He then relates this racially derived connection with the physical world to a specifically Negro-African epistemology, a form of black cognition that transcends the European distinction between subject and object. . . . *Négritude* may thus be related to a tradition of European vitalist thinking. . . . Black poetry, he believes, entails an unmediated expression of the cosmological life force. . . . He is attempting to elaborate an alternative, antipositivist form of reason and way of knowing. European modernism and irrational philosophy were engaged in a similar critical project. Senghor's move, like those of a number of cultural anthropologists of this period, was to define this difference in biocultural terms. This may be a conceptually indefensible and politically dubious gesture.[11]

Through excellent translations of some important passages, Wilder reestablishes the textual case in support of Senghor's own judgment of the importance of Bergsonian vitalism to his thought. While I shall try to add to this textual support, I shall focus on broadening the critical discussion beyond the problem of naïve biologism, which Christopher Miller has shown did not infect all of Senghor's contemporaries.[12] For a properly deconstructive analysis, the problems of antipositivist reason as well as irrationalism need to be explored with the limitations of their antitheses. To discuss Senghor's ideas critically, I have found myself in dialogue with

Abiola Irele's "What is *Négritude?*" first published in 1977.[13] His ground-breaking essays are referenced, though not often quoted, but the crispness of Irele's formulations of Senghor's key ideas facilitates the critical engagement with vitalism I shall encourage.

A dialectical thinker, Irele attempts to free Senghor's thinking from common misapprehensions and stereotypes, the better to hone in on the real difficulties. Of Senghor's rigid essentialization of the African personality and recourse to traditional African values, Irele grants that the objections of critics such as Stanislas Adotevi and Marcien Towa may well be valid. Indeed, he sharply summarizes the counterarguments to Senghor's position:

> The criticism that *Négritude* itself proceeds from an insufficient under-standing of the dynamic nature of African sociological realities finds its corollary in this objection on the practical plane. Because it postulates a narrow and rigid framework of social expression in traditional African culture, it is also felt to offer little possibility of meaningful social action in the present. The recourse to traditionalism, to the value of the past as a global reference, gives *Négritude* the character of conservatism which is felt to be at variance with the exigencies of the moment. And the spiritualist terms in which even the theory of African socialism is cast in Senghor's writings give his ideas an air of unreality that seem to bear no relation to the practical issues of socio-economic and technological development. (84–85)

Yet Irele suggests that the critics had not understood how Senghor forged for a deprived group "a sustaining vision of the collective self and its destiny" and thereby allowed Africans "to project themselves beyond their immediate experience" and particular historical situation.[14] There is a suggestion here of the critics' ingratitude; we do not create art in conditions of our own making, and had Senghor not made the most of the horrific conditions into which he was thrown, the African spirit of resistance may not have survived to outgrow the framework of *Négritude*. It is not that Irele denies the force of Adotevi's and Towa's criticisms in strictly philosophical terms; simply put, he suggests that the criticisms are anachronistic, though Miller's important archival research now leaves no doubt that many of Senghor's contemporaries were wary of any assertion of foundational, ethnic identity on the basis of ancestral determinism, given their commitment to a historical materialism centered on exploitation and universal emancipation.

Reviewing the black press in French, Miller concludes that the writers "seem to ban the cataloging or celebration of *inherited culture*, the cornerstone of essentialism. The past appears to be nothing but ruins. The only road open to the reader is political."[15]

Senghor could have developed a historicist critique of the notorious (and still all-too-common) positivist alchemical conversion of temporary "race" differences, themselves products of a violent history and social conditions, into "empirical proof" of deep, inherited, and immutable divisions existing, as it were, outside of time. To be sure, while trapped by racial logic (here we have his troubling indulgence of Arthur de Gobineau, though it should be remembered that the aristocrat's theory of degeneration by interbreeding was not premised naturalistically on the belief in the differentially evolved humanity of the races, and Gobineau's cultural Aryanism was not viewed as anti-Semitic in the early twentieth century),[16] Senghor strove to turn hard differences into soft ones, the clash of cultures into their future communion. But Senghor accepted race differences as they were; it may well have seemed otherworldly to keep the faith that such differences would be dissolved at some abstract future date: the history of slavery, colonialism, and racism would not soon be magically overcome, as our present confirms. Moreover, a dialectical Marxist approach could seem to call for the sacrifice of his generation and its ancestors in the name of the future transcendent race. For Senghor, the task became to reinterpret the extant, not distance from it from some future, utopian point. The living and the dead had to be vindicated; it was not simply a matter of the liberation of future generations. As Irele notes:

> Senghor's aim . . . is to explain what constitutes the difference as far as the black African is concerned, and to demonstrate the originality of his culture and by implication of Negro subcultures in the New World: the originality and the *validity* of their fundamental spirit. . . . Senghor's advocacy of *Négritude* does not imply therefore a simple return to outmoded customs and institutions—the point needs to be stressed, I think—but rather to an original spirit which gave meaning to the life of the individual in traditional African society.
>
> (73)

Since Africans were dismissed through positivist freeze-framing as congenitally antitechnological and "pre-logical," Senghor seems to have felt that he had no option but to avail himself of the only theoretical vocabulary in which the validity of this putatively alien mode of cognition could be defended. As Irele argued in a crucially important passage, that vocabulary was found in the Bergsonian vitalist form of irrationalism and the anthropology it informed:

> The terms in which Senghor formulates his theory of *Négritude* resound with distinct echoes of the work of a whole group of writers, thinkers and scholars in the West who can be situated within a single perspective—that of the anti-intellectual current in European thought. The specific derivation of some of his concepts is easily identifiable—his notion of "vital force" for example, can be attributed to Father Placide Tempels' now classic study of Bantu philosophy, while that of "participation," as well as his distinction between the traditional forms of the collective mentality in Europe and Africa respectively, owes much to the work of Lucien Lévy-Bruhl. Both Lévy-Bruhl and Tempels derive in turn from Bergson: the former explored in his work the anthropological implications of Bergson's reflections, whereas the latter applied his categories, particularly the concept of the "life surge" (*élan vital*) specifically to the Bantu. It is not only in this remote way that Bergson figures in Senghor's *Négritude* but as a direct influence. To Bergson, Senghor owes the concept of intuition on which revolves his explication of the African mind and consciousness. Bergson abolished with this concept the positivist dichotomy of subject-object, and proposed a new conception of authentic knowledge as immediacy of experience, the organic involvement of the subject with the object of his experience. It is largely the epistemology of Bergson that Senghor has adopted in his formulation of *Négritude*.
> (80)

The evaluation of Senghor's work thus depends largely on what critical use he made of Bergsonism and whether he was himself trapped by its failings.

Irele makes clear that vitalism works here both as an ontology and an epistemology. Let me first turn to Irele's discussion of Bergsonian ontology:

> The essential idea in Senghor's aesthetic theory is that the African arrives at a profound knowledge of the world by feeling the material world to the cosmic mind of which it is an emanation, to the transcendental reality underlying it—what Senghor calls, in a modification of Breton's term, *la sous-réalité*. . . . The spirit of African civilization is resumed in a Negro-

African ontology, which identifies *being* with life, with "vital force." This vitalist philosophy which Senghor attributes to the African explains the traditional forms of religious experience and expression on the continent. By his emotive and mystical disposition, and by the very fact of his intimate insertion into an organic milieu, the African is naturally a religious being, in whom the sense of the sacred is acutely alive. He communes directly with nature and with the elements, and through these, with the absolute fountain-head of vital force, God himself.

(76–77)

Here Senghor's concept of *la sous-réalité* may be closer to *surrealism* and its synonym, *surnaturalism*, as first used in the literature by Apollinaire in the introduction to his play *Les mamelles de Tiréasias* [The Breasts of Tiresias], than it is to Breton's meaning in *Manifeste du surréalisme* (1924). Apollinaire attempted to illuminate the superreality beyond simply experienced reality. The emphasis is not on irrational layers of the self, which are explored in the unconscious, dreams, and humor (René Ménil would attend to these layers). There is thus an important distance between Senghor's *Négritude* and Breton's Dadaism. This distance also indicates Senghor's attempt to reinterpret the European irrationalist revolt against science and empiricism as a suprarationalism.

Here Senghor becomes an essentialist. His essentialization of the African personality has so much been the focus of critical attention that his essentialization of the object of cognition has escaped criticism. In an incisive reading, Janet Vaillant notes Senghor's essentialism but does not challenge it:

According to Senghor, the African perceives the outside world with all of his senses simultaneously. He approaches each object gently, anxious not to harm it, eager to comprehend it *whole*, for he assumes that he shares with it and all else in the world certain essential qualities. What interests the African is less the superficial appearance of an object than its inner meaning, less its external sign than its sense. And the sense is not its use in a material way, but its moral and mystical significance. The black man goes beyond and behind daylight reality to the *essence* beneath. To this extent, he might seem to share the aesthetic of the modernist poet or the Surrealist in his rejection of the importance of superficial appearance. Unlike the European Surrealist, however, who downplays the importance of external appearance because he thinks that all experience is subjective, the African minimizes the importance of external appearance because he knows that is only the surface manifestation of *an underlying reality*. That underlying reality, not his own mind, is the focus of his interest. Knowledge of material objects is simply a means to understand the *essence* and order of the world. That order is *the only* important reality, and has an existence quite apart from any of its individual manifestations, including himself.[17]

Senghorian epistemology is conservative because it claims that there is in fact an important underlying reality and that knowledge of it is possible, but this suggests (as Nelson Goodman protested against Bergson) that since there is an ultimate reality behind our representations there cannot in fact be many ways the world is, with multiple correct versions each capturing only one of the many ways the world is.[18] There is a devaluation here of the constitutive power of language to make reality in multiple ways, leaving us with no metaphysical presence on the basis of which to arbitrate our conflicting ways of worldmaking.

Senghor was beholden to this theological belief in an ultimate underlying reality, and it was vital force into which both matter and life were dissolved. Senghor was a pantheist. God, pantheistically and immanently defined, remained the supreme object of knowledge. The Jesuit Placide Tempel's ethnophilosophy seemed to reveal the vitalist nature of African "ontotheology" (Tempels confirmed the earlier findings of Leo Frobenius, whose ethnography had already been enthusiastically assimilated). Being, Tempels argued, is life force for the Bantu. All is being, and force operates differentially through different kinds of beings, with the human being representing the greatest medium of the life force.

Senghor had already put *Négritude* on vitalist foundations in the 1930s through his embrace of Frobenius's ethnographic evidence for the popular African acceptance of animist beliefs. Indeed, as I shall discuss in greater detail below, the early *Négritude* thinkers welcomed the findings of Frobenius just as the early modern Germans had celebrated the rediscovery of Tacitus. Referred to as the *maitre á penser*, Frobenius was indeed the Tacitus of the *Négritude* thinkers.[19] One remembers that the partisans of the German Empire had read Tacitus very differently from the way he was read by Pope Pius II, who, according to Bruce Lincoln, focused on the descriptions of the Germans as "rude barbarians, whose material and cultural existence was severely impoverished in order to argue German knowledge of all higher things had come through the influence of the

Church wherefore an appropriately grateful German empire ought to submit to the Roman pontiff." The partisans, however, focused on Tacitus's description of "German honor and integrity, physical prowess, courage and beauty, their defense of liberty against Rome." As Lincoln notes, Tacitus's text bolstered northern pride by breaking the Mediterranean monopoly on antiquity.[20] Frobenius's text seemed to break for the *Négritude* thinkers the Western monopoly on cultural validity and creation. But in fact, Frobenius and Tempels read Western vitalism and its romantic revolt against positivism and mechanism into African culture, shaping its animism into an antidote to the malaise of their own cultures and inscribing a vitalist epistemology into the African personality itself.

Vaillant describes well Senghor's mystical univocal ontology:

> Africans believe there is a single life force that manifests itself in a variety of ways. Its enhancement is the highest good. Without it, nothing can exist. Everything visible in the world, rising from a grain of sand, through animals, to man, to his ancestors, finally to God, is connected to and dependent on it. All are part of a single whole. The life force itself, however, can appear only in and through these various forms of being and so is dependent on them in turn. Therefore the black African is careful to harm nothing and no one unnecessarily. Indeed his duty is to enhance all forms of life and through them to strengthen the life force upon which he also depends. The African goal is to live in harmony with all being.[21]

In *African Philosophy in Search of an Identity*, D. A. Masolo argues that the vitalist Bantu ontology (Tempels's understanding of which Senghor echoed) differs from Bergson's: "Bergson's dualism makes a clear distinction between the force and the matter on which it works change. In contrast, the Bantu, according to Tempels, appear not to be able to make this distinction; for them matter and force merge into a unity in which force subordinates matter under its dynamism. Being is force, declares Tempels."[22] As noted, Irele reads Tempels as a Bergsonian who does not seem to have been a dualist. Indeed, Bergson himself dismisses (at least at times) matter from his cosmology in order to reintroduce it as a myth projected on nature only for the purposes of technical mastery. Bergson, in fact, propounded a monism of a mnemic force that was most effective in the human being. Bergson attempted to dissolve the qualitative distinction between matter and mind in terms of degrees of duration, tension, and extensity. This ontological monism has rightfully confounded interpreters: the most difficult idea here is that as consciousness relaxes, it approaches matter in its extensity and separateness. The mind can thus get into the inside of matter because mind and matter only differ in degree.[23]

Here is the crucial passage from Bergson's *Creative Evolution*:

> The more we succeed in making ourselves conscious of our progress in pure duration, the more we feel different parts of our being enter into each other, and our whole personality concentrates itself in a point, or rather a sharp edge, pressed against the future and cutting into it unceasingly. It is in this that life and action are free. But suppose we let ourselves go and, instead of acting, dream. At once the self is scattered; our past, which till then was gathered together into the indivisible impulsion it communicated to us, is broken up into a thousand recollections *made external to one another*. They give up interpenetrating in the degree that they become fixed. Our personality thus descends in the direction of space. It coasts around it continually in sensation. We will not dwell here on a point we have studied elsewhere. Let us merely recall that *extension admits of degrees*, that all sensation is extensive in a certain measure, and that the idea of unextended sensations, artificially localized in space, is a mere view of the mind, suggested by an unconscious metaphysic much more than by psychological observation. No doubt we make only the first steps in the direction of the extended, even when we let ourselves go as much as we can. But suppose for a moment that matter consists in this very moment pushed further, and that physics is simply psychics inverted.[24]

Reversing eighteenth-century materialism, Bergson argues for the logical and even historical priority of psychics to physics, but how could matter be understood as a byproduct of life, which, after all, is only a recent, isolated, and sadly fleeting efflorescence in a vast cosmos of inorganic bodies? The bizarre idea is that by self-intuition of our most relaxed states of mind, in which the past is not condensed and thereby interpenetrated with the present as in our truly characteristic actions, we can understand from the inside the nature of matter! Matter and mind are reduced to *durée*. If for Bergson force is most relaxed in matter and tightly coiled in only the free subject, the Bantu (according to Tempels and after him Senghor) also understood being in terms of a hierarchy of force. For Senghor this suprarational, ontological commitment to an all-pervading force allowed the human, as highest form of being, to take itself and all other beings, whether trees, winds, or animals, into fellowship and apply the skills of social interaction.[25] As Senghor wrote in this essay of 1939, "Ce que l'homme noir apporte":

> People speak of their [Negro-African] *animism*; I will say their anthropo-psychism. Which is not necessarily negrocentrism, as we will see below. Thus, all of Nature is animated by a human presence. It humanizes itself, in the etymological and the real senses of the word. Not only animals and the phenomena of nature—rain, wind, thunder, mountain, river—but also the tree and the pebble become men.[26]

Senghor's vitalist ontology was radically egalitarian and noninstru-mental, but it also had the same damaging consequences of Bergsonism generally—a devaluation of the scientific aptitude and technological skills on which the African future inevitably depended and the access to which Afri-cans had been denied through the centuries of slave trade and colonialism.

As is well known, Senghor shared in this widespread rejection of in-strumental, Western reason and argued for the higher truth value of African participant reason. As noted, Senghor essentialized both the object and the subject. I shall soon turn to the latter, but I want to dwell on Senghor's "epistem-the-ology" aimed at the essence of the object. What is cognitively superior about participant reason? Irele's answer is still the best available:

> Senghor has singled out, as the dominant trait of this [African] conscious-ness, its emotive disposition. He presents the African as being, in his physi-cal constitution, a being of emotion.... The African's response to the ex-ternal world in Senghor's conception is an upsurge in sensibility, at the level of the nervous system, an intense, engulfing experience in which the whole organic being of the self is involved.... However, notwithstanding the profound association between [the African's] constitution and his emotiv-ity, the African's response to reality is not a mere instinctive reaction, but is an expression of an intention.... In other words, the emotive response of the African is an act of cognition, in which the subject and object enter into an organic and dynamic relationship, and in which the intense perception through the senses culminates in the conscious apprehension of reality.... The African's apprehension amounts to "living the object" in the depth of his soul, penetrating to the sensuous perception of its essence.[27]

This essentialism of the object or, rather, identification with the essence of the object does not read well in light of Nietzschean perspectivism and

Derridean deconstruction. But Irele's insistence that Senghor not be understood as an instinctualist remains important to our understanding of the thinker. Senghor highlights the cognitive importance of affectual response for the dance with the object by which it alone can be known; for Senghor, a person is not a substance but someone with whom one has a relation, and in the animist worldview, fauna, weather patterns, and animals can all be persons and related to as such. With animism as its ontological presupposition, participant reason enters into or intuits the life of the object, follows its fluid movement, and cognizes the creative evolution of life's respective forms. Senghor lyricized what he referred to as the African's participatory conception of reason and thus participatory relation to the objectival world and life itself. In extolling an African mode of knowledge, which "coincides here with the being of the object in its originating and original reality, in its discontinuity and indeterminacy: in its life," Senghor means nothing other than Bergsonian immediacy: participant reason is intuition by another name.[28]

Having underlined this debt to Bergson, I would qualify Emmanuel Chukwudi Eze's claim that Senghor is well understood as "Africa's Kant."[29] In his thoughtful study of the relation between philosophy and race, Eze justifies this interpretation by intimating that Senghor attempted to deuniversalize Kantian a priori categories by specifying and biologizing the determinate "physical and psychological structures of [African] perception."[30] For Eze, the influence of Lévy-Bruhl's *Primitive Mentality*, a work Senghor himself cited, is clear. One should not, however, conflate Lévy-Bruhl's conception of participation with Senghor's own anti-Cartesian conception. For the former, the primitive mind is governed by the law of participation between the physical and mystical worlds. Senghor does not (I think) mean to extol this, and he is not best understood as having simply made positive the image of the primitive mind in colonial anthropology, which was instead loosely used to deuniversalize the dominant Western modes of apprehension and to give confidence to Africans that their ways of knowing were not simply inferior and less truthful and no less capable of development than Western ways—and perhaps even more capable, because they were not burdened by scientist and objectivist assumptions that the development of science was undermining.

So by extolling participation, Senghor intends a critique of the spectator view of the world that Dilthey had already developed and, drawing from him, Merleau-Ponty and others would later elaborate. As Dilthey is best understood as a descendant of German Idealism, it is important to

remember that Senghor was convinced of the familial relationship between German and African epistemology under the sign of the Ethiopian
cultural type.[31] A persistent critic of ocularism and opsis, Dilthey located
the source of the problem in the same place as Senghor: Descartes, whose
excessively detached and spectatorial account of our relation to reality results in perception becoming, as Eric Matthews has put it, "a window on
to things, as if we were locked in a room in a house from which we were
gazing on to the world outside, a place in which we ourselves played no part
at all." Rather than building bridges to the world, Dilthey invoked that in
Erlebnis one was as certain of the outside world as one is of himself. One's
living experience of objects was quite different from that of the observa-
tion of "the dead and passive objectivity which resembles images in the
mirror."[32] Rather than objects simply causally affecting our sense organs,
our conative and affective sides affect, and indeed are constitutive of, the
lived experience of objects. As a result, our experience is inherently meaningful; experientially implicit meanings, interests, and values are at work
in perception, not simply superadded to it, and they are as real, factual,
and objective as the purely physical processes that science attempts to dis-
close.[33] Life, thus, became not a call for irrationalism but for a richer understanding of perception and lived experience as they actually are, richer
than what is captured in the scientific renderings of abstract-mathematical
and classificatory discourse. As Eric Matthews has put it:

> The "meanings" that we find in the world are no longer, as they were for
> Descartes and his empiricist and intellectualist heirs, the simple result of
> causal processes whereby situations in the world give rise to processes in
> the central nervous system that we experience as sensations of pleasure
> and pain. Instead, they become part of a reciprocal relationship in which
> the human body becomes the expression of a certain way of being in the
> world.[34]

What Senghor calls participant reason, Merleau-Ponty referred to as a
"vertiginous proximity [that] prevents us from both apprehending ourselves as a pure intellect as separate from things and from defining things
as pure objects lacking in all human attributes."[35]

To put the point another way, Senghor shared in what Martin Jay has
called the critique of the ocular, in particular of Bergson's implicit linking
of the domination of the eye with the deathlike rigor mortis.[36] Productive
of a cold and calculating objectification of the environment and distance

between spectator and the object seen, vision thus (putatively) undermines a "more harmonious, benevolent and empathetic awareness of our surroundings," while hearing and touch establish "the possibility of genuine intersubjectivity, of a *participatory communion* of self and other" through shared immersion in feeling and sound.[37] As Senghor, doubtless reflecting the sensibility of a poet who has touched his listeners with the spoken word, himself wrote:

> Until the twentieth century, the European always separated himself from the object in order to know it. He kept it at a distance. I add that he always killed it, and fixed it in his analysis to be able to use it in practice. . . . However paradoxical it may seem, the vital force of the Negro African, his surrender to the object, is animated by reason. Let us understand each other clearly; it is not the *reasoning-eye* of Europe, it is the *reason of touch*, better still, the reasoning embrace, more closely related to the Greek *logos* than to the Latin *ratio*. For *logos*, before Aristotle, meant both reason and the word. At any rate, Negro-African speech does not mold the object into rigid categories and concepts without touching it; it polishes things and restores their original color, with their texture, sound, and perfume; it perforates them with its luminous rays to teach the essential surreality in its innate humidity—it would be more accurate to speak of subreality. European reasoning is analytical, discursive by utilization; Negro-African reasoning is intuitive by participation.[38]

Senghor's critique of visual realism is not simply irrationalist. His ideal is less antiocularism than synaesthesia, the working together of different senses in our experiencing of reality. At one level, then, Senghor and the other *Négritude* poets were not instinctualists but intuitionists, with intuition working as a middle category between reason and instinct; they also tried to do away with the spectator model of perception for a participatory one and with mechanistic explanations, which always did violence to the phenomena of lived experience. There was nothing inherently reactionary about this part of their program insofar as it attempted to open up cognitive possibility rather than essentialize African perception as the simple other of a caricatured West. Often, for the *Négritude* poets, art was simply to bring to light those aspects of being in the world as experienced without theoretical presuppositions that did violence to them.

Bringing together anti-Cartesian philosophy, Western ethnography, and African cultural forms and cadences, Senghor grappled with philosophical and poetic language to capture this way that we actually are in the world prior to any distortion that resulted in the alienation of subject from object and subject from subject. For dubious physicopsychological reasons, Senghor believed that Africans were the least predisposed to Cartesian ocularism. Indeed, he maintained not that Africans experience life as participation between mystical and earthly forces but that Africans experience the oneness of life.

Searching for the basic continuity not so much in our individual psychic lives but between ourselves and others, Senghor seems to have sought it in the fact that we all participate in life and that in lived experience we are not alienated. Simply not properly appreciated (perhaps out of a mischievous cultural relativism) is the extent to which Senghor is best understood as the African Bergson and the father of a racial modernism. This contradicts Jean-Paul Sartre's interpretation of Senghorian *Négritude* as "spermatic"; however, like Lawrence, Senghor often heroically fails to prevent the collapse of his "participatory reason" into irrationalism and biologism. It has become commonplace to dismiss Senghor's famous juxtaposition of African emotion and Greek reason as antirationalist and emotivist; in a more generous reading, as I have been suggesting, Senghor, who privileged *logos* (the word) over *ratio*, here is only anti-intellectualist and intuitionistic, closer to Dilthey in important ways than a caricatured Dionysian Nietzsche.

To so expand the reach of the cognitive, Senghor's epistemology was, to put it another way, subtractive or, rather, it expanded the reach of the cognitive through subtraction. Here Bergson proves important yet again. For Bergson, intuition is actually an active (and difficult) mental operation meant to make experience immediate. It is not a form of irrationalism, much less instinctualism. To then free Senghor from the charge of instinctualism and simple irrationalism, it is important to understand how Bergson theorized the intuiting of the immediate. To recall from the last chapter, Milič Čapek has argued that for Bergson the immediate was exactly not what constitutes our sensory data as in empiricist philosophy but only that sensory data in as much as it is "freed from irrelevant and extraneous elements which, so to speak, 'mediatize' it."[39]

In other words, an immediate relation to other objects does not come through the casting off of cognitive equipment in a frenzied return to instinct. Senghor would surely would not have agreed that intuition or what he called participant reason has nothing in common with emotion, but he did share with Bergson the interest in freeing ourselves through concentrated

[handwritten marginalia: Bergson / mistaken / in the exclusion / of spatial ways]

mental action from dependence on ordinary tools for thought—the linearization of time, the logic of solid bodies, and the epistemological privileging of sight over hearing and touch. These tools do not allow us to experience flows in time but frame experience in terms of space. Objects are solidified into separate beads on a necklace, and to know something is to see it and place in a grid of categories. But for Bergson, reality is motion and the interpenetrated unity of an always unfolding duration ceaselessly yielding qualitative change. To recall another point from the last chapter: if, for example, mathematical or clock time is endlessly repetitious, as it *is* a string of homogeneous, infinitely divisible moments juxtaposed and mutually external to one another, the musical refrain is evidence of time's dynamic heterogeneous multiplicity of succession without separateness.[40] Even the repetition of notes in the same homogenous unit of time introduces a qualitative change, since time is experienced not as discrete multiplicity or as juxtapositions in metaphoric space but as continuity, as interpenetration.

Senghor's poetry explored the epistemological advantages that intuition as a mode of cognition had over rationalism and scientism: an appreciation of singularity and uniqueness; an awareness of the holistic nature of things and of their interconnection with other things; a comprehension of underlying, more fundamental processes of which ordinary things are only reifications, of life as a process and as a dynamic principle pervading the universe; and an access to the true flows of nature, love, music, and personal duration, allowing one to create and innovate rather than re-present the world as frozen and fixed. In this sense, Senghor's *Négritude* remains historically important as a salvo in an open anthropology of the senses. As he writes:

> *The Negro today is richer with gifts than with works. . . .* The very nature of emotion, of the sensibility of the Negro, explains his attitude before the object, perceived with such an essential violence. It is an abandon that becomes need, active attitude of communion, indeed of identification, as small as the action—the personality of the object, I was going to say— maybe. *Rhythmic* attitude. May we retain the word.[41]

Unlike other mystics, Senghor did not maintain that the way the world is cannot be expressed to justify a retreat into silence. But Senghor's epistemology has to be freed from Bergsonian absolutism, which can only interfere with the play of language and devalue the importance of scientific and technological framing as less true than participant reason. The gift of

rhythm may qualify blacks for poetry and music, but such an essentialization of the African personality threatens to validate our colonial disquali-
fication in science, technology, and even aesthetic experimentation. The
epistemological subtraction of the quasi-Kantian thought form of linear
time need not allow us to know the essence of things in order to remain
important for the cognitive enrichment it may enable.

I shall now turn at last to Senghor's controversial and more openly
contested essentialization of the subject. Here the problems are profound
and intractable, and again Bergson proved crucial as both inspiration and
source of error, though this has yet to be explored in the vast literature on
Négritude. As I have shown in the last chapter, one of Bergson's most powerful ideas is that while individuals appear to be acting from self-interest,
they are unaware that the self whose interest they try to promote is constructed for pragmatic social and instrumental reasons; unaware of this,
they identify with this "self" as something truly individual and personal—in
short, as "themselves."[42]

For Bergson, free action is true to individual character, and truth to
character requires creative fidelity to one's personal history, understood
not in linear or sequential terms but in terms of an interpenetrated whole.
Freedom is a matter of re-possessing oneself. Here it is important to remember that the animate can be distinguished from the inanimate precisely by
its mnemic force or ability to condense the past. Over the course of the eighteenth and nineteenth centuries, each birth came to seen less like the engendering of an unique work of art and increasingly understood in terms
of reproduction.[43] Once distinguished by its ability to reproduce, life could
be defined as that which physically embodies a physical memory by means
of which the present is bound to the past. Biology opened up the possibility of defining life in terms of memory. Bergsonian mnemic vitalism paradoxically demanded a creative fidelity to heritage or a renewal of tradition, insofar as the passage of homogeneous time itself did not guarantee
its efficacy. Senghor's *Négritude* was meant to recover the Bergsonian *moi
fondamental* for the African, yet—and this is a crucial difference—his theory of fundamental character breaks decisively with the solipsistic elements
in Bergson's. Indeed, Senghor's strident anti-individualism, which was meant
as a vindication of African communalism, eerily echoes the corporatist doctrine embraced by right-wing thinkers and mystifies the basis of social conflict within African societies. Senghor radicalizes the Bergsonian conception
of the past to include the living and dead ancestors of one's "race." In short,
he depersonalized the past.[44]

In a later work, Abiola Irele captured this aspect of early *Négritude* writing:

> The ideology of race . . . promoted by the theories of Africanism . . . [goes] hand in hand with movements of racial solidarity [and sustains] in the literature a form of Romanticism that seeks to legitimize and underwrite a myth of universal Black identity. In the African context this had had the largely salutary effect (though not without its problems and contradictions) of a revaluation and celebration of indigenous cultures, a process exemplified in the *gravitas* that writers as different as Senghor and Achebe ascribe to the universe of life that they posit as their true antecedents (what Senghor called *le royaume d'enface*, the realm of childhood) and which they stake their sense of origins. That the process of revaluation also embraces the modes of expression associated with the traditional world gives rise to what I have called an aesthetic traditionalism, a poetics of indigenism that shapes the formal structure of much of the imaginative literature. . . . The immediate import of these imaginative projections and intellectual efforts is perfectly clear: as counterdiscourses, they represent not only a repudiation of the negative representations of the "native" in the imperialist ideology, they also articulate the claim to an alternative cultural history to the Western. It is especially in this connection that theories of Africanism assume an incisive relevance for Black intellectuals in the New World, in what has come to be known, by analogy with the Jewish condition, as the Black diaspora. They imply a reinvestiture of the Black self, a reincorporation, in the strong sense of the word, that establishes a new compact of the racial and historical community through congruence with its origins. For the Black intellectual in Africa and the African diaspora, severed from a sense of immediate connection, with the original community, an appeal to the background of African traditional life and history represents a form of spiritual homecoming, a *nostos*.[45]

I am more skeptical than Irele of the effects of the conservative Bergsonian theory of identity on *Négritude*, for what Senghor has arguably done is accept the Marxist myths of the primitive communism and technological aversiveness of African societies, that is, the myth that they had not changed as a result of and thus cannot be explained by internal class contradictions conditioned by productive development. It follows from the myths of primitive classlessness and technology that there did indeed exist, buried in the African soul, an essential African culture timelessly fixed by its environment. In this context, Senghor's attraction to Maurice Barrés' provincial loyalties is hardly surprising and deserves short mention, as it points to the dangers of depersonalizing Bergsonian concepts. Senghor would openly admit: "When I arrived in France, I was educated . . . by provincial priests. I was mostly a monarchist. I was very influenced by Barrés [who] helped me to know and love France better, but, at the same time, he reinforced me in the feeling of *Négritude*, by placing the accent on race, or at least on the nation."[46]

Marcien Towa would call on African intellectuals to abandon any such descent into the self. He emphasized that Africa is a continent so complex and mired in difficulties that one can hardly indulge an endless dialogue on the nature of its true identity. Thus Africans needed to focus on what they need to become, not what they uniquely are:

> The desire to be one's self immediately leads to the proud reappropria-tion of one's past, because the essence of the self is no more than the cul-mination of its past; however, when the past is examined and scrutinized lucidly, dispassionately, it reveals that contemporary subjugation can be explained by reference to the origins of the essence of the self, that is to say in the past of the self and nowhere else.[47]

Through his poetic calls for an African unity grounded in blood, Sen-ghor spoke, however, of mystically connecting the individuations of the absolute reality of the life force through mutual native sympathy rather than in (as Michael Weinstein has perceptively put it) "exchange, power, deference and obligation."[48] In Bergsonian terms, formal political order and contract were based on analysis—*ordre géométrique*—rather than an understand-ing of the deep, internal unity social reality—*ordre vital*. Drawing on the Bergsonian theologian Teilhard de Chardin, Senghor would later elaborate this vision of a creative activity at work in the world, yielding individual human beings as the highest achievement only to date. Senghor would survey the physical and social sciences for evidence that our individual and discrete personalities were not the ultimate products of this life force and that we were already witnessing, especially in newly emerging African so-cialisms, Teilhard's vision of a hyperpersonal order through which the personal wills of individual being are merged into a larger organismic spiritual unity. But in such a vision, the basis and reality of social disagree-ment are simply eliminated through mutual spiritual identification and collective spiritual identification with a perduring African essence.

The criticism here is of course not new, but that essentialism had roots in Bergson's mnemically vitalist theory of the fundamental self has been overlooked. Rather, essentialism has been critically explicated as strategic, defensive, or reductively petty bourgeois. But this is to miss its profound philosophical foundations. Irele long ago underlined the centrality of Bergson to Senghor's vision of *Négritude*, which was above all else a reckoning of what was living and dead in the philosophy of Henri Bergson. It is slowly coming to recognition today that Bergson was the most important philosopher of the last century in terms of aesthetic and social influence, but the intellectual and dramatic importance of Senghor's critical Bergsonism has hardly received the attention it deserves. Such rigorous attention will enable the theoretical and critical engagement with Negritude that its ambition, depth, and historical importance demands.

Connecting Epistemology and Cultural Morphology

Aimé Césaire's critique of reason combined elements from Bergson's and Nietzsche's vitalism. While by the end of the chapter I shall have insisted on the greater complexity of Césaire's poetics and vision in comparison to Senghor's, they both remain united by and committed to a rather strong form of racial identity, and in this section I shall explore the philosophical importance of ethnography to their shared vision of *Négritude*. As James Arnold has noted, Césaire's debt to Bergson is allusively but decisively noted in his paper "Poetry and Cognition," which was delivered in 1947 to a meeting of professional philosophers. Only one professional philosopher is spared in Césaire's general condemnation of accepted modes of reasoning. Bergson is the unmistakable guarantor of this enthusiastically proclaimed truth: "Surrender to the vital movement, to the creative élan. Joyous surrender."[49] Arnold notes that Bergson's influence shows in Césaire's insistence on the silences of scientific knowledge, in his critique of the law of noncontradiction, and in his defiance of academic neo-Kantianism. Michael Dash has referred to Césaire as poet of *verrition*—Césaire's own neologism for a sweeping or stripping away. In this essay, whose importance to the philosophical understanding of *Négritude* was unfortunately eclipsed by Jean Paul Sartre's introduction to *Black Orpheus*, we see Césaire recommending a sweeping and stripping away not of social forms but of discursive knowledge and scientific cognition, due to the contradictions and antinomies it creates (Zeno's paradoxes). Césaire calls here for an apocalyptic act of self-invention and a return to primordial reality via poetry. This is more than a simple primitivism, which is a call for a temporal *verilm to Bergson.*

escape to a prelasparian state. Césaire is also interested in a phenomeno-logical bracketing—that is, an attempt to connect with lived experience as it still and always is before reflective experience brings its logic of substances and abstract temporality to bear on it, a logic that can only yield the antinomies of the scientific mind and the conversion of motion into logical contradiction and impossibility. Still, there is a call for a new space-time, going to the past by a spatial return, a coming home to where an African tradition survives and can be recovered through a stripping away of the sedimented categories of colonial reason. Rising above the quotidian self, the poet, inspired during the creative act, can alone tap into the more substantial and original energies of the racial unconscious and the life force itself. The notion here converges on older "metaphysical notions of literal possession by gods and spirits in the act of true utterance."[50] Césaire has married a Sorelian poetics of volcanic aggression with a Bergsonian call for a mystical return to a more intuitive and contemplative view of nature. In both aesthetics and epistemology, I would say that Césaire was also influenced by Nietzsche, a judgment Arnold doubtless shares. For example, while the references to Bergson's *élan vital* and critique of the intellect are clear, the idea of joyful surrender is also suggestive of Nietzsche's *The Birth of Tragedy*, in which the Dionysian redemption promises "the shattering of the individual and his fusion with primal being. . . . In the union of human beings with each other through forms of communication like song and dance the power of individuation is broken and the natural affinities among people are affirmed."[51] Ofelia Schutte notes that Nietzsche understood the principle of individuation as discontinuity from life:

> The myth of Dionysus being torn to pieces by the Titans symbolizes the essential tragic insight that individuation is the cause of human suffering. Here the body of the god of life (Dionysus) represents the totality of existence, while the shattering of the totality into parts symbolizes the violent separation of the individual from the whole. Individuation separates one from the whole of life, and, as it were, condemns one to death. However, just as the state of individuation is regarded as one of suffering, so its transcendence or end is experienced as a source of joy.[52]

Arnold does indeed insist that the Césairean hero is a lyrical and dramatic Black Overman, the exemplary sufferer through whose sacrifice the community is reborn. Yet Césaire was not an elitist; the poet was to help a people be reborn as a community in which persons are not strongly individuated, in which their reason is not used to protect and advance their egos in alienation from the rest. Césaire's inspiration was surely the creation of a community without domination internal or external. This is the Nietzsche that Schutte elaborates, and it was doubtless Césaire's. For Nick Nesbitt, however, Césaire's Nietzschean dissolution of the self— "my hand puny" in the "enormous fist" of "my country"—leaves him defenseless against Stalinist worship of the totalitarian state, by which, he speculates, Césaire was inspired, and my criticism of Senghor's strident anti-individualism or corporatism is similar in this regard. It is indeed important to challenge whether Césaire summoned sufficient appreciation for the autonomous personality who must shoulder responsibility for his actions in the face of powerful desires to be freed from the constraints of individuality, to immerse oneself in the stream of life and to lose one's identity. Yet I want to underline the generally ecstatic nature of Césaire's anti-individualism, for the communal ecstasy shared in dance and song (rather than mass torch-lit rallies) does not threaten to obliterate the individual in a violent, intolerant crowd, much less a machinic and statist communism in which surrealistic poets faced the same fate as did their species in *The Republic*.[53] We should not collapse Césaire's ecstatic politics for LeBon's crowd psychology of lynch mobs that, through ritual, ensconce invidious group identities. Astoundingly, our most vital experiences are ones in which we have minimal experience of self-consciousness. Vitalism gives recognition to such radically deindividualizing experience.[54] Speaking of a celebration in an unimposing little church on a Christmas eve, Césaire writes: "And not only do the mouths sing, but the hands, the feet, the / buttocks, the genitals, and your entire being liquefies into sound, voices, and rhythms."[55] Such experience is then contrasted to the lassitude of everyday life in an impoverished colony: "At the end of daybreak, life prostrate, you don't know how to / dispose of your aborted dreams, the river of life desperately tor- / pid in its bed, neither turgid nor low, hesitant to flow, pitifully / empty, the impartial heaviness of boredom distributing shade / equally on all things, the air stagnant, unbroken by the bright- / ness of a single bird."[56] At the poem's beginning, Césaire had already described quotidian existence under colonial rule as lifeless. Michael Dash notes that the oppressive nature of colonialism is symbolized in the "three statues of Césaire's *Cahier*, where the conquistador d'Esnambuc, the empress Josephine, and the liberator Schoelcher are frozen in white marble."[57]

Just as vitalism in biology served as a powerful reminder of the limits of mechanistic and reductionist science, Césaire's cultural vitalism evokes the dimensions of human experience outside the grind of daily life and beyond the reach of self-conscious, monadic agents. Here Césaire has a clear debt to Nietzsche, and he seems to have read him as Heidegger did. Schutte helpfully outlines the Heideggerian interpretation of Nietzschean self-overcoming as the intensification of life:

> Zarathustra . . . interprets all of existence as a process of will to power as self-overcoming. Here it is crucial to notice that in the process of intensification of life the boundaries of the self are not only dissolved but lose their authoritative and controlling function over the organism. . . . What is at stake is the overcoming of the schematizing self, the self which in terms of knowledge defines itself in contrast to the body and the passions, and which in terms of knowledge defines itself as the measure of all things, including the maxim that guarantees the validity of this measure. Nietzsche's thesis of the will to power as self-overcoming is at once an affirmation of life through the notion of its intensification and a critique of the metaphysical notion of the self. Self-overcoming means the intensification of life by which all divisive (even if conserving) boundaries on life are destroyed or transcended. Self-overcoming involves the overcoming of the Apollonian principle of individuation and drive to permanence in favor of the greater reality of the Dionysian flow of existence in which the boundaries between the subject and object, time and eternity, disappear. Language, caught in the metaphysics of the self, must also be exposed for the ideology it perpetuates through its metaphysics of subject/predicate and its reification of boundaries. The task for the "artists' metaphysics" with which Nietzsche meant to supplant the metaphysical tradition is the construction of a theory of meaning in which language no longer takes on this alienating function. [58]

True to Dionysian experience, Césaire was also compelled to criticize language itself as both an impediment and inadequate to such experience. Nietzsche's vitalist critique of language—that is, his contrast of life and language—was especially important to Césaire's exaltation of the poetic as a cognitively superior mode. In all the studies of Nietzsche, the Hegelian philosopher Stephen Houlgate has provided us with perhaps the best sense of Nietzsche's vitalist critique of the discursable, and I shall quote it at length:

> In his writing, Nietzsche always endeavors to emphasise the prelinguistic life that underlies his language; the real Nietzsche is his body, blood,

instinct, and will, and language and intellect are mere vehicles of that physiological reality. Yet Nietzsche is also obsessed with the idea that his words alone cannot adequately communicate his fundamental physiological sense of experience of life's complexity. Nietzsche's texts are not therefore designed to introduce the reader to utterly new thoughts and experiences. His words are meant to serve as signs to remind us of thoughts we have already had, but which perhaps we have suppressed. Nietzsche's personal experience of life, it seems, can only be communicated in a very imperfect way, but if we have had similar experiences, we can be reminded of them by Nietzsche and our understanding of those experiences can be deepened. The intensity of the reader's own experience of life is thus what entitles him to understand Nietzsche's truth. The reader is therefore intended himself to supply the experiences which give Nietzsche's metaphors substance. The metaphors themselves only lay down the limits of interpretation. In the first main speech by Zarathustra, for example, the metaphors of the camel, lion and child delimit the experience of self-burdening, of wild, of "leonine" freedom and of innocent wholeness, but the vagueness of the metaphors means that the reader must draw upon his own individual experience to give precise meaning to the text. It is the experiential base which is meant to provide the context for deciding the sense of Nietzsche's utterances. However, it also means that we can never *define* what Nietzsche's own experience of life is. Nietzsche's words do not take us "into" the complexity of his experience; they leave uneasily on the surface of his world. Only our own experience of life can take us "inside" Nietzsche's.

In all of his writings Nietzsche's pre-linguistic sense of life provides the authentic basis, the dogmatic conviction, from which he proceeds. Nietzsche's "truths," his metaphorical statements describing life, are thus nothing other than *truthful* expressions of his own experience of life. Nietzsche's personal experience is indeed his main criterion of "truth." This of course puts Nietzsche's philosophy beyond any rational criticism which is independent of the experience of life. Any terms of the public language which we might use as a frame of reference for such a criticism are repudiated by Nietzsche on the basis of unassailable experience.[59]

I believe that this precise concatenation of ideas animates "Poetry and Cognition," in which Césaire finds the way beyond the strictures of intellect not in a concentrated, Bergsonian act of nonsymbolic intuition, carried out in silence, but through the surrealist poetic tradition founded by

Baudelaire.[60] Because Césaire found truth and creativity in poetic language, he did not slip into the irrationalist, Bergsonian devaluation of language as a falsification of the *élan vital*. Truth is held to be beyond the discursable though within the reach of the poetic. Césaire would not find truth in silence or intuition.[61] Césaire elevates metaphor against the sterile precision of science in the introduction of "Poetry and Cognition." I have already discussed in the previous chapter why poetry and metaphor were alone vested with the power to describe life, for its movements, interdependencies, and metamorphoses bring discursive knowledge to silence by its own law of noncontradiction and the stable entities on which it depends: living things do not abide by the principle of $A = A$ and find themselves in the excluded middle that the logic of solid bodies evacuates.

Césaire's confidence and the optimism of *Négritude* in general were based on his belief that the African cultural legacy provided blacks with a heightened experience of life that would allow an understanding of the metaphoric depiction of the continuity of life, which poetry would then amplify. The textual proof of this animist sensibility was found in the ethnography of Leo Frobenius, whose importance to the early *Négritude* thinkers has been beautifully analyzed by T. Denean Sharpley-Whiting.[62] Whereas Schutte notes, "Nietzsche could not concretely imagine a universe where the continuity and flow of life would be part of one's daily social experience," whether in the areas of morality, social relations, or politics, Césaire was sure just such experience could be awoken by the African poet qua mystic.[63] The African's experiential base was understood as richer, closer to life. The *Négritude* poet-as-mystic would then help widen and deepen the intuitive, experiential mode only marginally recognized within European modernity and available only to poets and mystics.[64] Gregson Davis captures well Césaire's understanding: "the marvelous in its concrete, Caribbean incarnation was not, as it presumably became for the modern European, an artificially fabricated, escapist world of make-believe; rather it was present in the lived experience of people of African ancestry in their New World diaspora . . . the magical weapons turn out to be the cultural reserves of transplanted Africans."[65] But the poet Césaire needs the islanders of Martinique to serve as intercessors, for they still have contact with a living oral tradition. Yet the islanders also need Césaire, as the initiator of a communal task that revives group memory of their authentic ontology and instigates the invention of a new collectivity. Césaire and the islanders are "mutual intercessors, together engaged in the falsification of received truths" of African inferiority and the "'legending' of a people to come."[66] Take, for example, this stanza from the *Notebook*: "Blood! Blood! all our blood aroused by the male heart of the sun / Those who know about the femininity of the moon's oily body / The reconciled exultation of antelope and star / Those whose survival travels in the germination of grass."[67]

As the original recorder of this superior African ontology, Frobenius allowed the *Négritude* poets to repudiate a dialectical and linear scheme of history in which all gains are preserved and transcended, which allowed them to shatter the idea of objective progress, to find in African cultures, as the putative cradle of civilization, philosophical superiority in their recognition of the continuity and omnipresence of the life force. Frobenius's great interest in Africa was framed in typically German Romantic reactions. Africa was of interest because it represented a pure shepherding of being rather than its instrumentalization; Africa was in effect a contemporary realization of a cultural *Ursprung*, a living example of early cultural formations superior in the understanding of being to Western technological society. Where Bergson had written in neoprimitivist language of the need to return "to the dawn of our human experience," to "the world before man, before our own dawn," Césaire would proclaim that man had never been closer to the truth of being than at his birth.[68] In the face of the promise of Western decline, the *Négritude* thinkers refused a contemptuous dismissal of apparently anachronistic, though in fact coeval, ways of knowing: truth was not manifestly an end result, a dialectical outcome of the historical process. In short, an African vitalist ontology held out the promise of the radical democracy implicit in the belief in an all-pervading life force and the possibility for reconciliation with nature and ourselves as we take ourselves and nature into deindividuating fellowship and applied the skills of social interaction. It took, however, the catastrophic ending of the West to allow for the countenancing of the possibility that there had been a loss of objective capacities and truthful experience.

In "Leo Frobenius and the Problem of Civilization," Suzanne Césaire boldly revises the philosophy of history:

> In fact Frobenius has discovered that the idea of continual progress, dear to the nineteenth century, which showed civilization as progressing in a single line from primitive barbarism to the highest modern culture, is a false idea. Humanity does not possess a will to perfection. To emphasize this, it does not create civilization and then try to take it ever higher. On the contrary, it develops in multiple directions transformed by the inner

Paideuma, from one sudden "shock" to another, in the same way as the vital forces passes from one mutation to another through the diversity of living species.[69]

And Senghor would write:

> We had to wait for Leo Frobenius before the affinities between the "Ethiopian," that is the Negro African, and the German could be made manifest and before certain stubborn preconceptions of the seventeenth and eighteenth centuries could be removed. One of these preconceptions is that the development of every ethnic group, and of humanity itself, is linear, univocal, passing from the Stone Age to the age of steam and electricity and to the atomic age of today. . . . Frobenius tells us that, like individuals, ethnic groups are diverse, even opposed, like the Hamites and the Ethiopians, in their feelings and their ideas, their myths and their ideologies, their customs and their institutions; that each group, reacts in its own peculiar way to the environment and develops autonomously; that though they may be at different stages of development, Germans and "Ethiopians" belong to the same spiritual family. And he concludes: "The West created English realism and French rationalism. The East created German mysticism . . . the agreement with the corresponding civilizations in Africa is complete." *The sense of the fact in the French, English and Hamitic civilizations—the sense of the real in the German and Ethiopian civilizations!*[70]

To be sure, Frobenius's anthropological study of Ethiopian and Hamitic types may well have allegorized modern anti-Semitism; the Hamitic civilization was seen as the source of abstraction, while Cartesian rationalism produced analysis. Jews were often imagined as the destroyers of life; *Lebensphilosophie*, as I discussed in the last chapter, was often reducible to a veiled philosophical expression of anti-Semitism. Yet one suspects that Senghor was not attracted to Frobenius's cultural typology out of a prejudice toward Jews; fluent in German and having translated Goethe, Senghor was absolutely riven by the possibility of an affinity between early German Romanticism and the African world view. Yet, as the anthropologist Ita points out, Frobenius's elaborate topographies of African differences were often little more than a thinly veiled allegory of German nationalism—Germany's antagonists, France and Great Britain, would line up with the soulless Hamitic peoples, while life would be preserved by the Romantic nations. Of course, the idea of joining of the German and African spirit would have been repudiated by the European fanatics of race, and one suspects that Senghor was not innocent of—and may well have been amused by—how deconstructive of fascist racial theory his racial cultural pluralism was. More specifically, Senghor embraces the Ethiopian here to support values against the modern technoindustrial West, whether manifested in Hitler's Germany or imperial France. Both he and Suzanne Césaire obviously thought that Germany had lost its grounding in German mysticism.

A sympathetic reading of the *Négritude* thinkers would underline their sympathy with the *Frühromantiks,* by whose embrace they meant to articulate opposition to the colossal, imperial machine that Germany had become. As argued by Pheng Cheah and Michael Rosen, early German Romanticism, both as nature philosophy and political theory, is in important ways different from fascist ideology. The enthusiasm for Frobenius's Romantic anthropology should not be simplistically read as an acceptance of the premises of an inverted racism. Indeed, Senghor's sympathy with the *Frühromantiks* refracted here through Frobenius's ethnography undercuts any totalistic judgment against the West, hardly the nuance of Hiterlite racism.

And while *Négritude* is often understood, even here by Suzanne Césaire, as a relativist defense of beleaguered people and culture, Senghor and Aimé Césaire did not simply think that African culture implicitly carried epistemological and ontological assumptions that were perfectly legitimate for it alone; rather, their vindication struck deeper. African culture was thought to be superior to others in important respects: it was a living carrier of what had been lost in the course of Eurasian historical development and of what could be regained if the human catastrophes of cold, mechanical, and murderous civilizations were not to mount further. In this sense, *Négritude* was less an abandonment of reason than reason applied to itself, which is similar to, as Eze has perceptively noted, Horkheimer and Adorno's *Dialectic of Enlightenment. Négritude,* in short, was not a simple variant of cultural relativism, one of many branches of a Darwinian bush: the defiant particularism of *Négritude* was paradoxically underwritten by its universalist aspirations for truth.[71]

At this point, it becomes clear why Lukács' understanding of vitalism does not apply to the colonial context. Lukács wrote, of earlier forms of vitalism, that they had been mainly concerned with rejecting "moribund formations" of social being and confronting them with "the vivacity of total subjectivity as the organ of the conquest of life." Where Lukács found that the earlier vitalism had divided human beings into "two classes, the one living out life and the other torn from it," he argued that the cleft that appeared after the First World War was now within the subject, resulting eventually in what Adorno called the jargon of authenticity—the sometimes pathetic and often violent search for authentic, vital modes of being.[72] But for colonial intellectuals, the cleft remained social and had indeed become world historical with their living cultures, organically conceived, standing against the moribund West.

Indeed, the *Négritude* poets also exuded confidence that their emergent cultures would transcend the fatal dualism between art and life that, according to the young Romantic Lukács, Western thought tragically had not been able to do. That tragic sense of dualism is worth considering at length for the contrast it provides, and it is well related here by one of Lukács' last students, György Márkus:

> The relationship between life and the soul, the soul's great power over life and the transcendence of alienation that is represented by art (and by every other valid cultural "work"), cannot of itself solve the immediate problems of life raised by its dualistic, antagonistic nature. Art transcends the alienation of ordinary life, it also inevitably breaks away from it, and breaks away sharply, simply because it is totally self-enclosed, a complete universe in itself. It is a new life, which, as it is self-contained and complete in itself, has (and can have) no point of contact with anything beyond itself from the moment it comes into being. The relationship between the work of art and life (the reception of art), therefore, can never be anything but momentary contact between different spheres, through which "inauthentic life" can never be redeemed. One can perceive a meaning in life in and through the work, but that does not mean that one can order one's own life accordingly or invest it with meaning.
>
> Equally, art cannot abolish the inadequacies of human communication that isolate the individual—not only because of the inevitably elitist character of artistic communication (the concept of "genius" is one of the young Lukács' basic categories) but also because of its inherent nature. The work of art forges a universally valid link between creator and audience, since the link is created exclusively by the form objectified in the work. For precisely this reason, however, the link can never be adequate as far as content is concerned, partly because the world view objectively embodied and expressed in the form of the work does not necessarily stand in any relationship to the views and intentions of its creator (according to

the aesthetics of the young Lukács, intention and completed work are separated by an irrational leap) and partly because the experiences evoked by the work are *eo ipso* the receiver's own experiences. The quality of these experiences—that which makes the experiences unique to the receiver and the effect of the work of art immediate and particular—can never correspond in any way to that of the experiences of the artists.

This process of self-discovery through the work, the experience of being affected by it at the innermost and most personal level—whose endless repeatability forms the basis of its eternal influence—precludes any possibility of a sharing of experience between creator and audience. The possibility of misunderstanding, which in empirical reality was only *verite de fait*, becomes here a *verite eternelle*. The inadequacy of everyday processes of communication, the possibility of "misunderstanding," is not abolished by art; it is merely eternalized. It is changed from an empirical to a constitutive category.[73]

The *Négritude* poets believed that they were uniquely positioned to overcome two crucial dualisms: the tragic separation between audience and creator of which Márkus so eloquently speaks and the essential gap that separates representation from its object. As for the first contradiction, these colonial intellectuals felt that despite their elite origins, they were indeed bearers of a communal cultural tradition. As just noted, this was certainly the case for the intellectuals of *Négritude*, for whom the belief in a shared, animist, African cultural experiential base, a vitalist ontology with their countrymen, provided the basis for their visionary cultural nationalism. In this understanding, politics, art, culture, and the social are mutually constitutive elements. The work of art could finally have a socially valid existence.

Yet the postcolonial generations would soon tire of such views of traditional culture, to which the *Négritude* thinkers had putatively given precedence over real political and economic conflicts in the national culture of the riven present.[74] In fact, *Négritude*'s claim to cognitive superiority came to be understood as a romantic nostalgia for the past—a nostalgia that was itself a Western projection. Marc Augé would write of romantic anthropologists who:

> are concerned to delineate the phantom of an ideal primitive society, full of meaning, still close to the most basic of desires and removed from the repressions that as yet only haunt it: the negative or lost world of a world (our own) that lives only for writing, axiomatics and capital. Thus the

others gradually come to assume no other form in these authors' remarks than that of the shadow of our own remorse and anxiety. They are a western product meant for the use of the West . . . [75]

But *Négritude* thinkers did not seek to consign African cultures to a lost past from which we can now only learn but to see them as the living basis for cultural renewal.

As already implied, James Arnold contests *Négritude*'s self-presentation as a neo-Africanist poetry, arguing that the cultural prism that these artists qua Western subjects inherited and through which they perforce saw the world was the product of European modernism. Arnold is surely correct that Césaire "did not dredge up Mother Africa from some atavistic racial memory."[76] Writing against the Africanist critic Jahn, who saw the poetics of *Négritude* as the modern incarnation of *Muntu*, the aesthetic invocation of an African "life force," Arnold explains that it would be foolish to read Césaire as a neo-African artist whose poetics were the equivalent of African word-magic. Arnold avers—and I obviously follow him here—that it is a simpler and more probable hypothesis that Césaire's critique of Western metaphysics did not derive from a racial memory of African Hantu but rather a meditation on Bergson's *Essai sur les donnees immediates de la conscience*.[77] Indeed, Césaire's Africa is a constructed one, drawn from ethnographic texts and not mainly from a lived exposure to the culture, and the ethnographic texts themselves often projected nonrational, Western philosophies onto Africans. Arnold goes on to draw from Césaire's biography, noting that he had far too literate an early education to have been fully immersed even in the folkloric tradition of Martinique; thus, the African retentions he alludes to had to be for all practical purposes inaccessible to him. Césaire, he concludes, is "culturally a white poet"—a modernist—because his Africa is not a dictation from his unconscious but from his creative readings of ethnography.[78]

To be sure, the uncanny familiarity of animist belief systems for the *Négritude* thinkers may have resulted neither from African survivals and racial memory (as the *Négritude* thinkers sometimes fantastically believed) nor only from irrationalist Western philosophy (as Arnold suggests) but also from their thorough enmeshment as modern subjects in the fetishistic world of commodities. If animism allows things and natural processes to be endowed with will, intent, and purposiveness, we moderns handle those inanimate things called commodities as carriers not only of various respective concrete use values but of the supersensuous attribute of value itself, a mysterious property that fluctuates independently of the will of people and that no physical inspection or chemical analysis has yet found the material basis thereof. The vogue and popularity of the "magical real" is not only a result of the modern subject's yearning for a "lost" connection with nature or states of enchantment; it is also symptomatic of our own disavowal of the contemporaneity and persistence of animistic and fetishistic worldviews in our daily lives—modernity is itself an enchanted world.[79] The penchant for primitive worldviews derives from modern entanglements, not from the kind of inherited, quasi-biological, racial memory invoked at times by Bergson, Freud, Jung, and the *Négritude* poets.

Rather than search for the reasons for the hold of archaic belief systems in antimodern and irrationalist philosophy or in the incompleteness of modernization itself, it would be more productive in accounting for the uncanny familiarity of animist beliefs to follow Adorno in rejecting our false, Weberian understanding of the modern as disenchanted. Yet the irony remains that having taken as a given the division between the disenchanted world of abstraction and the world of the enchanted primitive, the modernist avant-garde (*Négritude* included) yearned to return to an age of fetishes.

However, whatever the motivations to study ethnography, it oversteps, I believe, to imply that *Négritude* did not learn from those early attempts, however flawed and marred by the times, to understand African beliefs in their integrity. The *Négritude* thinkers were right not to dismiss African worldviews as naïve or mythical or simply inferior, nonreflective forms of minor Western philosophies. It simply misses the depths of the Western crisis not to recognize that *Négritude* poets thought it unassailable in the light of the West's apocalyptic violence, now turned on itself, that its form of reason was itself based on myth: myths of the manipulability of nature as dead matter and of the Cartesian individual as an isolated, self-subsistent atom and thus paranoid and instrumental in relations. Such European haughtiness about the singularly rational basis of Western thought and its annihilative power over any alternative form of thought would have been at best risible to those witnessing Western implosion.

Moreover, one can understand the Hellenomania of nineteenth-century Europe as rooted not in an atavistic racial memory or even purely in romantic nostalgia but also in both the continuing influence of Greek art on modern conceptions and the unsurpassable nature of its achievements in, say, the epic form. For the *Négritude* thinkers, the vitalist African worldview was not drawn simply from consanguinity but rather because it was believed to be more enhancing of life; relatively immune to a triumphant Western historical narrative and contemptuous racist dismissal of African beliefs, the *Négritude* poets opened themselves to anthropology and to non-Western knowledge systems, to what had not been absorbed in the dialectic of history. As noted, Arnold underlines that Césaire's knowledge of Africa was mediated through Western Romantic anthropology, though African belief systems may well have organized those folktales that had survived the Atlantic holocaust. (Césaire and Ménil, we should remember, did publish a collection of folktales and may have had more exposure to these traditions than Arnold allows.) Yet one need not accept the neo-Herskovitsian thesis of African retentions, which simply stated that Mother Africa had something to teach and that her living culture had not been completely obliterated in the course of colonialism and the middle passage.[80]

Césaire's Returns

While Dipesh Chakrabarty has poignantly heralded Senghor as the precursor of the postcolonial ideal of an incarnate subject, one who inhabits his natal tradition with openness to cross-fertilization, the more interesting figure for me is Césaire.[81] Césaire understands the incarnate subject through the Bergsonian expression *le negré fondamental*, dismissed by Confiant as the myth of an inherited African substratum only overlain by a European veneer. In an interview with Rene Depestre, Césaire would implicitly dismiss the influence not only of European modernism but also Antillean Creole culture:

> I reasoned in the following fashion: I said to myself, "If I apply the surrealist approach to my particular situation, I can call up the forces of the unconscious." For me this was the call to Africa. I told myself: "It is true that superficially we are French, we are marked by French customs. We are marked by Cartesianism, by French rhetoric, but if one breaks through this, if one descends to the depths, one can discover the fundamental African."[82]

In *Notebook*, the Caribbean Césaire speaks of "a river of turtledoves / and savanna clover which I carry forever in my depths of height- / deep as the twentieth century floor of the most arrogant houses and as a guard against the putrefying force of crepuscular surroundings, surveyed night and day by a cursed venereal sun."[83] Césaire calls upon "these tadpoles hatched in me by my prodigious ancestry!"[84] Of *Négritude* he cries out: "Make me resist any vanity, but espouse its genius / as the fist the extended arm! / Make me a steward of its blood . . ."[85]

Yet *Notebook* reveals against manifest authorial intention some ambivalence about simply being fundamentally black, for Césaire rejects so many black identities, one persona after another, masks that his own Antillean displacement and Nietzschean radicalism disallows him, unlike Senghor, from ever wearing comfortably. That Césaire insists on the plural form of black (*negre*) suggests already the distance from an essentialist and reductionist idea of blackness. For this sensitive reading of Césaire's work, we are indebted to Gregson Davis's study of Césaire's poetics. He writes of *Notebook*:

> It is consonant with the poem's figurative texture to conceive it as a drama of self-exploration in which the speaker typically *impersonates* differing versions of the self and holds them up to merciless scrutiny. It will be useful to think of these discrete identities as masks (in the ritual-dramatic sense) that the poet assumes and discards at the dictates of his plot. From this perspective, *Negritude*, which many readers might regard as the defining theme of *Cahier*, can be interpreted not as a static datum or essence, but as a plastic concept in the process of construction. . . . In a word, the poem undogmatically explores the "fit" of various racial selves (masks of *Negritude*, so to speak) from contingent vantage points.[86]

Césaire stages a turning away from *persona*, which in Roman jurisprudence originally derived from the function of an actor's stage mask; the mask enables the actor to conceal his real identity and to conform to the role written for him. To our postmodern sensibilities it is comforting—though, alas, misleading—to underline that Césaire's narrator actually tries on and searingly rejects black personae while only proclaiming a fundamental African identity. Gregson Davis puts the point brilliantly in his discussion of the poem's ending:

> Despite the intimation of apotheosis implied in the motif of a ritual ascension, the poem's finale re-focuses our perception of *Negritude* as a *process* of self-exploration and recuperation. This re-focusing is mainly facilitated by the mention of "the great black hole" (*grand trou noir*) in which the speaker previously wished to drown, but from which he now

wishes to "fish out the baleful tongue of night." For partial illumination of the "black hole" figure the reader may recall of one of earlier pseudo-definitions of *Negritude* offered in the poem, where it was described as an *activity* of excavation ("it penetrates [*troue*] the dark debasement of its righteous patience"). The black hole (*trou*), then, may be read as an internal cross-reference, signifying, among other things, the spiritual space uncovered by the poet's persistent probing of the depths of plural black identity. In this account, the figure of "fishing" in the black hole points to the never-quite-concluded quest for an authentic self—a search that is not without the danger of "drowning" in a vast sea of racial consciousness. The poem's closure, then, is intimately bound up with the complex thematic trajectory it has followed throughout. The liberation that *Cahier* envisions is ultimately the freedom to re-examine ready-made identities—fragmentary models of the self—and to remake them into an integrated whole with the connivance of an engaged reader.[87]

Davis suggests that this vitalist understanding of *Négritude* not as a thing or a predicate noun but as a verb, as living activity, is implicit in Césaire's syntax:

> *Negritude* is positively defined not by predicate nouns (like its opposite number) but by verbs (*plonge, troue*: delves, penetrates). The shift to verbs strongly indicates that *Negritude* is not be regarded as a state, but an activity—an activity of self-exploration, of "delving" into the psycho-social unconscious. *Negritude* is nothing less than the ongoing process itself, the subterranean interior journey.[88]

For Nick Nesbitt, this dynamic of identity formation through negation, laid bare in dramaturgical terms by Davis and already outlined by Sartre in *Black Orpheus*, suggests a Hegelian influence mediated via Kojève's emphatic focus on the struggle for recognition in the dialect of master and slave. Brent Edwards has recently revised Nesbitt's challenging reading:

> Nick Nesbitt's recent study *Voicing Memory* offers the most thorough consideration of the work of negation in the poetics of the *Cahier*. Nesbitt argues convincingly that the subject of Césaire's poem can be read as a sort of "aesthetic analogue" to the "heroic subject" in Hegel's *Phenomenology of Spirit*. The intellectual world of Paris in the 1930s, Nesbitt points out, was very much animated by the rediscovery of Hegel, especially through

the highly influential lectures being given at the *Ecole des Hautes Etudes* by the philosopher Alexandre Kojève, whose reading of the *Phenomenology* emphasized the work of what Hegel termed "determinate negation" in the achievement of self-consciousness. Hegel argues that the Subject is "in truth actual only in so far as it is the movement of positing itself, or is the mediation of its self-othering with itself." . . . Such "self-othering" involves not a pretension to a secure and self-contained identity, but instead the continual confrontation with what is not the self: in other words, self-consciousness requires "the tremendous power of the negative [*ungeheure Macht des Negativen*]." . . . In his lectures of 1934–35, Kojève elaborates at length on the importance of "determinate negation" in the achievement of true or "revealed" Being through what Hegel calls "speculative logic": "The negation of A has a positive or specifically determined content because it is a negation of A, and not of M or N, for example, or of some undetermined X. Thus, the 'A' is preserved in the 'non-A'; or, if you please, the 'A' is 'dialectically overcome' (*aufgehoben*) in the 'non-A.' And that is why the non-A is not pure Nothingness, but an entity that is just as 'positive'— i.e., determined or specific, or better, identical to itself—as the A which is negated in it: the non-A is all this because it results from the negation of a determined or specific A." In other words, negation does not annihilate or destroy the negated element; instead that quality is preserved as that which defines the Subject (through what it is not). The parallel with the *Cahier* should be evident: Césaire defines *Negritude* in the anaphoric passage I quoted earlier ("my *Negritude* is not a stone . . .") through precisely this understanding of negation as the creation of a "positive" content by its differentiation from a series of items of "determined" symbolic valence within technocratic Western modernity ("stone," "leukoma," "tower," "cathedral"). As Kojève puts it, "The freedom which is realized and manifested as dialectical or negating Action is thereby essentially a creation. For to negate the given without ending in nothingness is to produce something that did not exist; now, this is precisely what is called 'creating.' . . . What is involved is not replacing one given by another given, but overcoming the given in favor of what does not (yet) exist, thus realizing what was never given." . . . One might argue, indeed, that determinate negation becomes a crucial element in Césaire's understanding of literary expression more broadly.[89]

This is very powerfully argued indeed, and all the more powerful, I believe, because it does not focus, as Nesbitt at points does, on Hegel's dialectic of master and bondsman as the *locus classicus* of the Hegelian notion of determinate negation. If the emphasis had been on this aspect of Kojève's reading of Hegel, then the self-consciousness of *le negre* would have been dependent on the recognition of that asserted self-consciousness as a human self-consciousness by the self-consciousness of those who had already denied the humanity of *le negre*. The dialectic of reflection, by which self-consciousness is engendered, is inherently mutual for Hegel, yet the predication of self-esteem on the recognition of the master race is a tragically destructive act, an act sure to yield only shame and violence, internal and external.

Yet, if recognition is a perilous goal, what of the other element of the Hegelian master-bondsman dialectic: work? Though Fanon clearly adopts in *Black Skins, White Masks* a Hegelian view of identity as a struggle for mutual recognition rooted in death-defying desire, he acknowledged in an usually ignored footnote that the white colonial master never depended on the recognition of the slave; he only wanted him reduced to a work animal. That is, he understood Hegel's ideas as too deeply rooted in the possibility of eventual reconciliation to capture the actual violence of the colonial system. As Fanon writes: "For Hegel there is reciprocity; here the master laughs at the consciousness of the slave. What he wants from the slave is not recognition but work."[90] Paul Gilroy, however, seizes on the Hegelian dialectic exactly for its acknowledgement of the irreconcilability of contradiction, slaves thereby having to emancipate themselves forcibly.[91] In this important reading, the struggle for recognition has indeed been displaced, but the role of work has been elided. While for Hegel the bondsman becomes conscious to his own meaning in the product of his labor and is thereby allowed to recover a sense of fulfillment, it is absurd to think that slave labor on the New World plantations served any such educative function and that black intellectuals would embrace the fear and service that Hegel thought the bondsman must endure in order to become objective to himself.[92] The Hegelian dialectic simply does not seem to fit the experience of African slaves in the New World: it is nonsensical that chained and whipped slaves could see in work a vehicle for self-realization, much less in their whips and chains the necessary conditions for the compulsion of the labor by which their humanity is to be achieved.

Emancipation depended rather on the emancipation from work, work being that bounded and alienated part of life activity. Césaire in particular would seem to be anticipating Jacques Lacan in the rejection of work *tout court*, as for Césaire—as well as Horkheimer and Adorno—it represents an instrumental framing of the world at odds with a heightened poetic sensibility of the pulsating life force pervading the universe.[93] Rather than preach a salvific change in the modes of practical labor, Césaire calls for a transformation in cognitive modes. For this reason, James Arnold is correct that Césaire's later sympathy for Marxism is at odds with his early idealist vision.

The Césaire of *Notebook* simply cannot be seen through the Hegelian-Marxist dialectic of recognition and labor, for he simply could not have found in slave labor the possibility of *Bildung*. Nor could have he believed that any master would confer, or was even interested in conferring, recognition on the slave. Moreover, if the slave has to struggle for recognition, it is doubtful that it can achieved. Recognition seems not to fall into the class of things that can be won through struggle; if it is imposed, it is simply not genuine.[94] A civil right as a right is not like the recognition of self-consciousness by another self-consciousness. Césaire would have dismissed as Sisyphean if not pathetic the slave's cry for recognition.

He simply does not care one whit about the recognition of the other (or the educative function of gang labor!). Here—and the irony cannot be lost—Nietzsche, an often crude exponent of eugenics, emboldened Césaire to rise above the need for confirmation, which can only imply conformation. Here are the roots of what is often perceived as the volcanic aggression of his poetics and the unapologetic call for violence in his student Fanon. I am not even convinced that Césaire attempted *first* to see himself from the perspective of others only to reject parodically inherited and imposed identities. Césaire is more sympathetically understood as someone who took himself to be affirming in the first place positive difference, not even engaging in Hegelian determinate negations. The poem is more than just the staging of the rejection of various internalizations of hostile others' phenomenal reality of one's self or one's "race." Césaire is better understood as an aristocrat in Deleuze's Nietzschean sense than as a Kojèvean Hegelian subject. In her masterful analysis of Deleuze's anti-Hegelianism, Judith Butler has written:

> For Deleuze as for Nietzsche, the Hegelian subject is the false appearance of autonomy; as a manifestation of slave morality, this subject is *reactive* rather than self-generating. Nietzsche finds the ideal of autonomy better satisfied in the will-to-power of what, in the *Genealogy of Morals*, is understood as an aristocratic value of life-affirming physical strength, the moral position beyond envy. . . . If the subject only exists through the assimilation of an external opposition, it therefore is dependent upon this

negative relation for its own identity; hence, it lacks the power of self-assertion and self-affirmation characteristic of the "strong" person, the *übermensch*, whose relations with others transcend radical dependency. The Nietzschean will, on the other hand, does not affirm itself apart from a context of alterity, but differs from Hegelian desire in its fundamental approach to alterity. Because distinction is no longer understood as a prerequisite for identity, otherness no longer presents itself as that to be "labored upon," superseded or conceptualized; rather, difference is the condition for enjoyment, an enhanced sense of pleasure, the acceleration and intensification of the play of forces which constitute what we might well call Nietzsche's version of *jouissance*.[95]

For Nietzsche, *ressentiment* is in essence a need to direct one's view outward instead of back to oneself; indeed, he emphasized that slave morality always first needs a hostile external world—that is, it needs, physiologically speaking, external stimuli in order to act at all. Michael Hardt would also emphasize the centrality to Deleuze's thought of Nietzsche's critique of Hegel's dialectics in the name of positive difference.[96] Deleuze always underlined his debt to Marx, and Marx's critique of Hegel's notion of the negation of the negation does anticipate Deleuze's. Bhikhu Parekh summarizes Marx's view:

> Following Feuerbach, Marx argues that although the negation of the negation is a necessary stage, it is not the goal of the dialectic. The entity resulting from the negation of the negation is not self-grounded, self-originating, and valid for itself. It postulates its existence through what it negates, and is therefore burdened with its opposite. In other words the negation of the negation is a negative and parasitic stage, and does not represent the true or the absolute positive. . . . The negation of negation thus plays the self-contradictory and peculiar role of both preserving and abolishing an entity, of securing both its denial and preservation, denial and affirmation. Since Hegel rejects an entity at one level to reinstate it at another, his negation of the negation never involves its annulment or abolition, and only sanctifies the status quo.[97]

For Marx, the vision of communism as the negation of its negation, private property, was ultimately destructive, because communists would then as a matter of identity be forced to destroy everything that is not being capable of being possessed by all, for example, talents. Marx tied an almost Nietzschean kind of *ressentiment* to Hegel's negation of the negation. As Butler notes, Deleuze also considered Hegel's dialectic anti-life, arguing that it serves to bury life-affirming desire.[98] The subject is after all forced to submit to the patient labor of the negative, which entails an acquiescence to the necessity and *rationality* of what already is if only then to negate it. The Hegelian subject has not a sufficiently vigorous sense of self to begin with its own self-transcending fecundity; rather, its sense of self is derived from the negative evaluation of the other, its beginning point.

Vital Difference

I can now elaborate on why I am uncomfortable with the idea that Césaire's poetics were structured by a Kojèvean idea of determinate negation other than there being no real evidence that he had read or heard of Kojève or had read Hegel carefully. Nesbitt records Césaire's note to Senghor that he had read the *Phenomenology of Spirit*, but this was after 1939, the year the *Notebook* appeared. Césaire's later enthusiastic discovery of Hegel also seems to weaken the argument that he had already been aware of Kojève's rendition of this philosophy when he conceived the *Notebook*.[99] Césaire was simply not a Hegelian. While negation and critique imply the determinate negation of given or inherited identities, they proceeded for Césaire only upon a prior affirmation of fundamental African selves. Césaire's fundamental black is fundamental in two ways: fundamental in terms of the retrieval of real, living heritage against a false tradition in which social roles are given as things, and fundamentally true to lived experience beneath concepts and reason. The *Négritude* poets imagined themselves as carriers of positive difference and affirmed the productivity of their own desire. In this way, Césaire was more than a poet of revolt; he attempted to create a line of flight. In other words, his flight does not take the form of "flight *from* something." It is rather "a pure movement *out* of something . . . a matter of *taking flight*."[100] Césaire's return is a fishing into and a moving out of a great black hole—the images at the end of the *Notebook*.

Yet Césaire's blackness does not simply fit any dominant conceptual categories, not even those of the homeland to which he is ostensibly returning but from which he has become natally alienated, to use Orlando Patterson's conception in a very different context. Nor can his blackness be defined as simply determinate negation in which the negated cannot but be carried over. His *Négritude* has at points all the attributes of the singular, the vital, and the multiple, because his return is meant to affirm and

Bergson's Virtual?

liberate the active force of a new way of being—at once modernist and neo-African and yet neither, a way of being that his society (and perhaps ours) was unable to recognize.[101] For Césaire understood, unlike Senghor, that the profound African self to which he inspired "a return" was indeed a construct not given simply in and through a Bergsonian duration but also through his own creation over the lacunae that history had violently created for the New World African, the gaps and breaks caused by the Atlantic slave trade. Just as for Gaston Bachelard duration was an active construct, so was it too for Césaire: the fundamental break with Bergson is on the same point, explicitly for Bachelard and implicitly and incompletely for Césaire.[102] To be sure, he equivocates on the ontological status of the living African heritage as both an already existing entrenched legacy and a reconstitution, that is, "a reinvention of ghosts past despite ruptures that have broken linear continuity."[103] As Robert Bernasconi has incisively shown, it was just this tension in Césaire's work between the myth of inertial tradition and modernist experimentation with which Frantz Fanon would struggle.[104] As we will see, Césaire is as interested in exposing wish fulfillment as what that entrenched legacy is to the reality principle as he is in recovering the African heritage as it in fact is. And in this double operation he does show the legacy to have the contingent character of "something constantly constructed and reinvented."[105]

And Césaire's *Négritude* is modernist in yet another way, for he claimed above all else "the freedom to transgress the limits of what one is presently capable of being or doing, rather than just the freedom to be or do those things"[106] and transgress those boundaries not first and foremost through determinate negation but affirmation of positive difference. An active force in Deleuze's Nietzschean sense, *Négritude* affirms positive difference as a multiplicity and difference from inherited blackness and thus self: difference is made the object of enjoyment and affirmation, and, as Gregson Davis has shown, the poem opens itself to plural black identities. In this sense, Césaire's return is much more open ended and radical than the young Marx's Schillerian sense of communism as a double return: return as a regaining at a higher level of the point from which man originally started and as a reappropriation of all that man has alienated from himself in the course of history. As Davis has noted, there is little sense in saying Césaire's epic hero has returned not simply because the starting point no longer exists but because the hero, like Odysseus, has himself been so transformed through his discarding of personae as to cast into doubt his identity over time. Moreover, Césaire suffers no illusion in history as fated for the happy ending of dealienation, of returning to man the powers he has alienated in blindly making history.

The idea of return to a native land is thus misleading, because it suggests above all else not the *terminus ad quem* of the reoccupation of old territory (*pays natal*) but the very process of deterritorialization in which the black body was to become, to use Deleuze and Guattari's awkward expression, without organs, that is, to achieve a form of somatic existence free from colonial, racist rule and no longer tortured, humiliated, semioticized, and degraded but liberated to resist the identity imposed by the territorializing processes of the imperial *Socius*. Césaire's poetics retain their significance because they represented more than a crack in rigid colonial society—cracks there had long been; Césaire transformed that crack into a full rupture, shattering the image of colonial black subjects in both form and content and freeing them to take a place on the plane of creativity, desire, possibility, experiment, and even death and destruction. Long before Deleuze and Guattari, Césaire had celebrated what Nik Fox has called "the death of the majoritarian individual subject by invoking experimental modes of consciousness which are excluded from normalizing reason such as those esoteric and Dionysian practices which involve rapture, excess and intoxication."[107]

> Reason, I crown you evening wind.
> Your name voice of order?
> To me the whip's corolla.
> Beauty I call you the false claim of the stone.
> But ah! My raucous laughter
> Smuggled in
> Ah! My saltpeter treasure!
> Because we hate you and your reason, we claim kinship with
> Dementia praecox with the flaming madness of persistent
> cannibalism[108]

To be sure, Césaire shied away from what he was doing. And the poem does speak of a conservative, if not Heideggerian, rejection of faraway places for an authentic *Dasein*. That is, Césaire's return is a gambit that greater possibilities are to be found in the history of a rooted people that looks back beyond the birth of a single individual than in the insights of contemporary foreign writers. Despite the geographical import of the return to a native land, the poem presumes that the life of black *Dasein* involves time more crucially than space simply because "tradition is handed down over time, not across space."[109] Césaire's return to African roots does not, in the end, fail to effect what Roberto Esposito has called a triple enclosure of subjects to the demands of their physiognomic specificities, their imagined community, and their fabulated genealogy; the triple enclosure is symbolized in the multiple references by Senghor and Césaire to blood (*sang*), which implies this more ramified, biocultural inheritance that cannot be symbolized by today's "gene," our contemporary synecdoche for the whole of intergenerational transmission.[110] So enclosed by blood, stuck inside an "Afrocentric reverie," and obsessed with a return, *Négritude* proved an obstacle to the appreciation of the non-African elements of Caribbean culture that blacks enjoyed, had made, and were making with others.[111]

Césaire's Nietzschean antidialectics created such problems; indeed, these problems are only comprehensible once we understand how far Nietzsche took Césaire from Hegel. As already suggested, Sartre defined *Négritude* in dialectical or Hegelian terms, as self-annulling negation and as a self-dissolving form of antiracist racism. But this logic of negative determination misses the function of affirmation in *Négritude*'s relationship to Africa. Yet if affirmation refuses the Hegelian external negation of existing forces in search of selfhood through a conceptual dialectical process, then affirmation has to somehow begin with itself, with an irreducible, original foundation. This is the only way to escape mediation by others. There has to be the possibility of an immediate affirmation of specific, immediate qualities. For Deleuze, the strong man's affirmation of himself is "rooted in his own feeling of power and vitality."[112] Césaire is certainly aristocratic in this sense. Or, to put it another way, Césaire is not the sheep of Nietzsche's *On the Genealogy of Morals*: he does not attempt to define *Négritude* in terms of what Africans hate and then impose anti-Western values on whom they hate; rather, he attempts to affirm in the first place who Africans are. Césaire's *Négritude* is modeled on Nietzsche's eagle, whose own self-affirmation determines its difference from the sheep: the eagle's sense of the sheep's baseness only affirms its own self-affirmation.[113] The problem, however, is with the metaphor of the invisible inside, the internal noumenal that is productive of the difference of *Négritude*. Rooted internally and defined outside mediation, it easily collapses into a biological substratum, even though Césaire struggled throughout his career to avoid this tragedy with his noble attempt not to have blacks defined even negatively by a culture that had despised and dehumanized them. However, this descent to the biological indeed haunted Césaire's work, and James

Arnold and Nick Nesbitt are quite severe in their criticism of Césaire. Even Gregson Davis thinks Césaire does not fully escape the problem.[114] Butler locates the same problem in Deleuze's posing as "an ahistorical absolute" his "arcadian vision of precultural libinidal chaos."[115] What I have tried to understand—and here I am indebted to the protocols of deconstructive reading—is how Césaire could be led back at times against his own predispositions to an ahistoric naturalism of racial biologism and noumenal racialism, not through a simple failure to break with racist culture but paradoxically through his very attempt to rise vigorously and vitally above the oppressive racial culture that he had inherited. The price of immanence was a naïve biologism, and Césaire's heroic poetics reveal race to be the tragedy that it is.

Yet I cannot agree with Nesbitt's argument that there is a fascist dimension to Césaire's poetics: "While manifestly antithetical to social oppression in hindsight, Césaire's references to pre-rational immediacy and 'Negro blood' in 1942 and 1945 merely invert and hence participate in the ideological categories of Hitlerian fascism."[116] It short-circuits the argument to dismiss prerational immediacy or prerational intuition as simply fascist, even though such irrationalism did often prove itself politically retrograde. Yet what makes this charge inapposite are the implications of Césaire's affirmation not of just what is vital in black life but in of all black existence.

While Gary Wilder has argued that Césaire's *Notebook* refuses to accept "the empirical coordinates of given reality" and turns to "the imagination as a refuge from the given world," the poem actually dwells on death, petrifaction, hunger, and disease—the lifeless existence of a cadaverous *Négritude*.[117] Césaire declaims: "I will withhold nothing." He tears away the softening veils of beautiful idealizations of Antillean life for a look at unvarnished reality:

> I refuse to pass off my puffiness for authentic glory.
> And I laugh at my former childish fantasies.
> No, we've never been Amazons of the King of Dahomey, nor
> princes of Ghana with eight hundred camels, nor wise men in
> Timbuktu under Askia the Great, nor the architects of Djenné,
> nor Mahdis, nor warriors. We don't feel under our armpit the
> itch of those who in the old days carried a lance. And since I
> have sworn to leave nothing out of our history (I who love nothing
>   better than a sheep grazing his own afternoon

shadow), I may as well confess that we were at all times pretty mediocre dishwashers, shoeblacks without ambition, at best conscientious sorcerers and the only unquestionable record that we broke was that of endurance under the *chicote* . . . [118]

One of the most famous scenes of the poem is Césaire's encounter with a broken black man ridiculed by fellow passengers on a tram. In giving a mirror to his complicit loathing, Césaire enacts a turning away from colonial racism and a return to all of black existence, affirmed without idealization of a great or royal African past or overlooked due to a mental escape for future utopia. He has instead exaggerated a history of abject mediocrity. Césaire even implores his readers to recognize that resistance does not always yield rewards. He recalls that the history of the diaspora has been marked by "monstrous putrefaction of stymied revolts." He writes bitterly that during the century-long era of slavery acts of historical agency could only be ascertained in the "good" (docile) nigger's ability to endure the whip. All of it, he tells us in a refrain, "I accept, I accept it all."[119] To use Robert Wicks's most important distinction, Césaire has affirmed not life but existence.[120]

For the fascist *Lebensphilosophs*, lives haunted by such brokenness, tragedy, damage, and spiritual sickness were lives not worth affirming but already dead, and they could therefore be put to death. As Roberto Esposito puts it:

> that death is juridically irreproachable not so much because it is justified by more pressing collective demands, but because the persons whom it strikes are *already* dead. The meticulous lexical research of those expressions that correspond to their diminished situation—"half-men," "damaged beings," "mentally dead," "empty human husks" (*Leere-Menschenhülsen*), "human ballast" (*Ballast-existenzen*)—has precisely the objective of demonstrating that in their case death does not come from outside, because from the beginning it is part of those lives—or, more precisely, of these *existences* because that is the term that follows from the subtraction of life from itself.[121]

Césaire is not implicated at all in a fascist thanatopolitics; on the contrary, he affirms the lives that fascists considered unworthy of life. He has none of that hardness toward the soft and weak, on whose destruction vitalist champions of cultural health had predicated the intensification of

life, the value on whose establishment the overcoming of modern nihilism, they said, depended. Césaire's existential affirmation even extends to
the living cosmos. Irele points to the "florid character of his evocations of
landscape, which attests to the fascination exerted upon his imagination
by the flourishing of life in all its forms in his environment and the aspect
of fantasy this imprints upon the tropical scene."[122] Yet Césaire's affirmation of nature does not depend on a fantasy of its idyllic or its benignly
profusive character; nor are the sufferings of nature red in tooth and
claw understood to serve a higher purpose, as in the theodicy of social
Darwinism. Nature is made neither a Father nor God substitute. Recall-
ing Nietzsche's Heraclitean view of nature, Césaire affirms the innocent
cruelty of a polymorphous and incessantly creative nature, powerfully
symbolized in Mt. Pelée's spewing out of volcanic lava. In "Poetry and
Cognition," Césaire would speak of the need for myth to restore our meaningful emotional responses to the sun, the moon, the rain, and the breath
and to rediscover in rapture and fear the pulsating, living newness of the
world. Yet even this call for myth is justified as a return to certain truths
lost since the first days of man. Césaire's primitivism is both mythic and
naturalistic.

The *Notebook* is indeed a work of myth, surrealist technique, and vitalism. But it is also a work of total, existential affirmation. Lukács argued
that the irrational *Lebensphilosophs* rejected existence for the affirmation
of life. He felt that the horrific effects of the First World War were registered
in the substitution of existence for the life concept: "The emphatic stress on
existence instead of life, even in contrast to life, expressed precisely this fear
of becoming inessential," and it indicated "a search for the core of genuine-
ness in subjectivity which, it was hoped, man could still endeavor to rescue
from the imminent general destruction."[123] Césaire's ability to affirm life,
however, is predicated on an affirmation of existence.

Césaire accepts his physical inheritance against colonial somatic prejudice, he accepts the ignominy of blacks' present condition against attempts to escape to a mythic past or transcendent future, and he accepts
the childlike violence and fecundity of the natural world of which he rightfully understands himself an evanescent and fragile expression.

. . . I accept

and the determination of my biology, not a prisoner to a facial
angle, to a type of hair, to a well-flattened nose, to a clearly

Melanin coloring, and negritude, no longer a cephalic index,
or plasma, or soma, but measured by a compass of suffering

and the Negro every day more base, more cowardly, more sterile,
less profound, more spilled out of himself, more separated from
himself, more wily with himself, less immediate to himself,

I accept, I accept it all

and far from the palatial sea that foams beneath the suppurat-
ing syzygy of blisters, miraculously lying in the despair of my
arms the body of my country, its bones shocked and, in its
veins, the blood hesitating like a drop of vegetal milk at the in-
jured point of a bulb . . .

Suddenly now strength and life assail me like a bull and the
water of life overwhelms the papilla of the more, now all the
veins and veinlets are bustling with new blood and the enormous breathing lung of cyclones and the fire hoarded in vol-
canoes and the gigantic seismic pulse which now beats the
measure of a living body in my firm conflagration.[124]

The narrator's return to the native land culminates in an affirmation of
dubious ancestral myths about a metaphysically vitalist inheritance, despite his attempt to define race less in terms of physiology than in terms of
a shared history of suffering. Contemporaneously with the early versions
of the *Notebook*, Césaire would write in an introduction to Frobenius's
writings: "But there flows in our veins a blood which demands of us an
original attitude toward life . . . we must respond, the poet more than any
other, to the special dynamic of our complex biological reality."[125] Yet
even this affirmation of what we know as pseudobiology speaks of a "passion for the real"; Césaire is attempting to awaken his readers from the
dreamscapes, ideologies, and imaginaries of the colonial world and to affirm black life and the cosmos just as they are—perfect.[126] Existence is
perfection: Césaire has radicalized Nietzsche's radical doctrine of *amor
fati* for a people whose history of enslavement and suffering are least suited
for it, and this is a measure of his accomplishment. For a people who have
been taught to loathe who they are and who seek otherworldly solace for
the stultification of their daily lives—yet who are in fact immobilized by the

disintegration of comforting cosmologies—Césaire creates a returning prophet who matches (as I suggest he was meant to) the description Nietzsche gave of a fictional messiah:

> Is this [great health] even possible at this time? . . . But sometime, in a stronger period than this rotten, self-doubting present is, he must come to us, a redeeming person of great love and contempt, the creative spirit, whose surging force always keeps him away from everything remote and beyond, whose solitude is misunderstood by the general population, as if it were an escape *from* reality—while it is only his sinking-into, burying-into, deepening *into* reality, so that, when he eventually comes back into the light, he can bring home the *redemption* of reality: its redemption from the cure laid upon it by the ideal that has been prevailing until now. This person of the future, who redeems us from both this prevailing ideal and *which will grow out of it*, from the great disgust, from the will to nothingness, from nihilism, this bell-stroke of noon and the great decision, which again frees the will, that gives back to the earth its goal, and gives back to people their hope, this Antichrist and antinihilist, this conqueror over God and nothing—*he must come some day.*[127]

Nietzsche had created Zarathustra in this image, and this black Zarathustra, the first-person narrator of *Notebook of a Return to the Native Land*, will certainly survive his creator, the great Aimé Césaire (1913–2008).

Acknowledgments

As a student in the Department of Comparative Literature at UC Berkeley, I began with an interest in modernist aesthetics and Frankfurt School critical theory but soon found myself deeply immersed in Middle High German and Latin. However, the great Maryse Condé made irresistible the study of Caribbean literature, and I was lucky to have had two other wonderful teachers: the late VéVé Clark and Julio Ramos, who encouraged me to turn my theoretical and linguistic training on postcolonial literature. At the same time, I attended Martin Jay's seminar on the philosophy of history and found myself filling up notebooks with his careful introductions to the major texts. As I was finishing coursework, I then had the greatest fortune of Judith Butler coming to Berkeley and taking me on as a graduate student. She allowed me to understand what rigorous theoretical argument really is, and in advising me, she showed me what intellectual commitment can be. She somehow found the time to read the Caribbean literature on which I was working simply to advise me; my debt to her critical reading of Deleuze is manifest.

I have had the great fortune of having taught at two great institutions—Princeton and Stanford. At both universities I had the support of invaluable colleagues. I am appreciative of Arnold Rampersad, an inspiration and great colleague at both institutions. At Princeton, Claudia Tate was my mentor and my friend, and I miss her dearly. I would be remiss not to recall the heady engagement of my senior colleagues Michael Wood, Eduardo Cadava, and Jonathan Lamb. I am also thankful to my dear friends and present colleagues Saydiya Hartman and Stephen Best for having chosen me to participate in a seminar on the theory of redress at the Institute for the Humanities at UC Irvine.

The sharpest comments I received on the present manuscript were delivered to me in conversations with Catherine Gallagher. They have led to much rethinking and revision, though of course she is not responsible for what the book has become. It meant the world to me that someone would be interested enough in the manuscript to articulate its contradictions and locate its potential. Snehal Shingavi also provided many helpful comments. My colleague Colleen Lye has been the closest of friends for almost a decade now—we read each other's dissertations, and on topics ranging from Frank Norris to racial mythology her thinking has shaped and directed mine. I would like to thank my department for the generous leave time I was granted, which allowed for the completion of this work and for a rigorous review of my work.

I am proud indeed to appear in the series that Amy Allen has edited, and her comments on this manuscript were insightful and helpful. I am very thankful to Wendy Lochner, who handled my manuscript expeditiously and found two excellent reviewers. Rob Fellman did an excellent job copyediting the text.

At Berkeley, I have been the lucky recipient of generous support from the Hellman Family Fund; without this help, my research budget would have been constrained. My mother has been with me every step of the way. My parents-in-law have provided important financial support and, more importantly, a wonderful extended family. My husband Rakesh Bhandari has been with this project since its inception and before; his interlocution has been invaluable. The book is dedicated to our two daughters, Avinashi and Aarushi: Avinashi's birth marked the conception of this book on life, and I finished it a few days before Aarushi's arrival. Children do remind us that our most astounding, involving, and vital experiences are those in which we have minimal experience of self-consciousness.

Notes

Introduction: The Resilience of Life

1. Ed Regis, *What Is Life? Investigating the Nature of Life in the Age of Synthetic Biology* (New York: Farrar, Straus and Giroux, 2008).

2. Nikolas Rose, *The Politics of Life Itself: Biomedicine, Power, and Subjectivity in the Twenty-First Century* (Princeton, N.J.: Princeton University Press, 2006).

3. Maurice Bloch, *Essays in Cultural Transmission* (Oxford: Berg Publishers, 2005); Luis Villarreal, "Are Viruses Alive?" *Scientific American* (November 2004), http://www.sciam.com/article.cfm?id=00077043-911C-119B-8EA483414B7FFE9F&colID=1.

4. Matthew Cobb, *Generation: The Seventeenth-Century Scientists Who Unraveled the Secrets of Sex, Life, and Growth* (New York: Bloomsbury Books, 2006).

5. Regis, *What Is Life?* 64.

6. Regis, *What Is Life?* 58.

7. John Maynard Smith and Eors Szathmáry, *The Origins of Life: From the Birth of Life to the Origin of Language* (Oxford: Oxford University Press, 1999).

8. Albert Jacquard "Human Rights and Human Nature," http://www.unesco.org/opi2/human-rights/Pages/English/JacquardE.html. Jacquard, however, reaches radically humanist conclusions. Underlining that the human metamorphosis into a self-conscious social person is not genetically programmed but the result of education, he argues for a special category of rights for human beings to ensure this fragile process of metamorphosis.

9. Rudolf A. Makkereel, "The Feeling of Life: Some Kantian Sources of Life-Philosophy," in *Dilthey Jahrbuch für Philosophie und Geschichte der Geisteswissenschaften*, bd. 3 (1985), 86–87, 101–102. A descendent of this argument is George Lakoff and Mark Johnson's thesis that our basic categories are metaphors (for example, inside/outside or up/down) rooted in lived bodily experience. See their *Metaphors We Live By* (Chicago: University of Chicago Press, 1980).

10. See Michel Foucault in *The Birth of the Clinic: An Archaeology of Medical Perception*, trans. A. M. Sheridan (New York: Vintage, 1973), 144; Leonard Lawlor, *The Implications of Immanence* (New York: Fordham University Press, 2006), 139.

11. The effects of violent death on the formation of black subjectivity are analyzed in Abdul JanMohamed, *The Death-Bound Subject: Richard Wright's Archaeology of Death* (Durham, N.C.: Duke University Press, 2005). For Wright,

the constant threat of physical violence and death in the age of lynching did not produce an indifference to worldly fate and thus resignation to extant social forms but rather a powerful, politically engaged form of existentialism. JanMohamed also draws on Orlando Patterson, who described slavery as a kind of living death or a social death resulting from natal alienation. There have been two kinds of death at the heart of the American black experience, and JanMohamed connects them in this stunning ways, see 18ff. in particular. See also Orlando Patterson, *Slavery and Social Death: A Comparative Study* (Cambridge, Mass.: Harvard University Press, 1982).

12. François Jacob, *The Logic of Life: A History of Heredity*, trans. B.E. Spillmann (Princeton, N.J.: Princeton University Press, 1993), 19–20.

13. M. H. Abrams, *Natural Supernaturalism: Tradition and Revolution in the Romantic Tradition* (New York: Norton, 1971), 431–432; see also his *The Mirror and the Lamp: Romantic Theory and the Critical Tradition* (Oxford: Oxford University Press, 1953). Of course, Abrams's identification of the Romantics with life and his aesthetic idealization of the organic form have been challenged. See, for example, Dominick LaCapra, *Soundings in Critical Theory* (Ithaca, N.Y.: Cornell University Press, 1989), 90–133.

14. Mark Antliff, *Avant-Garde Fascism: The Mobilization of Myth, Art, and Culture in France, 1909–1939* (Durham, N.C.: Duke University Press, 2007).

15. Roger Griffin, *Modernism and Fascism: The Sense of Beginning Under Mussolini and Hitler* (Basingstoke: Palgrave Macmillan, 2007), 317.

16. Luc Boltanski, "The Left After May 1968 and the Longing for Total Revolution," *Thesis Eleven* 69 (May 2002): 1–20.

17. Herbert Schnädelbach, *Philosophy in Germany, 1831–1933*, trans. Eric Matthews (Cambridge: Cambridge University Press, 1984), 139.

18. Alain Badiou, *The Century*, trans. Alberto Toscano (London: Polity Press, 2007), 13–14.

19. Michael Dash, *The Other America: Caribbean Literature in a New World Context* (Charlottesville: University Press of Virginia, 1998), 61–62.

20. Hilary Fink, *Bergson and Russian Modernism, 1900–1930* (Evanston, Ill.: Northwestern University Press, 1999).

21. Ernst Bloch, *Heritage of Our Times*, trans. Neville Plaice and Stephen Plaice (Berkeley: University of California Press, 1991), 319–320. In his richly allusive prose style, Bloch seems to argue that in his last book, *The Two Sources of Morality and Religion*, Bergson distanced himself from his entrepreneurial vitalism and acknowledged in a mystified way the need for rational social organization. But this reads Bloch's own wishes into Bergson's final work.

22. Quoted in R. C. Grogin, *The Bergsonian Controversy in France* (Calgary: University of Calgary Press, 1988), 199.

23. Heinrich Heine, "Differing Conceptions of History," quoted in Stathis Kouvelakis, *Philosophy and Revolution: From Kant to Marx*, trans. G. M. Goshigarian (London: Verso Press, 2003), 66–67.

24. Kouvelakis, *Philosophy and Revolution*, 67.

25. See Londa Schiebinger, *Plants and Empire: Colonial Bioprospecting in the Atlantic World* (Cambridge, Mass.: Harvard University Press, 2004). Schiebinger argues that mercantilists who found the key to the wealth of nations in the size of

the labor force blocked the importation of abortifacients discovered by rebellious slave women.

26. Michel Foucault, *History of Sexuality: An Introduction*, trans. Robert Hurley (New York: Vintage Books, 1990), 145.

27. Jürgen Habermas, *The Philosophical Discourse of Modernity: Twelve Lectures*, trans. Frederick Lawrence (Cambridge, Mass.: The MIT Press, 1987), 285.

28. Gilles Deleuze, *Foucault*, trans. Séan Hand (Minneapolis: University of Minnesota Press, 1988), 92–93; quoted in John S. Ransom, "Forget Vitalism: Foucault and *Lebensphilosophie*," *Philosophy and Social Criticism* 23, no. 33 (1997): 34–47. Ransom has provocatively challenged the claim that Foucault was a vitalist. He argues that his defenders, such as Deleuze, wrongly suggest that vitalism provides him with a normative foundation to critique institutions and disciplines and that his critics insist on his vitalism to charge him with irrationalism and the lack of a tenable normative theory. Ransom then points to Foucault's discussion of Georges Canguilhem and shows that Foucault disavows in a couple of passages vitalist critiques of the putative deadening effects of the philosophy of the concept and of extant configurations of power. This is a provocative argument, and I shall express similar skepticism about vitalism. But Ransom's argument is premised on the assumption that Foucault was aware of all the ways in which vitalism affected his thought and that he did not take or imply contradictory stances toward vitalism. Ransom also argues that Judith Butler's normative theory is predicated on Foucault's putative vitalism and based on the value of life's ever greater plenitude against any rigid system. I shall argue in the last chapter that this claim simply ignores the Hegelian elements in Butler's thought.

29. Enrique Dussel, "From Critical Theory to the Philosophy of Liberation: Some Themes for Dialogue," trans. George Ciccariello Maher (unpublished, 2004), 2–3, 9. Paper in the author's possession.

30. Dussel, "From Critical Theory to the Philosophy of Liberation," 19.

31. Giorgio Agamben, *Homo Sacer: Sovereign Power and Bare Life*, trans. Daniel Heller-Roazen (Stanford, Calif.: Stanford University Press, 1998).

32. Paul Rabinow, "French Enlightenment: Truth and Life," *Economy and Society* 27, no. 2/3 (1998): 194–200.

33. Aimé Césaire, *Notebook of a Return to the Native Land*, trans. and ed. Clayton Eshleman and Annette Smith (Middletown, Conn.: Wesleyan University Press), 11–12. See Giorgio Agamben, *State of Exception* (Chicago: University of Chicago Press, 2005).

34. Roberto Esposito, *Bíos: Biopolitics and Philosophy*, trans. Timothy Campbell (Minneapolis: University of Minnesota Press, 2008), 98, 128. Esposito offers the radical thesis that the metaphor of immunization is the *differentia specifica* of modern politics, but he dates the introduction of the paradigm to the early modern era while not showing that much was understood about biological immunization at that time or that the law about juridical immunity was well developed. Germ theory was, of course, introduced centuries later. Also to the extent that many contradictory things can be done in the name of the life of a people, the immunitary paradigm is necessarily underdetermined as to what a state actually does.

35. Rose, *The Politics of Life Itself,* 58.

36. Elizabeth Grosz, *The Nick of Time: Politics, Evolution, and the Untimely* (Durham, N.C.: Duke University Press), 260.

37. Michael Hardt and Antonio Negri, *Empire* (Cambridge, Mass.: Harvard University Press, 2001), 146. I thank Alberto Toscano for discussion of relevant passages.

38. Rosi Braidotti, *Transpositions* (London: Polity Press, 2006), 129–130. But Braidotti herself actually has the title of "Knight in the Order of the Nederlandse Leeuw."

39. A murderous bio-logic haunts us today with the objectification of immigrant workers as illegal aliens parasitical on the state and economy. Imagined as carriers of viruses, they are seen as a viral threat that must be fenced out and violently extirpated.

40. Paul Rabinow and Nikolas Rose, "Thoughts on the Concept of Biopower Today," http://www.molsci.org/research/publications_pdf/Rose_Rabinow_Biopower_Today.pdf.

41. Adorno as quoted in Alastair Morgan, "Petrified Life: Agamben, Adorno, and the Possibility of Life." The quotation comes from a prepublication version to which I am indebted to Professor Morgan for access.

42. Quoted in Eric Santner, *On the Psychopathology of Everyday Life: Reflections on Freud and Rosenzweig* (Chicago: University of Chicago Press, 2001), 22.

43. Of course, bodies that have lost that capability could still be enlivened by amplifying the electrical current, exactly what Dr. Frankenstein had to do in an act of assisted conception. Here Mary Shelley was drawing on and publicizing well-known experiments in which electricity was used to cause lifelike muscular contractions in corpses; in one experiment, electrical shocks to the chest resulted in a corpse blowing out a lighted candle. Electricity thus appeared as the vital principle, the spark of life. See David Channel, *The Vital Machine: A Study of Technology and Organic Life* (Oxford: Oxford University Press, 1991), 56.

44. Frederick C. Beiser, *German Idealism: The Struggle Against Subjectivism, 1781–1801* (Cambridge, Mass.: Harvard University Press, 2002), 541.

45. F. Abiola Irele, *The African Experience in Literature and Ideology* (London: Heinemann, 1981).

46. George Rousseau, "Traditions of Enlightenment Vitalism," in *The Crisis in Modernism: Bergson and the Vitalist Controversy*, ed. Frederick Burwick and Paul Douglass (Cambridge: Cambridge University Press, 1992), 50.

47. Leon Poliakov, *The Aryan Myth: A History of Racist and Nationalist Ideas in Europe* (London: Heinemann, 1974), 5.

48. Achille Mbembe, "Nicolas Sarkozy's Africa," http://www.africaresource.com/content/view/376/68. See an earlier, similar criticism: René Ménil, *Tracées: Identité, Négritude, esthetique aux Antilles* (Paris: R. Laffont, 1981).

49. Raymond Plant, *Hegel: An Introduction* (Oxford: Basil Blackwell, 1983), 236.

50. Abrams, *The Mirror and the Lamp*, 158.

51. Thanks to Roberto Gonzalez Echevarria for this reference.

1. On the Mechanical, Machinic, and Mechanistic

1. Jacques Louis Hymans, "French Influences on Leopold Senghor's Theory of *Négritude*, 1928–1948," *Race and Class* 7 (1966): 367; see also Jacques Louis Hymans, *Leopold Sédar Senghor: An Intellectual Biography* (Edinburgh: Edinburgh University Press, 1971).

2. Quoted in Rudiger Safranski, *Martin Heidegger: Between Good and Evil*, trans. Ewald Osers (Cambridge, Mass.: Harvard University Press, 1998), 54.

3. Senghor, "Prayer to the Masks," in Leopold Sédar Senghor, *The Collected Poetry*, trans. Melvin Dixon (Charlottesville: University of Virginia Press, 1998), 14.

4. Safranski, *Martin Heidegger*, 54.

5. I have in mind here Daniel Pick, *War Machine: The Rationalization of Slaughter in the Modern Age* (New Haven, Conn.: Yale University Press, 1993).

6. Georges Canguilhem, *Knowledge of Life*, ed. Paola Marrati and Todd Meyers, trans. Stefanos Geroulanos and Daniela Ginsburg (Baltimore, Md.: The Johns Hopkins University Press, 2009), 73. While Canguilhem focuses on the response to mechanism within biology, my focus will be on the wider cultural meanings of antimechanism.

7. Tom Quirk, *Bergson and American Culture: The Worlds of Willa Cather and Wallace Stevens* (Chapel Hill: University of North Carolina Press, 1990). This is a fine study of the spiritual needs Bergsonism met in a Godless world promised only entropy and heat death by science.

8. This is what Stephen Toumlin does for the sciences in "From Clocks to Chaos: Humanizing the Mechanistic World View," in *The Machine as Metaphor and Tool*, ed. Herman Haken, Anders Karlqvist, and Uno Svedin (New York: Springer Verlag, 1993), 139–153.

9. Sanford Schwarz, "Bergson and the Politics of Vitalism," in *The Crisis in Modernism: Bergson and the Vitalist Controversy*, ed. Frederick Burwick and Paul Douglass (Cambridge: Cambridge University Press, 1992), 277–305.

10. Bergson, "Laughter," in *Comedy*, ed. George Meredith (Baltimore, Md.: The Johns Hopkins University Press, 1980), 66–67.

11. Pheng Cheah, *Spectral Nationality: Passages of Freedom from Kant to Postcolonial Literatures of Liberation* (New York: Columbia University Press, 2003), 35.

12. E. J. Dijksterhuis, *The Mechanization of the World Picture: Pythagoras to Newton*, trans. C. Dikshoorn (Oxford: Oxford University Press, 1961), 70, 431ff.

13. René Descartes, *The World and Other Writings*, trans. Stephen Gaukroger (Cambridge: Cambridge University Press, 1998), 100. See also Susan Bordo, *Feminist Interpretations of René Descartes* (University Park: Pennsylvania State University Press, 1999); and Paolo Rossi, *The Birth of Modern Science*, trans. Cynthia De Nardi Ipsen (Oxford: Blackwell Publishers, 2001).

14. See the appendix on the history of vitalism in Guy Brown, *The Energy of Life: The Science of What Makes Our Minds and Bodies Work* (New York: The Free Press, 2000).

15. See Gaby Wood, *Edison's Eve: A Magical History of the Quest for Mechanical Life* (New York: Knopf, 2002). Her chapter "The Blood of the Android" has an excellent history of the mechanization of life.

16. Garland Allen argues that the defense of such explanatory or operational mechanisms does not depend on the ontological mechanism. He proposes that it is possible to commit to the former kind of mechanism while allowing for the unique and emergent properties of organisms. Garland Allen, "Mechanism, Vitalism, and Organicism in Late Nineteenth- and Twentieth-Century Biology: The Importance of Historical Context," *Studies in the History and Philosophy of the Biological and Biomedical Sciences* 36 (2005): 261–283.

17. See Hilda Hein, *The Origin and Nature of Life* (New York: McGraw-Hill, 1971).

18. David Channell, *Vital Machine: A Study of Technology and Organic Life* (New York: Oxford University Press, 1991), 54.

19. See also Stephen Rose, *Lifelines: Biology Beyond Determinism* (Oxford: Oxford University Press, 1998).

20. Jane Maienschein, *Whose View of Life? Embryos, Cloning, and Stem Cells* (Cambridge, Mass.: Harvard University Press, 2005), 26.

21. Stuart Shanker, "Descartes' Legacy: The Mechanist/Vitalist Debates," in *The Philosophy of Science, Mathematics, and Logic in the Twentieth Century*, ed. Stuart Shanker (New York: Routledge, 1996), 316.

22. Quoted in Evelyn Fox Keller, *Secrets of Life, Secrets of Death: Essays on Language, Gender, and Science* (New York: Routledge, 1992), 67.

23. Keller, *Secrets of Life, Secrets of Death*, 68.

24. Shanker, "Descartes' Legacy," 318–319.

25. The Great Chain of Being has at least two meanings. Shanker is focused on it as a continuum that links animal and human life; as we will see later, the Great Chain also implied the doctrine of plentitude, the idea that all the potential forms of life would be actualized in the course of evolution. Life is thus less a category of homeostasis or efficiency but maximalization and exuberance. The title of Bergson's major work, *Creative Evolution*, obviously suggests this meaning.

26. Nikolas Rose, *The Politics of Life Itself: Biomedicine, Power, and Subjectivity in the Twenty-First Century* (Princeton, N.J.: Princeton University Press, 2006), 21. Rose is summarizing an unpublished essay by Ian Hacking.

27. Carolyn Porter, "Reification and American Literature," in *Ideology and Classic American Literature*, ed. Sacvan Berkcovitch and Myra Jehlen (Cambridge: Cambridge University Press, 1987), 188–220.

28. J. W. Burrow, *The Crisis of Reason: European Thought, 1848–1914* (New Haven, Conn.: Yale University Press, 200), 35. Also, Georges Canguilhem has shown that while antivitalistic, the emergent chemistry of the nineteenth century initially "replaced the mechanical model of the organism proposed by Descartes with a model of antiquity: that of the flame. The organism had yet to be seen as a machine powered by heat, but it was no longer seen as one driven by weights (a clock), by springs (a watch), by air (an organ), or by a water (a mill)." Canguilhem as quoted by Bernard Doray, *From Taylorism to Fordism: A Rational Madness* (London: Free Association, 1988), 183.

29. See Mark Seltzer, *Bodies and Machines* (New York: Routledge, 1992), 143–144.

30. Doray, *From Taylorism to Fordism*, 84.

31. Raymond Williams, *Keywords: A Vocabulary of Culture and Society* (London: Fontana, 1988).

32. Colleen Lye, *America's Asia: Racial Form and American Literature, 1893–1945* (Princeton, N.J.: Princeton University Press, 2005), 95.

33. See the interesting discussion of Henri de Man and Ortega y Gasset in Stanley Pierson, *Leaving Marxism: Studies in the Dissolution of an Ideology* (Stanford, Calif.: Stanford University Press, 2001), 71.

34. Hans Jonas, *The Phenomenon of Life: Toward a Philosophical Biology* (Chicago: University of Chicago Press, 1982), 12. Jonas's attempt to fashion a neovitalist philosophy led him to a politics of ecology and an eventual countenance of authoritarian politics as necessary to prevent ecological destruction. See Richard Wolin, *Heidegger's Children: Hannah Arendt, Karl Lowith, Hans Jonas, and Herbert Marcuse* (Princeton, N.J.: Princeton University Press, 2001). But one should of course be careful not to equate any regulation on businesses and personal life in the service of ecological sustainability with authoritarianism.

35. See Maurice Godelier, *Perspectives in Marxist Anthropology*, trans. Robert Brain (Cambridge: Cambridge University Press, 1977).

36. See Susan Bordo, *The Flight to Objectivity: Essays on Cartesianism and Culture* (Albany: State University of New York Press, 1987). Bordo has also explored the connection between gender difference and Cartesian dualism. That reason is viewed as disembodied was taken to imply that those who could not free themselves of their bodies could not reason and act freely. Cartesian dualism became gender hierarchy. Yet this remains a controversial though provocative reading, indeed.

37. Cheah, *Spectral Nationality*, 32–33.

38. Cheah, *Spectral Nationality*, 47.

39. Cheah, *Spectral Nationality*, 94.

40. Cheah, *Spectral Nationality*, 59.

41. Canguilhem, *Knowledge of Life*, 72.

42. Friedrich Schiller, *On the Aesthetic Education of Man: In a Series of Letters* (London: Routledge Kegan Paul, 1954), 33–35. Schiller takes up the idea that, in the modern world, the growth of empirical knowledge, the division of labor, and the separation of ranks all mean that man has become specialized and divided, with the result that the "totality of the species" (*Totalität der Gattung*) becomes impossible to recover from its "fragments" (*Bruchstücke*), the individual members.

43. Michael Rosen, *On Voluntary Servitude: False Consciousness and the Theory of Ideology* (Cambridge, Mass.: Harvard University Press, 1996), 145. It can be noted in passing that Emile Durkheim later inverted Schiller's categories, in that the modern political economy, with its development of the division of labor, had created a universal interdependence resembling the organs of a living body, while primitive societies were understood as mechanical, in that parts being more or less mechanical copies of each other all could perform the same actions.

44. Cheah, *Spectral Nationality*, 29.

45. Rosen, *Voluntary Servitude*, 143.

46. Cheah, *Spectral Nationality*, 29.

47. Hymans, *Leopold Sédar Senghor*, 48–52.

48. Quoted in Gary Wilder, *The French Imperial Nation-State: Négritude and Colonial Humanism Between the Two World Wars* (Chicago: University of Chicago Press, 2005), 248.

49. Pope Pius XI, "Quadragesimo Anno," http://www.vatican.va/holy_father/pius_xi/encyclicals/documents/hf_p-xi_enc_19310515_quadragesimo-anno_en.html; Leopold Senghor, *On African Socialism* (New York: Praeger, 1964).

50. Max Horkheimer, "On Bergson's Metaphysics of Time," *Radical Philosophy* 113 (May–June 2005): 14–15.

51. Rosen, *Voluntary Servitude*, 154.

52. Marcien Towa, *Léopold Sédar Senghor: Négritude or Servitude?* (Yaoundé: Editions CLE, 1971).

53. Gilles Deleuze and Félix Guattari, *A Thousand Plateaus*, trans. Brian Massumi (Minneapolis: University of Minnesota Press, 1987), 499–503.

54. See Gilles Deleuze, *Negotiations, 1972–1990*, trans. Martin Joughin (New York: Columbia University Press, 1995). Deleuze argues: "It's organisms that die, not life. Any work of art points a way through for life, finds a way through the cracks. Everything I've written is vitalistic, at least I hope it is, and amounts to a theory of signs and events" (143).

55. Again, one should not conflate early Romantic organicism with totalitarianism.

56. Todd May, *Gilles Deleuze: An Introduction* (Cambridge: Cambridge University Press, 2005), 122–124.

57. Édouard Glissant, *Poetics of a Relation*, trans. Betsy Wing (Ann Arbor: University of Michigan Press, 1997).

58. Richard Lewontin has often challenged just this premise.

59. Robert J. Richards, *The Romantic Conception of Life: Science and Philosophy in the Age of Goethe* (Chicago: University of Chicago Press, 2002).

60. Richards, *The Romantic Conception of Life*, 539.

61. D. H. Lawrence, *Women in Love* (Boston: G. K. Hall, 1988), 327.

62. Elizabeth Grosz, *The Nick of Time: Politics, Evolution, and the Untimely* (Durham, N.C.: Duke University Press, 2004), 7–8.

63. In *Bergson and American Culture*, Tom Quirk has, as already noted, provided a penetrating study of the foreboding pessimism created by the assimilation of Darwinian naturalism.

64. The example is from John Maynard Smith, *The Problems of Biology* (New York: Oxford University Press, 1986).

65. Richard Lewontin, *It Ain't Necessarily So: The Dream of the Human Genome and Other Illusions* (New York: NYRB, 2001), 117.

66. Richards highlights this passage from *On the Origins of Species* in *The Romantic Conception of Life*, 83–84.

67. Paul Rabinow, "Artificiality and Enlightenment: From Sociobiology and Biosociality," in *Anthropologies of Modernity: Foucault, Governmentality, and*

Life Politics, ed. Jonathan Xavier Inda (Malden: Blackwell, 2005), 181–193, esp. 191.

68. I quote from the last paragraph of Charles Darwin, *On the Origin of Species* (New York: Oxford University Press, 1963).

69. Quoted in Ivan Strenski, *Four Theories of Myth in Twentieth-Century History: Cassirer, Eliade, Levi-Strauss, and Malinowski* (Iowa City: University of Iowa Press, 1987), 64.

70. Ernest Gellner, *Plow, Sword, and Book: The Structure of Human History* (Chicago: University of Chicago Press, 1989), 142.

71. Bruce Trigger, *Sociocultural Evolution: Calculation and Contingency* (Oxford: Blackwell, 1998), 60–61.

72. Gellner, *Plow, Sword, and Book*, 142.

73. Gellner, *Plow, Sword, and Book*, 142–144.

74. Henri Bergson, *Creative Evolution*, trans. Arthur Mitchell (New York: Modern Library, 1911), 64–75.

75. So argues his foremost disciple, Jacques Chevalier, in *Henri Bergson* (New York: Macmillan Books, 1928).

76. Léopold Senghor, "The Spirit of Civilization, or the Laws of African Negro Culture," *Présence Africaine* 8–10 (June–November 1956): 64. Emphasis added.

77. Gary Wilder, *The French Imperial Nation-State*, 251.

78. Georges Canguilhem, *A Vital Rationalist: Selected Writings from Georges Canguilhem* (New York: Zone Books, 2000). Canguilhem writes that Man "can look at nature in two ways. He *feels* that he is a child of nature and has a sense of belong to something larger than himself; he sees himself in nature and nature in himself. But he also *stands before* nature as an indefinable alien object. A scientist who feels filial, sympathetic sentiments towards nature will not regard natural phenomena as strange and alien; rather he will find in them life, soul and meaning. Such a man is basically a vitalist" (288–289).

79. See Arthur Lovejoy, *Bergson and Romantic Evolution* (Berkeley: University of California Press, 1914).

80. Defined by Hegel as variously without vivacity, vitality, or liveliness. See Michael Inwood, *A Hegel Dictionary* (Oxford: Blackwell, 1992).

81. Bergson, *Comedy*, 29.

82. Bergson, *Comedy*, 25–27.

83. See F. C. T. Moore, *Bergson: Thinking Backwards* (Cambridge: Cambridge University Press, 1996), 80.

84. Scott Lash and Celia Lury, *The Global Cultural Industry: Mediation of Things* (Cambridge: Polity Press, 2007), 184.

85. Bergson, *Comedy*, 117.

86. See Craig Brandist, *The Bakhtin Circle: Philosophy, Culture, and Politics* (London: Pluto, 2002), 127.

87. René Ménil, "Humour: Introduction to 1945," in *Refusal of the Shadow: Surrealism and the Caribbean*, ed. Michael Richardson, Krzysztof Fijakowski, and Philip Lamantia (London: Verso, 1996), 162–175.

88. Eric Santner, *On the Psychopathology of Everyday Life: Reflections on Freud and Rosenzweig* (Chicago: University of Chicago Press, 2001), 23.

89. Bergson, *Comedy*, 86ff. This is not an isolated instance of Bergson's colonial racism. His comments about contemporary primitive societies reproduces the worst colonial stereotypes of statis and savagery. See Henri Bergson, *Two Sources of Morality and Religion*, trans. R. Ashley Audra and Cloudesly Brereton (New York: Doubleday, 1935), 136–137. Bergson also thought African "savages" incapable of mobilizing the past for the purposes of the present; their memory was putatively only spontaneous, as their intellectual development had not gone beyond that of children. See also Henri Bergson, *Matter and Memory*, trans. Nancy Margaret Paul and W. Scott Palmer (New York: Zone Books, 1991), 154. I don't know of critical comments on this aspect of Bergson's thought in the neo-Bergsonist literature.

90. Ménil, "Humor," 173.

91. Aimé Césaire, *Notebook of a Return to the Native Land*, trans. Clayton Eshleman and Annette Smith (Middletown, Conn.: Wesleyan University Press, 2001), 4–5.

92. Leon Damas, "Hiccups [*Hoquet*]," in *Négritude: Black Poetry from Africa and the Caribbean*, ed. and trans. Norman Shapiro (October House: New York: 1970), 58.

93. Ménil, "Humour," 163.

94. Judith Butler, *Gender Trouble: Feminism and the Subversion of Identity* (New York: Routledge, 1990), 138–139.

95. Bourdieu's view of action is not quite mechanical, as he allows for some flexibility in action and strategy. But that freedom is quite circumscribed.

96. Pierre Bourdieu, *Pascalian Meditations*, trans. Richard Nice (Stanford, Calif.: Stanford University Press, 2000), 163.

97. That only living or animate labor can add new value is a vitalist premise that we find in classical political economy. See Catherine Gallagher, *The Body Economic: Life, Death, and Sensation in Political Economy and the Victorian Novel* (Princeton, N.J.: Princeton University Press, 2006).

2. Contesting Vitalism

1. The passage quoted as this chapter's epigraph is from Herbert Schnädelbach, *Philosophy in Germany, 1831–1933* (Cambridge: Cambridge University Press, 1984), 139.

2. I am even skeptical of—though genuinely moved by—Axel Honneth's important confrontation with the intellectual exhaustion of vitalism and Marxism and of his attempt to find new grounds for critical theory in the struggle for recognition, as will become clear in my discussion of Césaire in the last chapter. For what other than genuine recognition was Ralph Ellison's invisible man struggling? And do not his struggles illuminate what we mean by genuine recognition of our person?

3. Schnädelbach, *Philosophy in Germany*, 143.

4. Schnädelbach, *Philosophy in Germany*, 145.

5. Ofelia Schutte, *Beyond Nihilism: Nietzsche Without Masks* (Chicago: University of Chicago Press, 1984), 1.

6. Schutte, *Beyond Nihilism*, 36.

7. Friedrich Nietzsche, *Ecce Homo: How One Becomes What One Is*, trans. R. J. Hollingdale (London: Penguin, 2004), 109.

8. Eugene Halton has also traced the movement from *Naurphilosophie* as a bulwark against Western materialism to a vitalist overextension of inner feeling that gave voice to "the sense of inner superiority of German *Kultur* and the German state . . . and which, in its logical irrational endpoint contributed to the successful rise, domination, and self-destruction of German fascism." Eugene Halton, *Bereft of Reason: On the Decline of Social Thought and Its Prospects for Renewal* (Chicago: University of Chicago Press, 1995), 66. Halton argues for a new kind of identification with an incarnate, living cosmos, of which he sees D. H. Lawrence as a prescient exponent. I shall consider Lawrence in the next chapter.

9. Friedrich Nietzsche, *Beyond Good and Evil: Prelude to a Philosophy of the Future*, trans. Walter Kaufmann (New York: Vintage Books, 1989).

10. J. P. Stern, *Nietzsche* (Cambridge: Cambridge University Press, 1979), 108–109.

11. See Jean Gayon, "Nietzsche and Darwin," in *Biology and the Foundation of Ethics*, ed. Jane Maienschein and Michael Ruse (Cambridge: Cambridge University Press, 1999), 171. One could of course argue that Darwin's theory did not imply the utilitarianism and pragmatism against which Nietzsche rebelled. As discussed in the last chapter, Robert Richards and Elizabeth Grosz have attempted to recover a romantic Darwin.

12. See Ofelia Shutte, "Response to Alcoff, Ferguson, and Bergoffen," *Hypatia* 19, no. 3 (2004): 182–202.

13. Martin Jay, *The Dialectical Imagination: A History of the Frankfurt School and the Institute of Social Research, 1923–1950* (London: Heinemann, 1973), 47ff. Jay is analyzing Horkheimer's essays from the *Zeitschrift fur Sozialforschung* in 1933 and 1934. The former—a critique of Bergson—was only recently translated, just as I was finishing this manuscript. Max Horkheimer, "On Bergson's Metaphysics of Time," *Radical Philosophy 113* (May–June 2005).

14. Horkheimer, "On Bergson's Metaphysics of Time," 12. There are some similarities between Horkheimer's critique of *Lebensphilosophie* and Voloshinov's rather crude attack on Freud (1927), in which the work of Driesch and Bergson is bracketed with that of Freud, and they are each accused of betraying a "sui generis fear of history, an ambition to locate a world beyond the social and the historical, a search for this world precisely in the depths of the organic—these are the features that pervade all systems of contemporary philosophy and constitute the symptom of the disintegration and decline of the bourgeois world." V. N. Voloshinov, *Freudianism: A Critical Sketch*, trans. I. R. Titunik (Bloomington: Indiana University Press, 1987), 14.

15. I find no mention of the critical relation to vitalism in three excellent works on the Frankfurt School: Rolf Wiggershaus, *The Frankfurt School: Its History, Theories, and Political Significance*, trans. Michael Robertson (Cambridge, Mass.:, The MIT Press, 1994); the anthology *Foundations of the Frankfurt School*, ed. Judith Marcus and Zoltan Tar (New Brunswick, N.J.: Transaction Books, 1984); and Seyla Benhabib, *Critique, Norm, and Utopia: A Study of the Foundations of*

Critical Theory (New York: Columbia University Press, 1984). I am suggesting that both Adorno's and Horkheimer's critical philosophy is well understood as a critical encounter with the revolt represented by *Lebensphilosophie* as articulated by both Nietzsche and Bergson.

16. Georg Lukács, *The Destruction of Reason*, trans. Peter Palmer (Atlantic Highlands, N.J.: Humanities Press, 1981), 533.

17. Enzo Traverso, *The Origins of Nazi Violence*, trans. Janet Lloyd (New York: New Press, 2003), 98. Traverso is commenting on Walter Benjamin's insightful reading of Ernst Jünger.

18. First published in 1952 and translated by Peter Palmer and published by Merlin Press, in 1980. I rely here on two excellent critical discussions: H. A Hodges, "Lukács on Irrationalism," in *Georg Lukács: The Man, His Work and Ideas*, ed. G. H. R. Parkinson (New York: Random House, 1970); and Tom Rockmore, *Irrationalism: Lukács and the Marxist View of Reason* (Philadelphia: Temple University Press, 1992). The latter's scathing criticism is persuasive. Without the former, I doubt that I could have made sense of this sprawling text.

19. See János Keleman, "In Defense of *The Destruction of Reason*," *Logos* 7, no. 1 (Winter 2008), http://www.logosjournal.com/issue_7.1/kelemen.htm. Keleman does not discuss Lukács' critique of vitalism and racialism.

20. See the chapter by Adorno in *Aesthetics and Politics*, ed. Fredric Jameson (London: NLB, 1977).

21. Georg Lukács, *History and Class Consciousness: Studies in Marxist Dialectics*, trans. Rodney Livingstone (Cambridge, Mass.: The MIT Press, 1972), 110.

22. Georg Lukács, *The Destruction of Reason*, 416.

23. Georg Lukács, *The Destruction of Reason*, 414.

24. Todd May, "The Politics of Life in Deleuze's Thought," *Substance: A Review of Theory and Literary Criticism* 20, no. 3 (1991): 24–35. May was, perhaps, the first to argue systematically that life is the structuring principle of Deleuze's thought. But he makes no mention of this argument in his introduction to Deleuze written almost fifteen years later.

25. Gilles Deleuze, *Nietzsche and Philosophy*, trans. Hugh Tomlinson (New York: Columbia University Press, 1983), 101.

26. One of the most important recent debates about Deleuze has been conducted between Christopher Miller, Eugene Holland, and Ronald Bogue. Christopher Miller, "The Postidentitarian Predicament in the Footnotes of *A Thousand Plateaus*: Nomadology, Anthropology, and Authority," *Diacritics* 23, no. 3 (Autumn 1993): 6–35; Eugene Holland, "Representation and Misrepresentation in Postcolonial Literature and Theory," *Research in African Literatures* 34, no. 1 (Spring 2003): 159–173; Christopher Miller, "We Shouldn't Judge Deleuze and Guattari: A Response to Eugene Holland," *Research in African Literatures* 34, no. 3 (Fall 2003): 129–141; Ronald Bogue, *Deleuze's Way: Essays in Transverse Ethics and Aesthetics* (Aldershot: Ashgate Publishing Ltd, 2007).

27. Peter Hallward, *Out of This World: Deleuze and the Philosophy of Creation* (London: Verso, 2006).

28. Catherine Gallagher, *The Body Economic: Life, Death, and Sensation in Political Economy and the Victorian Novel* (Princeton, N.J.: Princeton University

Press, 2006), 96–97. The essay on Dickens is reprinted from a 1989 *Zone* article, and one can speculate that Deleuze derived the most powerful image of vitalism from Gallagher's reading.

29. See Gilles Deleuze, *Pure Immanence: Essays on a Life*, trans. Anne Boyman (New York: Zone Books, 2001), 9; and Elizabeth Grosz, "Deleuze's Bergson: Duration, the Virtual, and the Politics of the Future," in *Deleuze and Feminist Theory*, ed. I. Buchanan and C. Colebrook (Edinburgh: Edinburgh University Press, 2001), 214–235. Grosz's essay is perhaps the best analysis of what Deleuze means by virtuality.

30. Todd May, *Gilles Deleuze* (Cambridge: Cambridge University Press, 2005), 92.

31. Alain Badiou, *Briefings on Existence: A Short Treatise on Transitory Ontology*, trans. Norman Madarasz (Albany, N.Y.: SUNY Press, 2006), 68.

32. Peter Hallward, *Out of This World*, 44–45.

33. Henri Bergson, *Introduction to Metaphysics*, 22–24.

34. See David E. Cooper, *The Measure of Things* (Oxford: Clarendon Press, 2002), 92.

35. As Bergson insists: "All that which seems positive to the physicist and to the geometrician is actually a system of negations, the absence rather than the presence of a true reality." And later: "there are never any things other than those that the understanding has thus constituted." Bergson, *Creative Evolution*, trans. Arthur Mitchell (New York: Modern Library, 1911), 228, 271.

36. See John Rajchman, *The Deleuze Connections* (Cambridge, Mass., The MIT Press, 2000), 97.

37. See Peter Hallward, *Out of This World*, 19. Robert Wicks shares the same assessment; in fact, he considers Nietzsche's affirmation of life rather than existence the one source of the violence done for the most part mistakenly in his name. Robert Wicks, *Nietzsche* (One World Publications, 2007).

38. May, "The Politics of Life," 28. For Deleuze, the primary political problem is the very desire for these forms of life against life. As Deleuze writes: "Why are the people so deeply irrational? Why are they proud of their own enslavement? Why do they fight 'for' their bondage as if it were their freedom? Why does a religion that invokes love and joy inspire war, intolerance, malevolence and remorse?" Gilles Deleuze, *Spinoza: A Practical Philosophy*, trans. Robert Hurley (San Francisco: City Lights Books, 1988), 10. Critical theory is turned inward as we are led to investigations of why we reify social forms or why life subjects itself to death; on the other hand, Marx looked outward at the way in which reality itself deceives us due to the objective illusions generated by social forms, e.g., the objective appearance that value is inherent in the commodity, or that the wage is advanced and pays for the actual labor time performed, or that rent and profit represent the contributions to the total product made by land and capital, respectively. Desire is the pivotal category for Deleuze's theory of politics; objective illusion—think here of how a straight stick objectively does appear bent in water due not to any subjective failing but to the laws of refraction—is the foundation stone of Marx's theory of ideology. The movement from an objective science of society to a schizoanalysis of desire was brought about by the manifest inadequacy of Marxist science in

light of the French Communist Party's exteriority to the events of May 1968. In short, vitalism was a response to the failure of Marxism and not the horrified bourgeois response to the rise of scientific socialism as Lukács claimed about Nietzsche and fin de siècle *Lebensphilosophs*.

39. See John Rajchman, *The Deleuze Connections*; see also James Brusseau, *Isolated Experiences: Gilles Deleuze and the Solitudes of Reversed Platonism* (Albany, N.Y.: SUNY Press, 1998). Brusseau discusses Deleuze's ontology of the infinitive verb form. Deleuze himself writes: "Infinitives express becomings or events that transcend mood and tense." Gilles Deleuze, *Negotiations, 1972–1990*, trans. Martin Joughlin (New York: Columbia University Press, 1995), 34.

40. Quoted in Nik Fox, *The New Sartre: Explorations in Postmodernism* (New York: Continuum, 2003), 27.

41. On this, see the interesting comments by Christopher Norris, *Spinoza and the Origins of Modern Critical Theory* (Oxford: Basil Blackwell, 1991), 60–61. Norris argues that Spinoza's critique of Cartesian dualism led, on the one hand, to Louis Althusser's economically determinist theoretical critique of the illusions of the autonomous subject and, on the other hand, to a vitalist politics that refused the subordination of body to metaphysical abstractions (for example, the nation) and socialized exchange (the Oedipus complex). Again, Badiou's tantalizing argument is that this vitalist politics of the body is nothing other than asceticism, upon closer examination.

42. Badiou, *Briefings on Existence*, 68.

43. See Alain Badiou, *Metapolitics*, trans. Jason Barker (London: Verso, 2005).

44. See Georg Simmel, *Lebensanschauung* (München: Duncker and Humboldt, 1922). See also Rudolf Weingartner, *Experience and Culture: The Philosophy of Georg Simmel* (Middletown, Conn.: Wesleyan University Press, 1960).

45. Ernst Cassirer, however, argues (unpersuasively) that Simmel yearns to bypass the exteriorations of Spirit for a mystical relationship of Oneness with God. To him, this is no solution to the tragedy of culture, of which Simmel provided an enduringly important understanding. See Ernst Cassirer, *The Logic of the Cultural Sciences*. trans. S. G. Lofts (New Haven, Conn.: Yale University Press, 2000).

46. For a recent sympathetic reading of Bergsonian mysticism as developed by Muhammed Iqbal, see Souleymane Bachir Diagne, "Islam and Philosophy: Lessons from an Encounter," *Diogenes* 51, no. 2 (2004): 123–128.

47. Hallward, *Out of this World*, 82.

48. Michael Hardt and Antonio Negri, *Empire* (Cambridge, Mass.: Harvard University Press, 2000), 60.

49. Grosz, *Nick of Time* (Durham, N.C.: Duke University Press, 2005), 186.

50. Grosz, *Nick of Time*, 161.

51. Julien Benda, *The Treason of the Intellectuals*, trans. Richard Aldington (New York: W. Morrow & Co., 1928).

52. Shown brilliantly by Scott Lash and Celia Lury, *Global Culture Industry: The Mediation of Things* (Cambridge: Polity, 2007), 13. The vitalist production of difference turns out not to be the watchword of antibourgeois resistance but the advanced logic of capital itself.

53. From the *OED*'s entry on "Preformationism." See Hans Driesch, *The Science and Philosophy of the Organism* (London: MacMillan and Co., 1908).

54. See Steven Rose, *Lifelines: Biology Beyond Determinism* (Oxford: Oxford University Press, 1997). Rose describes the experiment well: "Wilhelm Roux, killed (with a hot needle) one of the two daughter cells resulting from the first division of frog's eggs. The result, in accord to mechanist beliefs, was that the surviving cell gave rise to only half the embryo. Embryological development was thus the mechanical unfolding of determinate stages, with irreversible differentiation of function between each cell. By contrast, his pupil Hans Driesch announced in 1891 that if he performed the same experiment with sea-urchin eggs at the two- or four-cell stage, he obtained perfectly sized adults, but each just one-half or one-quarter the normal size. For Driesch this seemed a complete refutation of the mechanist view of life—after all, if a machine is taken apart the individual pieces can never be turned into two or more complete functioning machines of the original type" (107). See also Anne Harrington, *Reenchanted Science: Holism in German Culture from Wilhelm II to Hitler* (Princeton, N.J.: Princeton University Press, 1996). Harrington provides an illuminating discussion of the antimechanist metaphysics that Driesch attempted to develop.

55. Ernst Cassirer, *The Problem of Knowledge: Philosophy, Science, and History Since Hegel*, trans. William H. Woglom and Charles W. Hendel (New Haven, Conn.: Yale University Press, 1978), 198.

56. Interesting here is Driesch's notion of "experimental indeterminism," in which entelechy only reveals what aspects of the organic life are inexplicable through mechanist methods.

57. Cassirer, *The Problem of Knowledge*, 199.

58. For Driesch, the entelechy was a force internal to each individual organism, while Bergson's *élan vital* was an external force working on all organisms.

59. Ben Ami Scharfstein, *The Roots of Bergson's Philosophy* (New York: Columbia University Press, 1943). Scharfstein documents Bergson's close attention to anti-Darwinian, vitalistic biological research.

60. Georges Canguilhem, *Knowledge of Life*, ed. Paola Marrati and Todd Meyers, trans. Stefanos Geroulanos and Daniela Ginsburg (Baltimore, Md.: The Johns Hopkins University Press, 2009), 72.

61. As discussed below, Bergson proved to be a key thinker in the reactionary French Celtic revival movements.

62. See R. C. Grogin, *The Bergsonian Controversy in France* (Calgary: University of Calgary Press, 1988).

63. This was a group to which Bergson and the chronophotographer Marey belonged.

64. See Alex Owen, *The Place of Enchantment: British Occultism and the Culture of the Modern* (Chicago: University of Chicago Press, 2004). She shows at many points the overlap between Bergson's critique of the intellect in the face of deeper life forces and various occultist and spiritualist movements.

65. An exception to this would be MacGregor Mathers, who was among the few prominent members from working-class origins.

66. At the same time, occultism did inspire a surge of social experimentation. It was intricately linked with British suffrage movement, animal-rights movements, and religious reform; spiritualism was connected with free love, transcendentalism, and vegetarianism. It is also important to note the global dimensions of late nineteenth- and early twentieth-century occult movements. See Gauri Viswanathan, "The Ordinary Business of Occultism," *Critical Inquiry* 27, no. 1 (Autumn 2000): 1–20. As Visvanathan points out, a great deal of the ritual content of nineteenth-century spiritualism was drawn from the writings of disillusioned British colonials detailing their encounters with Indian and East Asian esoteric traditions. Also, spiritualism or *espiritolismo* was also extremely popular in Latin America, particularly in the Spanish Caribbean, where, as in Europe, it was practiced mainly by the Creole middle class and elite. In the Latin American context, however, *espiritolismo* functioned as an esoteric buffer separating hermetic societies of whites from the societies formed around African-derived religions—*santería, palo monté,* etc.; these were practiced primarily by the Creole and mestizo working classes and Afro-Cubans. More often than not, the content of *espiritolismo* was explicitly European derived.

3. Bergson and the Racial *Élan Vital*

1. William James, *A Pluralistic Universe* (Cambridge, Mass.: Harvard University Press, 1977). I thank Abiola Irele for emphasizing the importance of James's engagement with Bergson's thought.

2. Suzanne Guerlac, *Thinking in Time: An Introduction to Henri Bergson* (Ithaca, N.Y.: Cornell University Press, 2006).

3. For a wide-ranging review of Bergson's influence, see R. C. Grogin, *The Bergsonian Controversy in France, 1900–1914* (Calgary: University of Calgary Press, 1988).

4. Judith Shklar, "Bergson and the Politics of Intuition," *Review of Politics* 20, no. 4 (October 1958): 645.

5. Richard Lehan, "Bergson and the Crisis of the Moderns," in *The Crisis in Modernism: Bergson and the Vitalist Controversy,* ed. Frederick Burwick and Paul Douglass (New York: Cambridge University Press, 1992).

6. For a full description of Bergson's influence, see Mark Antliff, *Inventing Bergson: Cultural Politics and the Parisian Avant-Garde* (Princeton, N.Y.: Princeton University Press, 1993), and Mark Antliff, *Avant-Garde Fascism: The Mobilization of Myth, Art, and Culture in France, 1909–1939* (Durham, N.C.: Duke University Press, 2007).

7. John Mullarkey, *Bergson and Philosophy* (Edinburgh: Edinburgh University Press, 1999), 66.

8. Mullarkey and I are speaking here of the last section of the chapter on "The Meaning of Life" in Henri Bergson, *Creative Evolution,* trans. Arthur Mitchell (New York: Henry Holt, 1911), 240–296.

9. Henri Bergson, *The Two Sources of Morality and Religion,* trans. R. Ashley Audra and Cloudesley Brereton (New York: Doubleday, 1935), 227.

10. Donald Verene, in Thora Ilin Bayer, *Cassirer's Metaphysics of Symbolic Forms*, intro. Donald Verene (New Haven, Conn.: Yale University Press, 2001), 36.

11. Bergson anticipates new Darwinist understandings of the power of myth. See John Maynard Smith and Eors Szathmary, *The Origins of Life: From the Birth of Life to the Origin of Language* (Oxford: Oxford University Press, 1999).

12. Guerlac, *Thinking in Time*, 9.

13. See Rushton Coulborn, "A Civilization in Decline? Lessons for Moderns from the Greeks and Romans," *Phylon* 2, no. 4 (1941): 377–387.

14. Wilhelm Dilthey makes the point nicely: "It is as if lines have to be drawn in continually flowing stream, figures drawn which hold fast. Between this reality of life and the scientific intellect (*Verstand*) there appears to be no possibility of comprehension, for the concept sunders what is unified in the flow of life. The concept represents something which is universally and eternally valid, independent of the mind which propounds it. But the flow of life is at all times unique [*überall nur einmal*], every wave in it arises and passes." Quoted in John Ermarth, *Wilhelm Dilthey: The Critique of Historical Reason* (Chicago: University of Chicago Press, 1978), 137. Dilthey offers a philosophical critique of the very possibility of a science of the lawlike consequences of a specific form of social life; that is, he attacks the very possibility of a social science that sees social consequences, whether beneficent or destructive, as inexorable tendencies of any kind of social organization. The Marxists argued that immiseration and business cycles, culminating in economic breakdown, were tendencies that would work themselves out with iron-clad necessity. Dilthey undercut the very possibility of such a positivist and predictive science of society in the name of life as an unfathomable process of unforeseeable creativity. That is, his critique works at a deeper level than empirical refutation. Ermarth convincingly shows that Dilthey's life philosophy cannot be equated with an irrationalist assault on scientifically controlled attempts at historical understanding but does not bring out the objective contradiction between Dilthey's *Lebensphilosophie* and positivist Marxist social science. In short, Dilthey's life philosophy allowed him to propose a more modest program of a science of historical understanding than offered by the then powerful currents of Marxist thought.

15. Eric Matthews, "Bergson's Concept of a Person," in *The New Bergson*, ed. John Mullarkey (New York: Manchester University Press, 1999), 122.

16. Sanford Schwarz, *The Matrix of Modernism: Pound, Eliot, and Early Twentieth-Century Thought* (Princeton, N.J.: Princeton University Press, 1985), 61. For good reason, Schwarz argues against an exclusive focus on the importance of Bergsonian vitalism for the development of modernism. But the richness and rigor of Bergson's thought—as well as his influence on the *Négritude* poets—encouraged my singular focus.

17. Henri Bergson, *Time and Free Will*, trans. Frank Pogson (New York: Dover, 2001), 231.

18. Hegel's *Phenomenology of Spirit*, as quoted in Ivan Soll, *An Introduction to Hegel's Metaphysics* (Chicago: University of Chicago Press, 1969), 102. But Hegel does not justify these judgments.

19. There is an obvious comparison to be made here between Bergson's superficial self and Martin Heidegger's categories of *das Man* and everydayness.

20. Judith Butler, *Gender Trouble: Feminism and the Subversion of Identity* (New York: Routledge, 1990).

21. See Joseph Chiari, "Vitalism and Contemporary Thought," in *The Crisis in Modernism: Bergson and the Vitalist Controversy*, ed. Frederick Burwick and Paul Douglass (New York: Cambridge University Press, 1992). Joseph Chiari argues for the value of Bergsonian philosophy in demonstrating the kind of truth that aesthetic expression can achieve.

22. The connection is also noted by Martin Jay, *Adorno* (Cambridge, Mass.: Harvard University Press, 1984). About the relation between Bergson and Adorno much more needs to be written. Kolakowski seems to point to the connection only to insinuate that Adorno was something of a plagiarist! Leszek Kolakowski, *Main Currents of Marxism: Its Rise, Growth, and Dissolution*, trans. P. S. Falla (Oxford: Clarendon Press, 1978), 3:367ff. However, in *Negative Dialectics* Adorno explicitly repudiates Bergson's distrust of language in the achievement of a nonidentical relation to the object as a cult of immediacy. Theodor Adorno, *Negative Dialectics*, trans. E. B. Ashton (New York: Seabury Press, 1973), 9–10.

23. Bertrand Russell, *A History of Western Philosophy, and Its Connection with Political and Social Circumstances from the Earliest Times to the Present Day* (New York: Simon and Schuster, 1945), 714–722.

24. Bergson, *Creative Evolution*, x.

25. See Theodor Adorno, *Minima Moralia: Reflections from Damaged Life*, trans. E. F. N. Jephcott (London: Verso, 1978). Adorno does indeed echo the idea: "things, under the law of their pure purposiveness, take on a form which limits intercourse of freedom of conduct or of the thing's independence, which would survive as the core of experience because it would not be consumed by moment of action" (43 [40]). For Bergson, that core of experience can only be appreciated through intuition.

26. Songsuk Susan Hahn, *Contradiction in Motion: Hegel's Organic Conception of Life and Value* (Ithaca, N.Y.: Cornell University Press, 2007), 40–41.

27. As quoted in Lucio Colletti, *Marxism and Hegel*, trans. Lawrence Garner (London: NLB, 1973), 159.

28. Rene Ménil, "Humour: Introduction to 1945," in *Refusal of the Shadow: Surrealism and the Caribbean*, eds. Michael Richardson, Krzysztof Fijakowski, and Philip Lamantia (London: Verso, 1996), 150. Ménil is probably unfair to Aristotle, whose prime philosophical examples were after all living and developing organisms and not the billiard balls of early modern physics.

29. See A. D. Lindsay, *The Philosophy of Bergson* (London: Hodder & Stoughton, 1911).

30. Jacques Chevalier, *Henri Bergson*, trans. Lilian Claee (London: Rider and House, 1928), 215.

31. Henri Bergson, "An Introduction to Metaphysics," in *The Creative Mind: A Study in Metaphysics*, trans. Mabelle Andison (New York: Philosophical Library, 1946), 192. As Elizabeth Grosz puts it: "The intellect functions primarily through recognition, through organizing material by what is already known. The intellect thus tends to submit the unknown to the principles of the known, not only to recognize but to precognize, anticipate in advance, what is to come." Elizabeth Grosz,

The Nick of Time: Politics, Evolution, and the Untimely (Durham, N.C.: Duke University Press, 2004), 192. For Adorno, instrumental rationality determined the nature of pre-cognizing. Todd May attempts to displace precognizing with a Deleuzean epistemology: "difference is the overflowing character of things themselves, their inability to be wrestled into categories of representation." Todd May, *Gilles Deleuze* (Cambridge: Cambridge University Press, 2005), 82. One of the first works to bring out these epistemological aspects of Bergsonism is Karin Stephen, *The Misuse of the Mind: A Study of Bergson's Attack on Intellectualism* (London: Kegan Paul, Trench, Trubner and Co., Ltd, 1922).

32. Max Horkheimer, "On Bergson's Metaphysics of Time," *Radical Philosophy* 113 (May–June 2005), 13.

33. Erik Krakauer, *The Disposition of the Subject: Reading Adorno's Dialectic of Technology* (Evanston, Ill.: Northwestern University Press, 1998), 77. Krakauer's defense of Adorno is among the most successful, because as a medical doctor one hears his own struggles to treat patients both in terms of general classifications and in terms of their own individuality, and the ways in which patients are non-identical to the categories into which they are fitted during diagnosis.

34. Henri Bergson, *An Introduction to Metaphysics*, trans. T. E. Hulme (New York: Liberal Arts Press, 1955), 69–71.

35. Bergson, *Creative Evolution*, 39.

36. Bergson provides a complicated, though I believe discredited argument, that even the highest achievements of the intellect, viz., the differential calculus with its basis in homogeneity and divisibility even if to an infinite degree, simply cannot represent true duration.

37. Henri Bergson, "Laughter," in *Comedy*, ed. George Meredith (Baltimore, Md.: The John Hopkins University Press, 1980), 117–118.

38. Guerlac, *Thinking in Time*, 78–79.

39. I thank Rakesh Bhandari for discussion here.

40. See C. Péguy, "Clio, Dialogue de l'histoire et de l'ame payenne (1909–1912)," in *Euvres en prose* (Paris: La Pléiade, 1968), 1:127–131, 180–181, 286, 299–300; quoted in Michael Lowy, *Fire Alarm: Reading Walter Benjamin's* On the Concept of History, trans. Chris Turner (London: Verso, 2005), 95.

41. Lucio Colletti attempted to the establish the similarity between G. W. F. Hegel's philosophy of nature, Friedrich Engels's dialectics of nature, and Bergson's idealist reaction against science. He argued that Bergsonian metaphysics underwrote the critique of reification as the product of intellect in the founding text of Western Marxism, Georg Lukács' *History and Class Consciousness*. See Lucio Colletti, *Marxism and Hegel*.

42. Bergson stands closer to the tradition of *Naturphilosophie* than to Enlightenment vitalism. Hans Peter Reill has put the contrast this way: "late Enlightenment thinkers argued that humans, being part of living nature, could acquire an intimate understanding of it through self-reflection, and vice versa, by examining living nature, humans could better understand themselves. But in this quest they emphasized the harmony between both, limited strictly the knowledge one could obtain, and usually excluded acquiring knowledge of dead matter through this epistemological procedure. The *Naturphilosophen* obliterated all these reservations.

Human reason and nature's processes were one. Or to put it more succinctly using Schelling's words: "Nature [is] visible mind; mind invisible nature.'" Hans Peter Reill, *Vitalizing Nature in the Enlightenment* (Berkeley: University of California Press, 2007), 201. For Bergson, the power of intuition justified the epistemological immodesty.

43. Bergson, *Creative Evolution*, 266.

44. Horkheimer, "On Bergson's Metaphysics of Time," 14.

45. Hilary L. Fink, *Bergson and Russian Modernism, 1900–1930* (Evanston, Ill.: Northwestern University Press, 1999).

46. See Daniel Cohnitz and Marcus Rossberg, *Nelson Goodman* (Chesham: Acumen Publishers, 2006), 13. They argue that Bergson was Goodman's implicit archenemy.

47. Richard Lehan, "Bergson and the Discourse of the Moderns," in *The Crisis in Modernism: Bergson and the Vitalist Controversy*, eds. Frederick Burwick and Paul Douglass (Cambridge: Cambridge University Press, 1992), 311.

48. See Michael North's discussion of the function of the African mask in *The Dialect of Modernism* (New York: Oxford University Press, 1994) and Henry Louis Gates Jr.'s discussion of the African mask as the embodiment of "contradiction" in *The Signifying Monkey: A Theory of Afro-American Literary Criticism* (New York: Oxford University Press, 1988).

49. Russell, *A History of Western Philosophy*, 716.

50. Lehan notes that Lawrence had direct knowledge of Bergson's *Creative Evolution*.

51. D. H. Lawrence, *Apocalypse* (London: Martin Secker, 1932), 64.

52. Ernst Bloch, *Principle of Hope*, trans. Neville Plaice, Stephen Plaice, and Paul Knight (Cambridge, Mass.: The MIT Press, 1986), 59.

53. Bergson, *The Creative Mind*, 190.

54. Alan Lacey, *Bergson* (London: Routledge, 1989), 144.

55. See Milič Čapek, *Bergson and Modern Physics: A Reinterpretation and Reevaluation* (Dordrecht: Reidel Publishers, 1971). The first half of Čapek's book is the clearest articulation of Bergson's psychological concepts available. It would be unfortunate if many humanists have neglected this text due to its misleading title.

56. Čapek, *Bergson and Modern Physics*, 86–88.

57. Michael Löwy and Robert Sayre, *Romanticism Against the Tide of Modernity*, trans. Catherine Porter (Durham, N.C.: Duke University Press, 2001), 41.

58. Bergson, *An Introduction to Metaphysics*, 22–24.

59. György Márkus, "Life and Soul: The Young Lukacs and the Problem of Culture," in *Lukács Revalued*, ed. Agnes Heller (Oxford: Basil Blackwell, 1983), 8.

60. Ernest Cassirer, "'Spirit' and 'Life' in Contemporary Philosophy," in *The Philosophy of Ernst Cassirer*, ed. Paul Arthur Schlipp (Evanston, Ill.: Library of Living Philosophers, 1949), 876. After the proofs of this book were completed, I came to read the brilliant discussion of Cassirer's critique of the philosophy of life in Edward Skidelsky, *Ernst Cassirer: The Last Philosopher of Culture* (Princeton, N.J.: Princeton University Press, 2008), 160–194.

61. Nelson Goodman, *Problems and Projects* (Indianapolis, Ind.: Bobbs Merrill, 1972), 31.

62. For a very helpful overview of the analysis of Bergson's influence on modernist aesthetics from Pound and imagist poetry to cubism, see Martin Jay, *Downcast Eyes: The Denigration of Vision in Twentieth-Century Thought* (Berkeley: University of California Press, 1993).

63. Of course, Marx's critique was that production had to be mediated by money not because the fetishistic powers of money allowed it to monopolize direct exchangeability but because the organization of social labor in the form of commodity production gave rise to the need for money's monopoly. Throughout the interwar years, antimonetary demagoguery, vitalism, and fascism converged. The Nazis were able to invoke this noxious brew while keeping intact the major institutions of commodity productions; once in power, their radicalism against the money men was quickly abandoned and displaced horrifically into the Judeocide. See Moishe Postone, "Anti-Semitism and National Socialism: Notes on the German Reaction to 'Holocaust,'" *New German Critique* 19, no. 1 (1980): 97–115. I thank the much missed Michael Rogin for this reference.

64. Herbert Schnädelbach, *Philosophy in Germany, 1831–1933* (Cambridge: Cambridge University Press, 1984), 145.

65. Richard Sieburth, "In Pound We Trust: The Economy of Poetry/The Poetry of Economy," *Critical Inquiry* 14, no. 1 (Autumn 1987): 142–172.

66. Sieburth, "In Pound We Trust," 158. Another valuable work on Pound's erratic economic writings is Peter Nicholls, *Ezra Pound: Politics, Economics, and Writing: A Study of the* Cantos (Atlantic Highlands, N.J.: Humanities Press, 1984).

67. Ezra Pound, *The Cantos of Ezra Pound* (London: Faber & Faber, 1987), 231.

68. Ezra Pound, *The Cantos*, 231.

69. Ezra Pound, *The Cantos*, 230.

70. Sieburth, "In Pound We Trust," 153.

71. The silence of the New Criticism era around Pound's fascist and anti-Semitic past has in recent years been thankfully broken by an increasing debate on the political and social themes in modernism, a debate to which this manuscript hopes to contribute. It is clear that anti-Semitism (as well as a vehement anti-Marxism) functioned as a rhetorical referent for Pound's deep aversion to money and monetarism. The figure of the Jew as the embodiment of abstraction is prevalent throughout Pound's work, and this figuration is usually achieved through the metonymic use of the name of the Jewish banking family Rothschild. In "Canto XLVI," which follows his almost biblical denunciations of the crime of usury, Pound presents a Mr. RothSchild as the agent of underhanded and usurious banking practices. Referred to alternately as "RothSchild" and "Roth-Schild," Pound insists on introducing a "generic" figure of the Jew to stand in as a sign for the sin of abstraction, "hell knows which Roth-Schild 1861, 64 or sometime." The Jew in this context is the embodiment of mobility; he is timeless and enigmatic. In short, as the pun on the German word *Schild* (shield) suggests, he functions as a cover for the workings of a corrupt monetary system. In the narrative of the Canto, "the

Jew" obscures the workings of capitalism with duplicitous language and sleight of hand: "Very few people will / understand this. . . . / The general public will probably not / see it's against their interest." Like paper money itself, the figure of the Jew stands in the way and obstructs our vision of the working of the economic.

72. An interesting comparison here is to Georges Sorel, who understood Bergson's vitalism as the metaphysics for a hysterically nationalist and anti-Semitic form of nationalism. Sorel asserted that Bergson's own Judaic heritage prevented him from understanding the implications of his own vitalist thought (one can also add that this is what prevented the Nazis from a full endorsement of his thought). In other words, Sorel claimed that he understood Bergson better than he understood himself. As will become clear, I think Sorel is quite correct that Bergson did not acknowledge—in fact, in his own political practice worked against—the rising antiliberal and nationalist mythology of his day, to which his philosophy indeed gave a powerful voice. See again the brilliant and painstaking study by Mark Antliff, *Avant-Garde Fascism*.

73. See Wyndham Lewis, *Time and Western Man* (London: Chatto and Windus, 1927).

74. Gertrude Stein, *Three Lives* (1909; repr. New York: Penguin, 1990), 57–168.

75. See Russell Berman, "German Primitivism/Primitive Germany: The Case of Emil Nolde," in *Fascism, Aesthetics, and Culture*, ed. Richard Goslan, 56–66 (Hanover, N.H.: University Press of New England, 1992). See also Simon Gikandi, "Race and the Modernist Aesthetic," in *Writing and Race*, ed. Tim Youngs, 147–165 (London: Longman, 1997).

76. Arthur Lovejoy, *Bergson and Romantic Evolution* (Berkeley: University of California Press, 1914), 17.

77. Stephen, *The Misuse of the Intellect*, 64–65.

78. See Bergson, *Time and Free Will*, 231.

79. One of course remembers here Wyndham Lewis's horrified response in 1927 to the penetrating and merging of duration with its "emotional urgency and visceral agitation" and preference for "the distinct, the geometric, the universal, non-qualitied" and things standing apart—"the wind blowing between them and the air circulating freely in and out of them." Wyndham Lewis, *Time and Western Man*, 428. The criticism that I shall be developing is radically different.

80. Lovejoy's early encounter would seem to have been a key point in the career of his ideas. He had already noted Bergson's similarity to the romanticism and *Naturphilosophie* of Schelling, the analysis of whose thought is the dénouement of Lovejoy's study of the concept of plentitude and the great chain of being. Lovejoy would return to Bergson at the very end of his career as well.

81. Arthur Lovejoy, "Practical Tendencies of Bergsonism," *International Journal of Ethics* (1913).

82. Keith Ansell-Pearson, "Bergson and Creative Evolution/Involution," in *The New Bergson*, ed. John Mullarkey (New York: Manchester University Press, 1999), 149–150. Pearson is quoting from Bergson, *Creative Evolution*, 4–5.

83. May, *Gilles Deleuze*, 43.

84. Deleuze, *Bergsonism*, trans. Hugh Tomlinson and Barbara Hubberjam (1966; repr. New York: Zone Books, 1988), 26.

85. How does Bergson's duration compare to William James's stream of consciousness, as analyzed by Franco Moretti in *The Modern Epic: The World System from Goethe to Garcia Marquez*? I am trying to emphasize here how interpenetrated the moments are, or, in other words, how misleading Bergson thought it was to think of time as any kind of succession or form of space. The past thus has a much greater role; it is indestructible, though not always present even in its effects. If, as Jameson suggests, the Bergsonian duration is a modernist trope in an age of incomplete modernization, then the analysis of the stream of consciousness has more contemporary relevance, especially in a world of loosely related advertising images meant to whet appetites for commodities.

86. Bergson, *Creative Evolution*, 7–8.

87. "We believe that so far as time is taken to be a pure continuity, devoid of any discreteness, the variety of temporal manifestations is left unintelligible. Any novelty implies discreteness of appearances, since if they were blended with the previous phases of time, they could not present a real novelty, being already tied to the past. If nothing distinctly different occurs, nothing can occur at all. For a temporal transition is a passage to something, which has not yet been possessed in the past or the present. Otherwise, as a strife for obtaining that which is already obtained the situation would simply be nonsensical and impossible." Andrew P. Uchenko, *Logic of the Event: An Introduction to the Philosophy of Time* (Berkeley: University of California Press, 1929), 119–120.

88. See Martin Heidegger, *On Time and Being*, trans. Joan Stambaugh (New York: Harper and Row, 1972).

89. Since Bergson's thought can only be vague given that its propositional content is about the ineffable, the meaning of his thought can be productively sought in its aesthetic and political uses. Such studies (Antliff's being the most important one) reveal that Bergson's thought has had many, even contradictory, meanings, almost all of them disturbing. Of course, it is possible that Bergson was misread in his own time and that posthumous readings such as Gilles Deleuze's, Milič Čapek's, Guerlac's, and Elisabeth Grosz's have taught us to read Bergson anew. But there does not seem to be at this point a self-conscious effort to read Bergson against himself and Bergsonism, even though many scholars do read Marx, Nietzsche, and Heidegger in this critical way. See Mark Antliff, "The Fourth Dimension and Futurism: A Politicized Space," *The Art Bulletin* 82, no. 4 (December 2000): 720–733; and Mark Antliff, "The Jew as Anti-Artist: George Sorel, Anti-Semitism, and the Aesthetics of Class Consciousness," *Oxford Art Journal* 20, no. 1 (1997): 50–67.

90. Guerlac, *Thinking in Time*, 83.

91. J. W. Burrow, *The Crisis of Reason: European Thought, 1848–1914* (New Haven, Conn.: Yale University Press, 2000), 168.

92. Guerlac, *Thinking in Time*, 104.

93. Keith Ansell-Pearson, *Philosophy and the Adventure of the Virtual: Bergson and the Time of Life* (London: Routledge, 2002), 71.

94. Keith Ansell-Pearson, *Philosophy and the Adventure of the Virtual*, 377. For Lukács, Nietzsche's controversial doctrine of eternal recurrence was meant as a critique of the possibility of radical innovation. I find this interpretation doubtful.

95. Löwy, *Fire Alarm*, 12. Lowy is quoting from Benjamin's *Arcades Project*.

96. Grosz, *Nick of Time*, 170.

97. Guerlac, *Thinking in Time*, 149.

98. On the coherence of the multiple selves, see Graham Parkes, "A Cast of Many: Nietzsche and Depth Psychological Pluralism," *Man and World* 22 (1989): 453–470. Guerlac presents Bergson as an alternative to Hegel, but Nietzsche is an alternative to both.

99. Jonathan Crary, *Suspensions of Perception: Attention, Spectacle, and Modern Culture* (Cambridge, Mass.: The MIT Press, 2001), 327. Crary's reading of Bergson is one of the most perceptive. I am more skeptical of whether Bergsonian metaphysics in fact underwrites freedom in a meaningful sense and allows for irreducible novelty.

100. A fine introduction to Deleuze's theory of identity can be found in John Rachjaman's chapter on "Life" in *The Deleuze Connections* (Cambridge, Mass.: The MIT Press, 2000), 79–112. It seems to me that Peter Hallward has shown that Deleuze is a utopian more than a mystic.

101. Leonard Lawlor, *The Challenge of Bergsonism: Phenomenology, Ontology, Ethics* (New York: Continuum, 2003), 67–69.

102. Grosz, *Nick of Time*, 196. At other points, Grosz critiques the emphasis on heritage and tradition and embraces the importance of Nietzsche's emphasis on forgetting as a precondition for creative action. In other words, Grosz does not explore the differences between Nietzsche and Bergson, who are both subsumed under the category of philosophers whose reflections on the productivity of time were themselves untimely.

103. May, *Gilles Deleuze*, 50.

104. Frederic Jameson, *A Singular Modernity: Essay on the Ontology of the Present* (London: Verso, 2002), 142. I cannot but wonder here whether a Bergsonian conception of duration structures the temporal sense of so-called third-world migrant workers who are periodically returning to their villages after working in modern agriculture and cities. One awaits a study of the simultaneity that Jameson finds in Proust and Joyce in contemporary migrant literature. Here the spatial crossing of the border may indicate a temporal fusion of two worlds, the past and present.

105. See George F. Putnam, "The Meaning of Barrèsisme," *Western Political Quarterly* 7, no. 2 (June 1954): 161–182. Putnam does not see the homology between Barrès' theory of freedom and Bergson's theory of duration.

106. Bergson, *Creative Evolution*, 219.

107. Mark Antliff, *Inventing Bergson: Cultural Politics and the Parisian Avant-Garde* (Princeton, N.J.: Princeton University Press, 1993), 178–179. Antliff is drawing here from Eugen Weber's *Peasants Into Frenchmen*. However, outside of Weber's vision was the importation and use of Algerian peasants; they did not become Frenchmen—except, of course, as conscripts.

108. See Jonathan Lear, *Happiness, Death, and the Remainder of Life* (Cambridge, Mass.: Harvard University Press, 2000), 141–155. Lear provides an insightful and important Freudian reading of Freud's own mythmaking about racial memory in *Moses and Monotheism*.

109. A. James Arnold, *Modernism and Négritude: The Poetry and Poetics of Aimé Césaire* (Cambridge, Mass.: Harvard University Press, 1981), 161.

110. Grosz, *Nick of Time*, 178.

111. See Thomas Trautmann, *Aryans and British India* (Berkeley: University of California Press, 1997). Trautmann provides a most brilliant study of this assimilation and its tremendously destructive consequences; his work builds on the pioneering work of George Stocking.

112. Simon Critchley, *Continental Philosophy: A Very Short Introduction* (New York: Oxford University Press, 2001), 68–72. See also Simon Critchley, *Ethics, Politics, Subjectivity: Essays on Derrida, Levinas, and Contemporary French Thought* (London: Verso, 1999), 129–130.

113. David E. Cooper offers a similar interpretation of Heidegger's *Being and Time*, especially section 74 of division 2, in which one finds references not to individual Dasein as such but to one's generation, time, and *volk*: "birth refers to our Being-towards-the beginning. This 'beginning' is what he calls 'heritage,' that which has been 'handed down' to us as historically located creatures. This heritage is not to be equated with the conditions into which we are 'thrown,' for these constitute our world as structured and articulated by the They, and the They inevitably ignores, distorts or trivializes our heritage. Either the They dismisses the past as old hat and 'seeks the modern,' makes it 'unrecognizable,' or reduces it to a repository of quaint traditions only to be disinterred on special occasions, like the trooping of the colour. Far from our heritage dictating the shape of everyday, inauthentic existence, it is precisely 'in terms of the heritage . . . that resoluteness . . . takes over' that the possibilities of authentic existence are 'disclosed.' . . . In properly taking over our heritage, we 'snatch' ourselves back from the 'comfortableness, shirking, and taking things lightly' of the They. This time, moreover we are left without guidance as to the possibilities on which to resolve, for the 'authentically historical' person who 'takes over' his heritage will draw these possibilities precisely from that heritage. For what the heritage offers are 'the possibilities of the Dasein that has-been-there,' the decisions and ways of life adopted by our forebears which are open to us to 'repeat,' for example by 'choosing a hero' from the past, and—with due appreciation of the new context—emulate. Indeed, 'revering the repeatable possibilities of existence' is to revere 'the sole authority' which people can pit against the dictatorship of the They and, in so doing, become free. . . . Only in the light of a heritage, Heidegger argues, are our horizons widened so that we can enjoy a 'clear vision' of the Situation in which we are placed and hence authentically respond to it. Dasein, recall, is essentially temporal in nature. In everyday, 'average' life, it is presently absorbed 'alongside' things in a world it is already 'thrown' into 'for the sake of' realizing its projects in the future. But we are now in a position to define an authentic mode of temporality or historicality: Dasein's being 'in the moment of vision for "its time,"' a vision of its Situation which requires both recall of its heritage and anticipation of its death. . . . The authentic person then is one who

is determined to make of his life an integrated whole, is able to understand and properly respond to the Situation he is in by bringing to bear upon it the lessons of tradition. A heritage of course is not mine alone, though how I take it over is my doing. The 'fateful destiny' to be gleaned from a heritage is that of a 'community, a people . . . [a] generation.' To live as an authentically historical person, then, is not to 'soar above' or 'float free' from my fellows but to 'exist essentially in Being-With-Others' who have also inherited such a destiny. Hence the dichotomy which Heidegger's choice between authentic and inauthentic existence seemed to imply— solipsistic alienation from society versus sheepish refuge in the They—turns out to be a false one. By taking over the heritage handed down to me, I at once 'snatch' myself from the comfortable embrace of the They and find a new 'home' in a people or generation which shares that inheritance. Heidegger's authentic person, though 'individualized,' is not the existentialist 'loner,' necessarily at odds with his society, who stalks the novels of Albert Camus. On the contrary, his 'resoluteness,' if it is to have any issue and direction, requires identification with 'a people's destiny,' and only then can Angst be transformed from a state of 'uncanniness' into one of 'unshakeable,' if 'sober,' joy at recovery from 'lostness in the They.' " David E. Cooper, *Heidegger* (London: Claridge Press, 1996), 48–50. Cooper argues that this jargon of authenticity does not contain *in nuce* Heidegger's later commitment to the Nazi political project. Be that as it may, it ties authentic existence to the recovery of what can only be the founding myths by which a people are imagined to be united and therefore implies a mythical and conservative response to the crises of modernity.

114. In a footnote to *Being and Time*, Heidegger dismisses Bergson's conception of time but does not seem to have understood it and thus the proximity of Bergson's vision to his. The fact remains that both thinkers contrasted the subjective experience of time to its objective conception in the physical sciences. While Rüdiger Safranski emphasizes Heidegger's debt to the Bergsonian critiques of rigidified forms, abstract temporality, and abstract subjectivity—and Safranski, overly apologetic of Heidegger, misses their most important similarity as a revolutionary traditionalists—there exists no detailed comparative study of quite probably the two most important continental philosophers of the twentieth century. But see Critchley's short note on their similar temporal conceptions in his essay "On Derrida's *Spectres of Marx*," reprinted in Simon Critchley, *Ethics-Politics-Subjectivity* (London: Verso Books, 1999), 155. Rüdiger Safranski, *Heidegger: Beyond Good and Evil*, trans. Ewald Osers (Cambridge, Mass.: Harvard University Press, 1998). One also wonders how to explain the much greater interest in Heidegger than in Bergson in the American academy. One hopes that with the scientism of American philosophy Bergson's mistakes about vitalism and Einstein's theory of relativity have not been seen as more embarrassing than Heidegger's political commitments. For my purposes, there is no doubt that Bergson's influence was many times more important than Heidegger's for aesthetic modernism. Of course, their shared importance for me was their success in making compelling cultural reaction.

115. Bergson lauded the interpretation of his work by Eduard LeRoy (*Une philosophie nouvelle: Henri Bergson*, 1912), a traditional traditionalist, and it was

this interpretation of Bergson that Lovejoy attacked as conservative in "Practical Tendencies of Bergsonism," *International Journal of Ethics* 23, no. 4 (July 1913): 419–443. But Bergson himself and more importantly Bergsonism are better understood in terms of radical traditionalism.

116. Paul Gilroy, *The Black Atlantic: Modernity and Double Consciousness* (Cambridge, Mass.: Harvard University Press, 1993), 192. Gilroy also suggests that Wright's antitraditionalism leaves him few resources against the embrace of technocratic modes of governance and echoes the earlier embrace of Western modernism by those benighted Africans who had made peace with imperialism. Gilroy's thinking, it should be remembered, has its own tradition—the dialectical analysis of the Enlightenment.

117. Gilroy, *The Black Atlantic*, 198–199.

118. Stephen Asma, "Metaphors of Race: Theoretical Presuppositions Behind Racism," *American Philosophical Quarterly* 32, no. 1 (January 1995): 13–29.

119. Asma, "Metaphors of Race," 22–23.

120. Lovejoy, *Bergson and Romantic Evolution*, 53–54.

121. George Bernard Shaw, *Back to Methuselah: A Metaphysical Pentateuch* (London: Constable, 1931).

122. May, *Gilles Deleuze*, 37.

123. See David Cooper, *World Philosophies: A Historical Introduction* (Oxford: Blackwell, 1996); David Cooper, *The Measure of Things: Humanism, Humility, and Mystery* (Oxford: Oxford University Press, 2002); David Cooper, "*Verstehen*, Holism, and Fascism," in *Verstehen and Humane Understanding*, ed. Anthony O'Hear (Cambridge: Cambridge University Press, 1996); and David Cooper, "Modern Mythology: The Case of 'Reactionary Modernism,'" *History of the Human Sciences* 9, no. 2 (1996): 25–37.

124. Enrico Cavacchioli, "Let the Moon Be Damned," in *Poeti Futuristi* (Milan: Nuova Accademia, 1963).

125. Ernst Junger, *Sämtliche Werke: Essays II, Der Arbeiter* (Stuttgart: Klett-CottaVerlagsgemeinschaft, 1981), 160.

126. Oswald Spengler, *Man and Technics: A Contribution to the Philosophy of Life*, trans. Charles Francis Atkinson (New York: Knopf, 1932), 85–86. See Jeffery Herf, *Reactionary Modernism: Technology, Culture, and Politics in Weimar and the Third Reich* (New York: Cambridge University Press, 1984).

127. Robert Wicks, *Nietzsche* (Oxford: Oneworld, 2002), 41–43.

128. See the discussion in Emmanuel Eze, *Achieving Our Humanity: The Idea of a Postracial Future* (New York: Routledge, 2001).

129. Frantz Fanon, *The Wretched of the Earth* (New York: Grove Press, 1965).

130. Cooper, "Modern Mythology," 302.

131. For a useful collection of Dilthey's writings, see Wilhelm Dilthey, *Pattern and Meaning in History: Thoughts on History and Society* (New York: Harper, 1962).

132. Cooper, "Modern Mythology," 295.

133. Lucien Lévy-Bruhl, *Primitive Mentality*, trans. L. A. Clare (New York: MacMillan, 1978).

134. Robert Bernasconi, "Lévy-Bruhl Among the Phenomenologists: Exoticisation and the Logic of the 'Primitive,'" *Social Identities* 11, no. 3 (May 2005): 229–245.

135. In an attempt to underline how radical the break represented by modern science was, Gaston Bachelard would argue, for example, that the primitive mentality predominated among even the first exponents of the scientific revolution.

136. Messay Kebede, "*Négritude* and Bergsonism," *Journal on African Philosophy* 3 (2003). This piece represents a highly stimulating attempt to develop our understanding of these two intellectual movements beyond the seminal formulations by Abiola Irele, whom I discuss in the next chapter. I am obviously much more critical of Bergson, Bergsonism, and *Négritude* than Kebede, but we share the belief that they need to be understood in their mutual implications.

137. Henri Bergson, *The Two Sources of Morality and Religion*, 136–137. Of course, the only remedy for this evolved monstrosity is, as implied on the next page, openness to colonial rule.

138. Aimé Césaire, *Notebook of a Return to the Native Land*, trans. Clayton Eshleman and Annette Smith (Middletown, Conn.: Wesleyan University Press, 2001), 35–36.

139. For an important criticism of *Négritude*, see Patrick Taylor, *Narrative of Liberation: Perspectives on Afro-Caribbean Literature, Popular Culture, and Politics* (Ithaca, N.Y.: Cornell University Press, 1989), 171.

4. *Négritude* and the Poetics of Life

1. Michel Rolph Trouillot, *Silencing the Past: Power and the Production of History* (Boston: Beacon Press, 1995), 17.

2. Bruce Lincoln, *Discourse and the Construction of Society: Comparative Studies of Myth, Ritual, and Classification* (New York: Oxford University Press, 1989).

3. Aimé Césaire, *Cahier d'un retour au pays natal*, trans. Abiola Irele (Columbus: Ohio State University, 2000), li.

4. Senghor erases here the fundamental difference between a vitalist and existentialist ontology, as my reading of Césaire will show. Léopold Sédar Senghor, "The Spirit of Civilization, or the Laws of African Negro Culture," *Présence Africaine* nos. 8–10 (June–November 1956).

5. Sylvia Washington Bâ, *The Concept of Négritude in the Poetry of Léopold Sédar Senghor* (Princeton, N.J.: Princeton University Press, 1973), 55.

6. Janice Spleth, *Léopold Sédar Senghor* (New York: Twayne Publishers, 1985), 42.

7. Jean-Paul Sartre, *Black Orpheus*, trans. S. W. Allen (Paris: Présence Africaine, 1976), 44–47. An important critical treatment of Sartre's influential essay can be found in Belinda Elizabeth Jack, *Négritude and Literary Criticism: The History and Theory of "Negro-African" Literature in French* (Westport, Conn.: Greenwood Press, 1996), 60–79.

8. Michael Kimmelman, "For Blacks in France, Obama's Rise Is Reason to Rejoice, and to Hope," *New York Times* (June 17, 2008), http://www.nytimes.com/2008/06/17/arts/17abroad.html.

9. A. James Arnold, *Modernism and Négritude: The Poetry and Poetics of Aimé Césaire* (Cambridge, Mass.: Harvard University Press, 1981).

10. A. James Arnold, *Modernism and Négritude*, 70.

11. Gary Wilder, *The French Imperial Nation-State: Négritude and Colonial Humanism Between the Two World Wars* (Chicago: University of Chicago Press, 2005), 262–263.

12. Christopher Miller, "Involution and Revolution: African Paris in the 1920s," in *Nationalists and Nomads: Essays on Francophone African Literature and Culture* (Chicago: University of Chicago Press, 1998), 9–54.

13. Abiola Irele, *The African Experience in Literature and Ideology* (London: Heinemann Educational Books, 1981), 67–88.

14. Miller, "Involution and Revolution," 37.

15. André Pichot, *The Pure Society: From Darwin to Hitler*, trans. David Fernbach (London: Verso Books, 2009), 256, 268.

16. Janet Vaillant, *Black, French, and African: A Life of Léopold Sédar Senghor* (Cambridge, Mass.: Harvard University Press, 1990), 253–254.

17. See Daniel Cohnitz and Marcus Rossberg, *Nelson Goodman* (Chesham: Acumen Publishers, 2006), 13. They argue that Bergson was Goodman's implicit archenemy.

18. See János Riesz, "Senghor and the Germans," *Research in African Literatures* 33, no. 4 (2002): 25–37.

19. Bruce Lincoln, *Theorizing Myth: Narrative, Ideology, and Scholarship* (Chicago: University of Chicago Press, 1999), 48.

20. Lincoln, *Theorizing Myth*, 48.

21. Vaillant, *Black, French, and African*, 254.

22. D. A. Masolo, *African Philosophy in Search of Identity*, Bloomington: Indiana University Press, 1994), 49.

23. In explaining Deleuze's indebtedness to Bergson here, Ronald Bogue, drawing on Čapek, has given us as sensible an interpretation as one could expect. See Ronald Bogue, *Deleuze on Cinema* (New York: Routledge, 2003), 16–21.

24. Henri Bergson, *Creative Evolution* (Mineola, N.Y.: Dover Press, 1998), 220–221.

25. See here Nurit Bird-David, "Animism Revisited: Personhood, Environment, and Relational Epistemology," *Current Anthropology* 40 (February 1999): S67–S91.

26. Translation mine with assistance from Kea Anderson from "Ce que l'homme noir apporte," *L'Homme de couleur* (Paris: Librairie Plon, 1939), 24. This 1939 essay, which appeared in this volume edited by Cardinal Jean Verdier, meant to address the question of race relations in the French colonies. Works such as *L'Homme de couleur* were part of an explosion of writings from both Anglophone and Francophone corners written from various discursive vantage points—ecclesiastic, ethnographic, and political—in an effort to gain a better understanding

of "subject" peoples who, following the Great War, were gaining greater understanding of the possibilities of their own sovereignty and cultural identities.

27. Irele, *The African Experience in Literature and Ideology*, 74–75.

28. Léopold Sédar Senghor, *On African Socialism*, trans. Mercer Cook (New York: Praeger, 1964), 71.

29. Emmanuel Chukwudi Eze, *Achieving Our Humanity: The Idea of the Postracial Future* (New York: Routledge, 2001), 124.

30. Eze, *Achieving Our Humanity*, 126

31. Ermarth, however, emphasizes that Dilthey's attacks on science and empirical study were much less radical than those of many of the *Frühromantiks*. See Michael Ermarth, *Wilhelm Dilthey: The Critique of Historical Reason* (Chicago: University of Chicago Press, 1978).

32. Quoted in Ermarth, *Wilhelm Dilthey*, 117.

33. Dilthey's own example is powerful: "There is no man or no thing which would only be an object for me and not a hindrance or a help, a goal for striving or an instance of will, importance, a demand for attention, closeness or opposition, distance or strangeness. The vital relation, whether momentary or lasting, makes men and objects into bearers of happiness, expansion of my existence, extension of my power or that they restrict the horizon of my existence, exert a restriction upon me, and lessen my potentiality." Quoted in Ermarth, *Wilhelm Dilthey*, 118–119.

34. Eric Matthews, *The Philosophy of Maurice Merleau-Ponty* (Chesham Bucks: Acumen Publishers, 2002), 59.

35. Maurice Merleau-Ponty, *The World of Perception*, trans. Oliver Davis (New York: Routledge, 2004), 66.

36. Martin Jay, *Downcast Eyes: The Denigration of Vision in Twentieth-Century French Thought* (Berkeley: University of California Press, 1992), 198.

37. Tim Ingold, *Evolution and Social Life* (New York: Cambridge University Press, 1986), 246–247. Emphasis mine.

38. Léopold Sédar Senghor, *Nationhood and the African Road to Socialism*, trans. Mercer Cook (Paris: Presence Africaine, 1962), 70–74.

39. Milič Čapek, *Bergson and Modern Physics* (Dordrecht: Reidel, 1971), 88.

40. See Henri Bergson, *Time and Free Will*, trans. F. L. Pogson (1913; repr. Mineola, N.Y.: Dover Books, 1990), 231.

41. Senghor, "Ce que l'homme noir apporte," 24.

42. There is an obvious comparison to be made here between Bergson's superficial self and Martin Heidegger's categories of *das Man* and everydayness.

43. François Jacob, *The Logic of Life: A History of Heredity*, trans. B. E. Spillmann (Princeton, N.J.: Princeton University Press, 1993), 19–20.

44. Senghor, "Ce que l'homme noir apporte," 30: "In Negro society, man is tied to the collective owned object by the juridical tie of custom and tradition, also and above all by a mystical tie. Let us stop at this last one. The group—family, corporation or age group—has its own personality, which is felt as such by each member. The family is the same blood; it is, as we have seen, the same shared flame; the corporation is only a clan[ic] family, which has ownership of an 'art.' Man thus feels like a person—a communal one, I grant—before the object of ownership. But very often the object itself is felt as a person. This is the case of

natural phenomena: plain, river, forest. We have said it: the Ancestor, by living in the ground, is tied to it in the name of the family. And the Earth is a feminine genie; and the mystical marriage of the group and the Earth-Mother is celebrated 'solemnly.' "

45. Abiola Irele, *The African Imagination: Literature in Africa and Black Diaspora* (New York: Oxford University Press, 2001), 70–71.

46. Senghor, *Poésie de l'action*, quoted in Wilder, *The French Imperial Nation-State*, 356.

47. Quoted in Abiola Irele, "Contemporary Thought in French Speaking Africa," in *Africa and the West: The Legacies of Empire*, ed. I. James Mowoe and Richard Bjornson (New York: Greenwood Press), 143.

48. Michael A. Weinstein, *Structure of Human Life: A Vitalist Ontology* (New York: New York University Press, 1979), 93.

49. Arnold, *Modernism and Négritude*, 55.

50. Raymond Williams, *The Politics of Modernism: Against the New Conformists* (New York: Verso Press, 1989), 172. In his study of modernism, Williams unfortunately does not bring the colonial world into his view.

51. Quoted in Ofelia Schutte, *Beyond Nihilism: Nietzsche Without Masks* (Chicago: University of Chicago Press, 1984), 13–14.

52. Schutte, *Beyond Nihilism*, 14.

53. Césaire was read as antirealistic in the Soviet Union. See Janis Pallister, *Aimé Césaire* (New York: Twayne Publishers, 1991).

54. Georges Bataille is the vitalist thinker par excellence of such limit experiences. For an important critique of Bataille, see Martin Jay, *Songs of Experience: Modern American and European Variations on a Universal Theme* (Berkeley: University of California Press, 2005).

55. Aimé Césaire, *Notebook of a Return to the Native Land*, trans. Clayton Eshleman and Annette Smith (Middletown, Conn.: Wesleyan University Press, 2001), 8.

56. Césaire, *Notebook*, 9.

57. Michael Dash, *The Other America: Caribbean Literature in a New World Context* (Charlottesville: University of Virginia Press, 1988), 69.

58. Schutte, *Beyond Nihilism*, 86–87.

59. Stephen Houlgate, *Hegel, Nietzsche, and the Criticism of Metaphysics* (Cambridge: Cambridge University Press, 1986), 54–55.

60. Martin Jay perceptively notes that Bergson's epistemological embrace of poetry was later superceded by a critique of verbal images *tout court*. At the very least, Bergson's thought expresses an ambivalence toward the verbal image. See Bergson, *Time and Free Will*, 15. Bergson writes, "The poet is he with whom feelings develop into images, and the images themselves into words which translate them while we in our turn experience the feeling which was, so to speak, their emotional equivalent." After citing this passage, Jay then notes that in *Matter and Memory* Bergson claims that "sympathetic thoughts between two consciousnesses must be prior to the verbal images that communicate them." Jay, *Downcast Eyes*, 202.

61. See Jay, *Downcast Eyes*, 203. Jay shows how central this thesis was to modernism as such: "the widely remarked influence of Bergson on the Imagist

poetry of the modernist movement, transmitted by T. E. Hulme, of Anglo American poets like T. S. Eliot, Ezra Pound, and William Carlos Williams, should be construed as impelling them away from mimetic representation and toward the immediate presentation or evocation of lived experience through the arresting juxtaposition of verbal images."

62. T. Denean Sharpley-Whiting has written incisively and definitively of the importance of Suzanne Césaire in the circulation of Frobenius's ideas among the *Négritude* poets. See "Tropiques and Suzanne Césaire: The Expanse of *Négritude* and Surrealism," in *Race and Racism in Continental Philosophy*, ed. Robert Bernasconi with Sybol Cook (Bloomington: Indiana University Press, 2003), 115–128.

63. Schutte, *Beyond Nihilism*, 104.

64. One is reminded here of Dilthey. "Art, especially poetry, is closest to life, the truest, most comprehensive and at the same time most concrete representation of its coherence and meaning. Art is the organ for the understanding [*Verstehen*] of life." Dilthey quoted in Ermarth, *Wilhelm Dilthey*, 134.

65. Gregson Davis, *Aimé Césaire* (Cambridge: Cambridge University Press, 1997), 73–74.

66. Ronald Bogue, *Deleuze's Way: Essays in Transverse Ethics and Aesthetics* (Burlington: Ashgate Publishers, 2007), 100.

67. Césaire, *Notebook*, 36.

68. See also Henri Bergson, *Matter and Memory*, trans. Nancy Margaret Paul and W. Scott Palmer (New York: Zone Books, 1988), 60.

69. Suzanne Césaire, "Leo Frobenius and the Problem of Civilisations," in *Refusal of the Shadow: Surrealism and the Caribbean*, ed. Michael Richardson, trans. Krzysztof Fijalkowski and Michael Richardson (London: Verso, 1996), 82–87.

70. Léopold Sédar Senghor, "The Lessons of Leo Frobenius," in *Leo Frobenius: An Anthology*, ed. E. Haberland (Wiesbaden: Franz Steiner Verlag, 1973), xi.

71. Marxists often dismissed *Négritude* as particularist against the universal dialectic of a global proletariat against a cosmopolitan bourgeoisie. However, the PCF was particularist, being a nationalist expression of only one great power, the USSR. Césaire in particular thought the passage to the universal was safer through *Négritude* than through official Marxism.

72. Lukács, *The Destruction of Reason* (London: Merlin, 1980), 492–493.

73. György Márkus, "Life and Soul: The Young Lukács and the Problem of Culture," in *Lukács Revalued*, ed. Agnes Heller (Oxford: Basil Blackwell, 1983), 12–13.

74. Paulin Hountondji, *African Philosophy: Myth and Reality* (Bloomington: University of Indiana Press, 1983), 161–162.

75. Marc Augé, *The Anthropological Circle: Symbol, Function, History* (Cambridge: Cambridge University Press, 1982), 92.

76. Arnold, *Modernism and Négritude*, 52.

77. Arnold, *Modernism and Négritude*, 50.

78. Arnold, *Modernism and Négritude*, 105.

79. One of the most creative explorations of this dialectic is William Pietz, "Fetishism and Materialism: Limits of Theory in Marx," in *Fetishism as Cultural Discourse*, ed. Emily Apter and William Pietz (Ithaca, N.Y.: Cornell University Press, 1993).

80. See Dipesh Chakrabarty, *Provincializing Europe: Postcolonial Thought and Historical Difference* (Princeton, N.J.: Princeton University Press, 2000). Dipesh Chakrabarty has written eloquently against the narcissistic Western idea that its form of colonialism was so powerful as to have obliterated all other cultures. His critique may seem more persuasive in the case of old writing cultures than oral ones, however.

81. Dipesh Chakrabarty, "Legacies of Bandung: Decolonization and the Politics of Culture," *Economic and Political Weekly* 40, no. 46 (November 12, 2005).

82. Quoted in Davis, *Aimé Césaire*, 72–73.

83. Césaire, *Notebook*, 1.

84. Césaire, *Notebook*, 32.

85. Césaire, *Notebook*, 37.

86. Davis, *Aimé Césaire*, 27.

87. Davis, *Aimé Césaire*, 60.

88. Davis, *Aimé Césaire*, 50–51.

89. Brent Edwards, "Aimé Césaire: The Syntax of Influence," *Research in African Literatures* 36, no. 2 (2005): 7.

90. Frantz Fanon, *Black Skins, White Masks*, trans. Charles Lam Markmann (New York: Grove Weidenfeld, 1968), 220.

91. Paul Gilroy, *The Black Atlantic: Modernity and Double Consciousness* (New York: Verso, 1993).

92. Drawing on Jacques Lacan, Abdul JanMohamed is one of the few commentators who has focused on the role of work in Hegel's dialectic and who has underlined that Fanon, too, was critical of Hegel on these grounds. One remaining ambiguity is whether work is intrinsically incapable of educative effect or whether work only under oppressive conditions cannot be positivized. See Abdul JanMohamed, *The Death-Bound Subject: Richard Wright's Archeology of Death* (Durham, N.C.: Duke University Press, 2005).

93. That Hegel was able to privilege those who labor as vehicles of the Spirit does put him at odds with bourgeois sensibility. Hegel's thought admits of radical interpretation for both the left and right.

94. McCarney makes this point in his comments on Kojève's interpretation. Fanon makes the opposite point—that since the freedom of the Antillean black was not struggled for but simply granted, it is not genuine. True recognition must be conquered through life-and-death struggle, but McCarney seems to be correct that the imposition of respect for one's civil rights does not necessarily win one recognition as a self-consciousness by another self-consciousness. Fanon invidiously praises African Americans vis-à-vis Antillean blacks for their active struggle, but he is mistaken that the struggle resulted in true recognition rather than rights. African Americans were not less racially objectified than blacks on Martinique.

95. Judith Butler, *Subjects of Desire: Hegelian Reflections in Twentieth-Century France* (New York: Columbia University Press, 1987), 207–209.

96. Michael Hardt, *Gilles Deleuze: An Apprenticeship in Philosophy* (Minneapolis: University of Minnesota Press, 1993).

97. Bhikhu Parekh, *Marx's Theory of Ideology* (Baltimore, Md.: The John Hopkins University Press, 1982), 94–95.

98. Butler, *Subjects of Desire*, 21.

99. Nick Nesbitt, *Voicing Memory: History and Subjectivity in French Caribbean Literature* (Charlottesville: University of Virginia Press, 2003), 120.

100. Peter Hallward, *Out of This World: Deleuze and the Philosophy of Creation* (London: Verso Books, 2006), 58.

101. The refusal of the African radical response to submit to the dominant categories of dissent is beautifully explored throughout Brent Hayes Edwards, *The Practice of the Diaspora: Literature, Translation, and the Rise of Black Internationalism* (Cambridge, Mass.: Harvard University Press, 2003).

102. Gaston Bachelard, *Dialectic of Duration* (Manchester: Clinamen Press, 2000).

103. Steve Stern, "The Tricks of Time: Colonial Legacies and Historical Sensibilities in Latin America," in *Colonial Legacies: The Problem of Persistence in Latin American History*, ed. Jeremy Adelman (New York: Routledge, 1999), 148.

104. Robert Bernasconi, "The Assumption of *Négritude*: Aimé Césaire, Frantz Fanon, and the Vicious Circle of Racial Politics," *Parallax* 8, no. 2: 69–83.

105. Stern, "The Tricks of Time," 148.

106. Quoting Paul Patton, *Deleuze and the Political* (New York: Routledge, 2000), 85.

107. Nik Fox, *The New Sartre: Explorations in Postmodernism* (New York: Continuum, 2003), 30.

108. Césaire, *Notebook*, 17–18.

109. Michael Inwood, *A Heidegger Dictionary* (Oxford: Blackwell Publishers, 1999), 59.

110. On the imagery of blood, see Irele's introduction in Césaire, *Cahier*, lxv.

111. Christopher Miller, *The French Atlantic Triangle: Literature and Culture of the Slave Trade* (Durham, N.C.: Duke University Press, 2008), 329. Miller successfully softens this charge against Césaire's *Négritude*, but he puts the point very well. The criticism is made in Jean Bernabé, Patrick Chamoiseau, and Raphael Confiant, "Eloge de Creolite / In Praise of Creoleness" *Callaloo* 13, no. 2 (Autumn 1990): 886–909. The authors announce themselves "to be neither Africans, nor Europeans, nor Asiatics, we proclaim ourselves Creoles."

112. Quoted in Houlgate, *Hegel, Nietzsche, and the Criticism of Metaphysics*, 8.

113. I have in mind here the analysis of affirmative and negative forces throughout Gilles Deleuze's *Nietzsche and Philosophy*, trans. Hugh Tomlinson (Minneapolis: University of Minnesota Press, 1983).

114. ". . . on the recurrent charge that may have some degree of validity: that of biological essentialism. Confiant and his cohorts have not been the first to object to the notion of the 'fundamental black' (*le negre fondamental*), with its implication of an inherited racial substratum that is overlaid by a European cultural veneer." Davis, *Aimé Césaire*, 181.

115. Butler, *Subjects of Desire*, 215.

116. Nick Nesbitt, *Voicing Memory: History and Subjectivity in French Caribbean Literature* (Charlottesville: University of Virginia Press, 2003), 83.

117. Gary Wilder, *The French Imperial Nation-State*, 292.

118. Césaire, *Notebook*, 27–28.

119. Césaire, *Notebook*, 43.

120. Robert Wicks, *Nietzsche* (Oxford: Oneworld, 2006), 105–109. Wicks brilliantly traces much of what goes wrong in Nietzsche's thought due to his preference for life affirmation over complete existential affirmation.

121. Roberto Esposito, *Bíos: Biopolitics and Philosophy* (Minneapolis: University of Minnesota Press, 2008), 134.

122. Irele's introduction in Césaire, *Cahier*, lxvii.

123. Lukács, *The Destruction of Reason*, 493.

124. Césaire, *Notebook*, 43–44.

125. Césaire's introduction to Frobenius in *Tropiques* 5 (April 1942), translated and quoted by Arnold, *Modernism and Négritude*, 37–38.

126. See Alain Badiou, *The Century*, trans. Alberto Toscano (Cambridge: Polity, 2007). Badiou finds the meaning of the twentieth century in this passion for the real.

127. Friedrich Nietzsche, *On the Genealogy of Morals*, trans. Douglas Smith (Oxford: Oxford University Press, 1996), essay 2, paragraph 24.

Index

creativity (*continued*)
  Négritude and, 147, 149–51,
    161, 172, 176; racialism and,
    49–50; racial memory and, 102,
    105–6, 108, 111, 113–14, 116;
    technology and, 119–20; vitalism
    and, 93, 97–99
*Crisis in Modernism, The: Bergson
  and the Vitalist Controversy*
  (Burwick and Douglass), 4, 21, 83
Critchley, Simon, 114–15, 116
Crowley, Aleister, 75
cultural pluralism, 156–58
cultural relativism, 124, 145, 158
cultural vitalism, 4–5, 100–102,
  152–53
culture, as supraorganic, 124, 128

Damas, Leon, 54
Darwinism: as God substitute, 48;
  materialism, 43–50; Nietzsche's
  opposition to, 60–61; racialism
  in, 8, 47–50; social, 6, 8, 21, 80,
  82, 117, 176
Dasein, 115, 172–73, 205–6n. 113
Dash, Michael, 10, 150, 152
Davis, Gregson, 155, 164–65, 171,
  174
death: fascism and, 63; of the West,
  8, 24–25, 41
death-in-life, 3–4, 19
Decline of the West, The (Spengler), 8
Deleuze, Gilles, 4, 12, 17, 28, 41–42,
  104, 172–74, 174, 193n. 38,
  194n. 39; anti-Hegelianism,
  168–70; asceticism of, 68–69;
  depersonalization of Bergsonian
  past, 110–11; duration, view of,
  104, 106; as mystic, 69–70; on
  Nietzsche, 66; vitalism of, 41–42,
  57, 66–71

Deleuze: The Clamor of Being
  (Badiou), 109
Depestre, Rene, 163
depth psychology, 85–86, 108
Derrida, Jacques, 125
Descartes, René, 25, 30–37, 143;
  bete-machine, 32–33
Destruction of Reason, The (Lukács),
  63–64
Destruktion, 115
determinism, 28–29, 32, 37, 51,
  194n. 41; indeterminism, 103,
  113, 117, 195n. 56
deterritorialization, 172
dialectic, 25, 41–42, 62, 64–65, 82,
  101, 134–35, 156, 163, 166–70,
  173, 199n. 41, 207n. 116, 212n.
  71, 213n. 91
dialectical materialism, 12–13, 91
Dialectic of Enlightenment
  (Horkheimer and Adorno), 158
Dickens, Charles, 66
difference, 67, 70–71, 108–9,
  199n. 31; positive, 28, 168–71,
  173; racialized, 113–14, 133–35,
  157, 168–69; vital, 170–78
differentiation, 66, 77, 87,
  195n. 54
Dijksterhuis, E. J., 30
Dilthey, Wilhelm, 3, 64, 122–24,
  142–43, 145, 197n. 14, 210n. 33,
  212n. 64
Dionysianism, 172; Nietzschean, 39,
  61, 69, 132, 145, 151, 153
disapora, African, 148
DNA, 2–3
Doray, Bernard, 35
Douglas, Major, 101
Douglass, Paul, 4, 21, 83
drag, as parody, 54
Dreyfussards, 111

Pype → ud au Gibbsns
         to life phys,
         who life maslu